Conservation in the Age of Consensus

The conservation of the historic environment as an important goal of public policy has, over the last thirty years, become a rarely challenged consensus. This book explores beneath and beyond this consensus, looking at how the role of conservation has evolved in the planning system and how the values ascribed to heritage have changed in the process.

The practice of conservation is a highly modernist practice, premised on the discernment and judgement of experts protecting the 'intrinsic' cultural value of buildings and places. John Pendlebury charts the evolution of the relationship between conservation and state intervention in the post-war planning system from the high modernist period of the 1940s to the 1960s, through the tumult of the 1970s and into what might be termed the Age of Consensus that arrived in the 1980s. The text examines a number of key arenas; the ways that conserved heritage has become commodified, how much consensus extends to the wider population, and heritage at a global scale – through the medium of World Heritage Sites. These chapters illustrate the shifting values attached to conservation and heritage especially in terms of the instrumental purposes to which heritage is put and the benefits which are argued to derive from its protection.

This book innovatively marries an understanding and sympathy for modern conservation practice with the critical insights about the nature of heritage and conservation of recent academic study. It ends with a call for a greater critical reflexivity in conservation practice and the need for this to evolve in a socially progressive manner.

John Pendlebury is a Senior Lecturer in the School of Architecture, Planning and Landscape, Newcastle University. Before becoming an academic, he worked as a Conservation Officer.

Conservation in the Age of Consensus

John Pendlebury

Routledge
Taylor & Francis Group

LONDON AND NEW YORK

First published 2009
by Routledge
2 Park Square, Milton Park, Abingdon, Oxon OX14 4RN

Simultaneously published in the USA and Canada
by Routledge
270 Madison Avenue, New York, NY 10016, USA

Routledge is an imprint of the Taylor & Francis Group, an informa business

Typeset in Univers Light by
Florence Production Ltd, Stoodleigh, Devon
Printed and bound in Great Britain by
CPI Antony Rowe, Chippenham, Wiltshire

British Library Cataloguing in Publication Data
A catalogue record for this book is available from the British Library

Library of Congress Cataloging in Publication Data
Pendlebury, John R., 1963–
    Conservation in the age of consensus/John Pendlebury.
        p. cm.
    Includes bibliographical references and index.
    1. Historic preservation – Great Britain – Planning.   2. Historic
preservation – Social aspects – Great Britain.   3. Consensus (Social
sciences) – Great Britain.   4. Historic sites – Conservation and restoration
– Great Britain.   5. Historic buildings – Conservation and restoration –
Great Britain.   6. Cultural property – Protection – Great Britain.   7. Great
Britain – Cultural policy.   I. Title.
DA655.P46 2008
363.6'90941 – dc22   2008007500

ISBN10: 0–415–24983–X (hbk)
ISBN10: 0–415–24984–8 (pbk)
ISBN10: 0–203–89234–8 (ebk)

ISBN13: 978–0–415–24983–6 (hbk)
ISBN13: 978–0–415–24984–3 (pbk)
ISBN13: 978–0–203–89234–3 (ebk)

For Maria, Kasia and Finn.

My personal heritage.

Contents

Figures

Tables

Foreword and acknowledgements

This book was started as an equal partnership with my friend and colleague Tim Townshend. Time, circumstance and shifting interests have meant that ultimately it evolved into a solo project. Some specific acknowledgements for Tim's contributions are given below but first I must acknowledge his enthusiasm and belief in encouraging us to start this project, some years ago!

The impetus to write this book stemmed from an early career spent working in conservation followed subsequently by teaching and writing on the subject. Having trained as a town planner I found myself working within the conservation-planning system as a conservation officer. I held a feeling of rightness in what I was doing and, inspired by my friend John Sanders, gradually learnt the modern conservation 'way of seeing'.

At the same time I was aware that the values I held and advocated were by no means universal amongst the people I encountered in my professional daily life. There seemed to be a broad consensus that conservation was a 'good thing', but often in ways that did not fit with my professional perspective. I was aware that the reasons for conserving buildings were not always clear, whether in terms of cultural value or whether cultural values such as architectural or historic significance were indeed the most important considerations. This book is an attempt to explore some of these issues and in particular to look beneath the conservation consensus.

Many people have helped me during the years this book has taken to gestate. First and foremost I must thank Tim Townshend. Tim undertook early drafts of Chapters 4 and 6 and part of Chapter 5, and some of the text within these will originally be his. Parts of other chapters also derive from work we have undertaken jointly: specifically parts of Chapter 7 and the sections on inclusion and Byker in Chapter 10 (these latter also undertaken with Rose Gilroy). Part of Chapter 7 also relates to work undertaken with Peter Larkham, and I would like to thank him for comments on the draft of this chapter. Various other friends and colleagues have read drafts and provided helpful comments along the way. Above all I would like to thank Aidan While for going beyond the bounds of what I might reasonably have hoped for, but also Andrew Law and Andrew Ballantyne for helpful comments. Nick Shore kindly allowed me to draw significantly from his doctoral work undertaken in Gloucester in Chapter 10.

Foreword and acknowledgements

I am very grateful for the generosity of friends, colleagues and organisations who have let me use their photos free of charge and in some cases spent considerable amounts of time digging them out for me. In putting the text together Bernie Williams has been invaluable and I thank the various editors I have gone through at Taylor and Francis, Caroline Mallinder, Kate McDevitt, Ellie Rivers and Katy Low, for displaying the patience of Job. Ultimately, of course, the responsibility for any errors, bad ideas and possibly occasional useful insights is mine alone.

Chapter 1

Introduction

Conservation, culture and planning

Introduction

A study of conservation made in different historical periods would inevitably throw up quite different themes and emphases. So, for example, a cursory look at books produced on conservation in the early to mid 1970s would reveal books with such emotive titles as *Goodbye Britain* (Aldous 1975) and *The Rape of Britain* (Amery and Cruikshank 1975). Just reading these titles would suggest that conservation was, at the time, a contentious and hard-fought-over issue. It seems, writing in the mid 2000s, however, that perhaps the key characteristic of conservation in the thirty or so years since is how accepted it has become. Inevitably there is always 'surface noise', for example, debate about the extensiveness of protection of the historic environment, complaints about, and fears for, resources and individual cases to contest. However, that the conservation of the historic environment should be an important goal of public policy is generally accepted as a given. Such challenges that do occur to this basic premise are so unusual as to be regarded as iconoclastic. This consensus evolved through strife-torn development struggles in the 1960s and 1970s and the heritage-drenched 1980s and has endured into a new political era where terms such as 'new' and 'modernising' have been greatly emphasised. On the face of it this is 'the age of consensus'. What I seek to do in this book is examine and look beneath the surface of this apparent consensus. I look at what sort of activity conservation is and how its application to our towns and cities has evolved. I look at some of the ways that the nature and purpose of conservation have developed and changed and what its role is in contemporary society. Part of this discussion involves examining the function built heritage plays in society. I do this principally with reference to the United Kingdom, and often specifically England, although my discussion sometimes extends much further afield.

My particular principal concern is the protection and management of the historic environment by the national and local state. Within this I have a particular interest in the conservation of places, rather than, say, a focus on grand individual monumental buildings. The way protection and management of such places occurs is through the planning system.

Planning and protection

Within the sphere of the historic environment one can make a binary division between those heritage sites that are usually visited and experienced for their qualities as heritage and the 'other'. In the former one might include country houses cared for by the National Trust and ruined castles in the guardianship of English Heritage, as well as other places beyond the scope of this book, such as museums acting as repositories of cultural artefacts. Though I will occasionally touch upon heritage sites, my concern is more with the other: the historic environment that is experienced as part of everyday life. This includes a whole range of buildings and environments officially labelled as historic, from major architectural compositions to the commonplace and even mundane. There are few places in Britain where the conservation of this heritage is not a significant issue. With around 500 000 listed buildings, 9000 conservation

1.1
The protected heritage: Stonehenge, part of a World Heritage Site and a Scheduled Ancient Monument.
Source: author.

areas and 20 000 scheduled ancient monuments in England alone, it is a patrimony that extends the length and breadth of the country. Listing encompasses, for example, the grandeur of Bath, where the whole city is also inscribed as a World Heritage Site, and a pigeon cree in Sunderland. Conservation areas are designated around the internationally important and renowned towns and cities such as Bath, York and Chester and much more modest elements of the heritage such as former colliery villages and 'Metroland' suburbia, as well as such unusual designations as the Settle-Carlisle

Railway line (see Figure 1.4) and areas of field barns and walls in the upland countryside of the Yorkshire Dales. The sheer extensiveness of the protected heritage means that it is also subject to considerable ongoing change. This is not a heritage of castles and standing stones that can be 'preserved as found'. It covers hundreds of thousands of buildings that people live in and areas that are subject to major economic change.

The evolution of the relationship between conservation and planning is the focus of Chapters 3, 4 and 5 of the book. These three chapters are not an attempt at an even history: I focus on issues and events that are of especial relevance to the story I wish to tell. Nor do they give a detailed history of changes in legislation and public policy such as that given admirably in other books such as (Delafons, 1997a). Although the first conservation legislation in Britain dates back to the 1882 Ancient Monuments Act, it is in the post-Second World War period that the conservation-planning system as we know it today began to really evolve. For example, the Town and Country Planning Acts of

1.3
The diversity of the protected heritage: listed public urinals, Rothesay, Isle of Bute.
Source: author.

1.4
The diversity of the protected heritage: the Ribblehead Viaduct, part of the Settle-Carlisle Conservation Area, some 76 miles (122 km) long.
Source: author.

1944 and 1947 introduced the system of listing buildings. However, of equal relevance was the way that town planners began to become seriously engaged in the planning of existing towns and cities at this time, rather than being predominantly concerned with the layout of new development. The 1940s produced a series of remarkable 'advisory plans' or 'reconstruction plans'. In the case of historic cities these sought to reconcile sustaining character with the pressures of the modern world. Since the 'reconstruction plans' of the 1940s there has been an ever closer relationship between conservation and planning, sometimes fractious, sometimes harmonious. By the end of the 1960s conservation issues had started to assume the centre ground. Chapter 3 charts this evolution.

Chapter 4 moves the story into the 1970s and the seismic shifts of that period as development struggles were fought up and down the country and as the economy and property markets collapsed. It was a period of intense polemical activity, as noted at the beginning of this chapter, and conservationists fought for their cause both within and outside the machinery of the state. Gains were won by utilising, expanding and strengthening state protection through listing and the system of conservation areas, introduced in 1967. The European Architectural Heritage Year of 1975 was perhaps a high-point of the decade; towards of the end of the 1970s there were concerns that the conservation movement's achievements were endangered by governmental indifference and economic austerity.

Chapter 5 focuses on conservation during the Conservative governments in the 1980s and 1990s. It was during this period we can say that we arrived at the *Age of Consensus*. Ironically perhaps, it was during this period of government known for economic liberalisation that conservation became firmly established as a key element of planning policy. I document how conservation strengthened as a national policy objective in this period and some of the reasons why this might have been the case and go on to describe how contestation in the planning system effectively shifted from whether to conserve to *how* to conserve and develop historic areas.

Conservation has become a policy objective of central importance within the planning system in a way that would have been barely recognisable in earlier periods. However, it is worth noting that at the same time there has been tremendous continuity in the framework within which protected heritage is defined and in terms of the basic principles which government advises should apply to its management (Pendlebury 2004). The legislative definitions for listed buildings and conservation areas remain unchanged, since 1944 and 1967, respectively. The primary criteria for listing buildings have endured, focusing on architectural interest, historical interest, historic associations and 'group value', albeit these have been applied more and more generously. Similarly there is much continuity in the basic principles that have underpinned policy guidance on the historic environment since the first significant national guidance started emerging in the late 1960s, though again this has been within a context of conservation assuming more policy importance.

There is therefore tremendous continuity in the basic principles that *define* the historic environment and the way government considers it should be *managed*, since the late 1960s/early 1970s. These derive from a justification for conservation based upon cultural values relating to architectural quality, historic importance and archaeological significance: to defining places as *special*. However, what has shifted fundamentally in official pronouncements during this period is the *benefits* that are argued to derive from this activity. An official document such as *Preservation and Change* (Ministry of Housing and Local Government 1967) set out brief statements of the value of conservation relating to beauty and visible history. In the 1970s there was rhetorical emphasis on the social value of conservation, and in the 1980s stress on its economic potential. By the time of the government's policy advice document PPG15 (Department of the Environment and Department of National Heritage 1994) benefits were argued to include value in terms of national identity, quality of life, local distinctiveness, leisure and recreation and economic prosperity. *Force for Our Future*, a more recent government statement on the heritage was even more fulsome. It waxed lyrically and extensively about the role of conservation in establishing environmental quality and identity, local distinctiveness and continuity and as an active part of social processes, including community cohesion and social inclusion, and as a stimulus for creative new architecture (Department of Culture, Media and Sport and Department of Transport Local Government and the Regions 2001a). Furthermore, conservation was held to aid economic processes and economic regeneration in particular.

However, despite these sweeping statements, these are benefits that may (or may not) follow decisions to protect based upon essentially traditional criteria of specialness, and where guidance on conservation management decisions emphasises first and foremost the importance of sustaining cultural worth defined around issues of fabric and aesthetics.

The next section briefly introduces some conceptual assumptions used in this book.

Heritage, conservation and culture

A starting premise of most recent study of the concept of heritage suggests that its nature is not as a static inheritance to which fixed and enduring values are applied. Rather, for objects to be identified as heritage requires a process of identification, or 'heritage creation'. The establishment of value, however 'value' is defined, is central to the act of conservation; societies only attempt to conserve the things they value. In addition, the very act of conservation gives a building, object or environment cultural, economic, political and social value. Concepts of cultural, historical or social value are culturally and historically constructed; thus value is not an *intrinsic* quality but rather the fabric, object or environment is the bearer of an externally imposed, culturally and historically specific meaning that attracts a value status depending on the dominant frameworks of value of the time and place. Inherent in this is the idea that when we refer to the heritage we are talking about the *contemporary* use of the past. Heritage becomes a fluid phenomenon rather than a static set of objects with fixed meanings. Smith (2006) has taken this argument to its logical conclusion by arguing that there is no such thing as material heritage; heritage is essentially a cultural practice and social process.

Conservation of such heritage is in turn a bundle of processes, encompassing the political, cultural, social, economic and so on (Avrami *et al.* 2000). This may include the idea of conserving the fabric of the past for future generations, historically a strong principle in the field of architectural conservation. Privileging some element of the past as heritage over another necessarily involves a socially constructed process of selection. As what constitutes heritage is contingent on prevailing cultural, political and economic mores it is also inherent that what constitutes heritage can be contested. For example, different social or economic groups in a society may have quite different ideas both about what heritage is and how it should be managed. Furthermore, different groups may have radically different interpretations of, or lay claim to, what is ostensibly one piece of material heritage.

Heritage identification and creation are complex processes, and decoding precisely how and why this happens may be very difficult. However,

7

1.5
The wider historic environment: Sissinghurst, Kent; Grade 1 in the Register of Historic Parks and Gardens.
Source: author.

if we accept that heritage is not 'just there', but that an active process of identification and labelling occurs, then we can assume that this takes place for a purpose. Usually the idea of heritage is linked to cultural concerns (though the economic and social functions of heritage have become increasingly significant factors, as I will discuss). Developing from Williams' (1976) landmark discussion of culture, Mitchell held culture to be the patterns and differentiations of people, the way these develop and the way these mark off different groups (Mitchell 2000). It is also the way these patterns, processes and markers are represented and the way people organise these into hierarchies of significance or importance. Culture is thus a reflexive act of definition from inside or outside particular groups; in other words, culture is socially produced.

This definition applies usefully to the way that cultural heritage is defined. It is a medium through which identity, power, and society are produced and reproduced. Furthermore, cultural heritage is the heritage of somebody and thus, it has been forcibly argued, not the heritage of others (Tunbridge and Ashworth 1996). The historic environment is thus one manifestation of a particular set of markers of culture that has a variety of functions. For example, as discussed in Chapter 2, the very development of systems of heritage protection was intertwined with narratives of nationhood and the creation of the modern nation state, giving an explicit political function to the historic environment. Definitions and delineations of heritage emerge through debate, negotiation and struggle between different interests at a range of geographic scales. Heritage is rarely, if ever, 'neutral' and politically can be used for good or ill.

The idea of heritage extends far beyond the confines of built heritage or the historic environment. Despite Smith's recasting of heritage noted above, a common binary division is made between material and intangible heritage, the latter encompassing traditions, folk songs and so on. Material manifestations of heritage are again enormously diverse, including, for example, any of the vast range of objects that might be found in museums. This book focuses on a particular subset of this material heritage, historically known as the architectural or monumental heritage, historically reflecting a relatively discrete focus on major buildings and prehistoric monuments. However, as remarked upon above, heritage definition and conservation activity have undergone a phenomenal expansion over the last century or so, extending to a vastly wider range of material heritage. In the UK the term historic environment has been adopted to describe this, perhaps partly to avoid the term heritage, which, as I discuss later, became problematic in UK discourse. It also reflects the fact that not only buildings but just about any material artefact around us may achieve heritage status; the most recent new categories of state-protected heritage evolved in England have been for historic parks and gardens and historic battlefields.

Conservation values

The preoccupations of early conservationists were predominantly with protecting very special places for cultural reasons, which emphasised the stewardship of such places for future generations. Alois Riegl, at the time the Austrian state-appointed 'General Conservator', produced an influential early typology of heritage values in 1903 that attempted to produce a more refined understanding of the motives which lay behind the process of conservation (Jokilehto 1999). In summary, Riegl divided heritage values into two broad categories. The first was memorial values, such as age value, historical value and intended memorial value, and the second was present-day values, such as use value, art value, newness value and relative art value.

Many subsequent typologies have been produced. For example, Feilden and Jokilehto (1998) produced a typology of values for the management of World Heritage Sites, independent of the value-based criteria upon which sites are inscribed. They sustained the binary distinction employed by Riegl, distinguishing between cultural values (divided into identity value, relative artistic or technical value and rarity value) and contemporary socio-economic values (divided into economic value, functional value, educational value, social value and political value). As part of a major project on heritage values, de la Torre emphasised the division between sociocultural and economic values (Torre 2002).

Two specifically British 'official' statements on values have appeared in recent years. One was, rather unusually, produced as a British Standard (British Standards Institution 1998) and distinguished between stewardship motivations for sustaining the heritage and more contemporary cultural, economic and environmental objectives. The more recent English Heritage statements of *Conservation Principles* (English Heritage 2006; 2007) defined aesthetic, community/communal, evidential, historical and instrumental (such as economic, educational and recreational) values, though instrumental values were seen as being quite different in nature from the other 'intrinsic' values (English Heritage 2006; 2007). The British Institute of Historic Building Conservation has produced a list of twenty-three benefits gained from valuing the historic environment. Many of the traditional values in conservation were wrapped up in one category, 'intrinsic value', while the focus of much of the rest of the list stressed the economic and social benefits of heritage, including economic development and competitiveness, enhanced property values, social inclusion and local distinctiveness and pride (Institute of Historic Building Conservation 2005).

All these statements form a family of documents that seek to rationalise and justify orthodox or authorised versions of the importance of heritage protection, why it is an important activity demanding our attention. This forms what Smith (2006) has termed the 'authorized heritage discourse'. The development of modern conservation orthodoxies is the theme of Chapter 2, and it describes some of the key tenets that have evolved. Modern conservation is based upon a highly moralistic framework that stresses the importance of concepts such as authenticity. Although conservation is now often portrayed in terms of an anti-modern impulse it developed as, and remains, an intrinsically modern activity. Principles evolved principally in relation to particular buildings and monuments. Since the middle of the twentieth century architects, planners and conservationists have been struggling to translate these frameworks to, or evolve new frameworks for, the urban scale. The last part of Chapter 2 briefly discusses two of the principal frameworks that have been used in the UK to think about the management of place, townscape and urban morphology.

The espousal of conservation orthodoxy comes from the heart of the conservation movement. Chapter 7 discusses the nature of the 'conservation movement' or 'conservation community' at national and local levels and in terms of the wider public. It considers the evolution of the conservation movement and the mythology it has evolved, a central feature being its assertion that it speaks on behalf of the wider public. The second part of the chapter examines the limited empirical research that exists on the relationship between a wider public and the conservation-planning system. It concludes with a sketch of a schema of different levels of public involvement with conservation issues.

Chapter 8 considers the key articulation of authorised heritage values at the global scale: UNESCO-inscribed World Heritage Sites. Looking beyond the British experience throws relief on some of the contentious areas that are not always very visible in the UK; whether because they are absent or sublimated in Smith's 'authorized heritage discourse' is a matter of debate. The chapter considers the political function of World Heritage Sites, the impact of tourism and contestation over the 'ownership' of heritage using a range of international examples before focusing back on the UK and specifically on Blaenavon Industrial Landscape in Wales and Liverpool Commercial Centre and Waterfront.

The instrumentalisation of conservation

The development of the cultural sector, including heritage, as an 'industry' and the recognition that there are cultural, economic, political and social effects of supporting cultural programmes has led to a requirement that they must affect social and public policy outcomes, such as regeneration (Gibson and Stevenson 2004). This shift has put increasing pressure on cultural programmes to respond to (shifting) government objectives rather than responding to logics that are defined internally to the field (Strange and Whitney 2003; Pendlebury 2002). One principal driver has been the economic potential to be realised from the heritage.

A key motivation for achieving World Heritage Site status in both Blaenavon and Liverpool was the economic benefits that were assumed to follow from such status. The relationship between economic development and the conservation of the historic environment became a major focus in the UK in the 1980s and 1990s and is the principal theme of Chapter 6. Sometimes this was related to using heritage as part of focusing on cultural industries generally or 'place-marketing' (Bianchini and Parkinson 1993; Cowen 1990; Ward 1998). Increasingly, though, the focus came on the direct role of historic property, 'opportunity spaces' as I (with colleagues) have previously termed them (Pendlebury *et al.* 2004), in physical regeneration. This was evident in all kinds of locales including, for example, significant parts of city centres (Pendlebury 2002). This enhanced relationship between historic status and economic value in recent decades had also been reflected in more diffuse processes, such as the colonisation through gentrification of older housing stock.

While bodies such as English Heritage have been understandably keen to trumpet the regenerative potential of the historic environment, the development of more economically instrumental roles for the historic environment has not been pain-free for the conservation sector. The use of the historic environment as an economic good or commodity rests more on image than ideas of authenticity, central to the ideology of modern conservation. Thus the commodification of heritage and market-friendly, aesthetically constructed heritage has challenged conservation orthodoxies based upon truth to material. This postmodernisation process is one of the key themes of Chapter 9. Other products of postmodern influence on conservation practice have been more readily absorbed by the sector, such as more diverse concep- tions of protected heritage and the wider value frameworks used to establish importance, noted above.

In recent years there has been a re-emergent emphasis on the social potential of the historic environment, which had lain dormant since the 1970s. This has been evident internationally, although in the UK it has assumed distinctly New Labour dress, articulated around the key policy drivers of social inclusion/exclusion. Chapter 10 considers this growing emphasis on the instrumental social potential of heritage, together with the development of ideas about the socially constructed nature of heritage and its conservation.

Conservation in a new century

The evolution of a more critical perspective concerning the definition of heritage has naturally led to challenges to singular hegemonic definitions of heritage and its means of protection. There has been an erosion of the previously dominant notion of value understood as intrinsic to the object or environment and able to be revealed by correct processes of investigation that could only be conducted by a limited body of experts. In a pluralist democratic society, it is argued, definitions of value cannot be singular but must allow for plural interpretations and meaning.

However, the influence of such reconsiderations of value has been patchy across different academic heritage-related sub-disciplines and, thus far, has had limited impact on practice. Furthermore, it is difficult to see how the theoretical formulations of this debate will impact on the pragmatics of the conservation protection system; this is in turn embedded within the planning system, which is currently still premised on particular cultural constructions of architectural quality and historic importance.

In Chapter 11 I try to pull some of these threads together. In doing so, I seek to reflect my own positionality: my personal values and their origins. Briefly, I review how conservation planning has evolved, outline some key dimensions of conservation value, making distinctions between values concerned with the special and the ordinary, with time and place, with culture and economy, and between values that are ultimately fundamental to the conservation process and those that are more incidental in nature. The chapter then reviews what we might understand by the concept of 'good conservation' and the 'conservation community'. I argue that conservation as a practice needs to evolve reflexively; it needs to embrace new understandings of the social role of heritage and its conservation, while retaining and sustaining many of its core principles. This is a difficult challenge.

Chapter 2

Modern conservation

Introduction

This chapter explores briefly the history of conservation and the principles and practices that have developed from the eighteenth century onwards. The main emphasis is on *ideas* about conservation and, in particular, *architectural conservation*, with its focus on the individual building or monument. After a brief review of pre-eighteenth century antecedents it considers the dominant conceptions of the treatment of historic buildings that crystallised in the nineteenth century – stylistic restoration and conservative repair – the latter concept equating to the idea of 'modern conservation' (Jokilehto 1999).

The second part of the chapter then explores the relationship between modern conservation and modernity. It is part of conservation mythology that the apparent triumph of conservation as a political project in the 1970s, coinciding as it did with the downfall of architectural modernism, left a perception of conservation as antithetical to modernism. This rather simplistic conception is shared both by proponents and critics of the conservation lobby (Andreae 1996; Pawley 1998). Though conservation did become far more extensive in the wake of the collapse of modernism, it is argued that this conceals a more complex relationship with modernity. First, conservation is essentially a product of the modern age, defined as essentially stemming from the eighteenth century Enlightenment. Second, the particular approach to the treatment of historic buildings, dominant since the nineteenth century ('modern conservation' or the Ruskinian tradition), has a number of principles in common with the architectural Modern Movement. Third, though conservation existed in tension with the Modern Movement, both are closely interlinked and indeed at some periods have been pursued as one project. Finally, though modernism and the architectural Modern Movement appeared to collapse in the late 1960s and 1970s and conservation seemed to triumph, modernist concepts remain a key strand in conservation thought and action today.

In the last part of this chapter the emphasis shifts from architectural conservation to the development of thinking about the historic city and its conservation. Specifically, the focus is on the townscape tradition that has been of great influence in Britain. This is no less a modern tradition in its formation than the conservative repair movement, despite its shift in emphasis from fabric to visual composition. Finally and briefly, the discipline of urban morphology is considered, a further method of thinking about the historic city.

Principles and practice

Antecedents

The concept of 'modern conservation' became firmly established in the eighteenth century. However, there are observable antecedents, especially in Renaissance Italy where a renewed appreciation of the surviving artefacts of Imperial Rome in particular was evident. Collecting 'rediscovered' artefacts became a fashionable pursuit of rich patrons of the arts. Initially, fragments and mutilated statuary were displayed in the state in which they were found, but in the fifteenth century a trend developed for restoring statues by, for example, adding lost limbs. There was debate even from this early period about the correct treatment of such works: there were those who wanted to complete fragmented works of art to make them more pleasing, to achieve an aesthetic reintegration on the basis of conjecture over probable form; and there were others who placed greater significance on the quality of the original work itself. These debates extended to work on buildings; indeed distinctions between works of art at the scale of sculpture on the one hand, and of buildings on the other, were not clear cut. Thus there was an appreciation of the potential of both the cultural and aesthetic value of old buildings (Jokilehto 1999).

Interest in antiquity gradually spread out from Rome. An appreciation of indigenous historic buildings and artefacts began to develop throughout Europe and was evinced for example, in the seventeenth century Grand Tour of the English virtuosi. Another example was the English baroque architect Hawksmoor who, though classically trained, appreciated older Gothic buildings and argued for their retention, in particular at All Souls College, Oxford, in 1715 (Earl 2003).

Stylistic restoration versus conservation

Stylistic restoration and conservation have become a convenient dualism through which to represent a fundamental difference of thought about the appropriate treatment of historic buildings. It is potentially misleading to try and encapsulate complex debates and approaches to historic buildings, which have occurred across several hundred years and across many European countries, within two broad concepts. However, these concepts exemplify many of the competing ideas and notions. They have become especially associated with the mid-nineteenth century and with the French Eugène Emmanuel Viollet-le-Duc (stylistic restoration) – and the English John Ruskin and William Morris (conservation).

There are clear antecedents, however, for the positions advanced by Viollet-le-Duc, Ruskin and Morris. For example, in the early nineteenth century a full spectrum of treatments could be seen on major Roman monuments. So, for example, under different supervisors and administrations two distinct approaches were taken to work on the Colosseum. Initially the aim was to conserve the monument as a document from the past without any reconstruction. Later works were intended as a partial reconstruction. This represents the dialectic between conservation and stylistic restoration.

Viollet-le-Duc was an architect, whereas his English counterparts, Ruskin and Morris, were not. His most famous achievements encompass work to Vézelay, a major Romanesque church south-east of Paris (see Figure 2.1), the cathedral of Notre Dame, the fortified city of Carcassone and the castle of Pierrefonds. He believed that restorers required a good historical knowledge of architectural history and styles and that restoration was a process requiring critical assessment underpinned by systematic analysis. The aim of restoration was unity, the completion of an artistic idea. Therefore, 'To restore a building is not to preserve it, to repair, or to rebuild it; it is to reinstate it in a condition of completeness which may have never existed at any given time' (Viollet-le-Duc, 1866, cited in Jokilehto 1999: 151).

2.1
Vezelay Abbey; extensively restored and rebuilt by Viollet-le-Duc.
Source: Andrew Ballantyne.

Restoration was a creative process, and the achievement of unity could justify both removal of original fabric and any subsequent alterations. Sustaining use in buildings was important, and stylistic restoration was generally seen as more appropriate for 'living' monuments, such as churches where the original function was sustained, than for 'dead' monuments – ruins and remains from earlier civilisations. Viollet-le-Duc was recognised across Europe as a talisman of the process of stylistic restoration. He was nominated, for example, as an honorary member of the Royal Institute of British Architects.

The polemics of John Ruskin were effectively fuelled by the English equivalent of stylistic restoration, albeit rarely executed with the skill of Viollet-le-Duc. In the wake of the Gothic Revival the 1840s onwards saw the restoration of many historic buildings, and of ecclesiastical buildings in particular. Groups such as the Ecclesiological Society promoted the restoration of churches to their supposed original and best Gothic form, most often Decorated or Middle Pointed, sometimes Early English. Though buildings were often amalgams of different periods, preference was given to restoration in one particular style. George Gilbert Scott is often considered to be the English equivalent of Viollet-le-Duc, if for no other reason than the extensiveness of his commissions and practice. The comparison is reasonable: though Scott often advocated a more conservative approach in print, he tended to be interventionist in practice. For this he was often vilified, although he was by no means the most extreme exponent of restoration.

The reaction against restoration came initially, and principally, from Ruskin, a non-architect, a prolific and polemical polymath, and perhaps most notable as an art critic. This was not an alternative architectural creed but a critical reaction and it remained essentially a campaigning programme for some time. His key work of relevance was *The Lamp of Memory* in *The Seven Lamps of Architecture* (Ruskin 1849 (1886)). Ruskin believed a historic building was the unique creation of an artisan or artist. This material truth was central. Old fabric rather than modern replica was fundamental. Restoration and the removal of historic fabric were thus an act of destruction: '(Restoration) means the most total destruction which a building can suffer: a destruction out of which no remnants can be gathered . . .' (Ruskin 1849 (1886): 194).

Following Ruskin, anti-restoration was gradually taken up by others, including Sidney Colvin, Slade Professor of Fine Arts at Cambridge, and some architects such as J. J. Stevenson. Critical, however, was the intervention of William Morris. It was Gilbert Scott's restoration proposals for Tewkesbury Abbey that prompted Morris to write to *The Athenaeum* in March 1877 suggesting an association to act as a watchdog over such works. Within less than a month this had led to the formation of the Society for the Protection of Ancient Buildings (SPAB) by Morris together with other prominent anti-restorationists such as Ruskin and Colvin. Morris drafted a manifesto for the new society that became a benchmark for conservation practice and that remains an influential architectural conservation document today – 'the rock on which all modern conservation philosophies are founded' (Earl 2003: 25). Protection of historic buildings was to be based not on style but on a critical evaluation of the building, and historic buildings relied for their authenticity on their material fabric. Removing this, or restoring it or copying it would lead to a loss of authenticity and the creation of a fake.

SPAB had an important role in uniting those opposed to conjectural restoration and promoting maintenance and conservationist treatment. This was its key contribution: the principles outlined in the manifesto had all been articulated previously. Its formation crystallised conservation as a political movement. Dominated by non-architects it was first and foremost a campaigning body, initially in opposition to those with a different vision of the appropriate treatment of historic buildings. This was quickly to broaden and extend into a wider role, promoting the significance of architectural cultural heritage and campaigning against the demolition of buildings of a wide range of types, far beyond the initial focus on ecclesiastical buildings. It has been questioned whether or not the initial confrontational approach adopted by SPAB was effective in its early years in achieving its aims (Miele 1996), but this deliberate separation from vested interests in the architectural profession and the church was a distinctive feature. Early campaigns included unsuccessful resistance to the major restoration of St Albans Abbey by Lord Grimethorpe. More successful was the campaign against the rebuilding of the west front of San Marco in Venice, though whether this was due to the influence of SPAB is a matter of debate (Miele 1996; Jokilehto 1999).

One of the defining characteristics of 'modern conservation' is the stress that it places on a moral and ethical approach. Morris and the formation of SPAB played an important part in beginning to move conservation from an 'ethics-orientated' morality (Foucault 2000), individualistic in nature, to a morality that has become more closely related to codes of behaviour and subsequently, in the twentieth century, to charters, laws and policies which seek to enforce these codes. In other words, this is a shift from the Ruskin polemic to the didactic instruction of the Venice Charter (see below). Conservation principles of action are perceived as founded upon the key uniting factor of integrity (Warren 1996). Another fundamental concept at the heart of modern conservation is *authenticity*, which is discussed further below.

Competition between conservative repair and restoration approaches has continued to the present day. Within different countries the stress has varied. According to Jokilehto (1999), in England and Italy the emphasis has been on conservation, in France on restoration. Italian architects have influenced the development of international codes of practice, which have emphasised a broadly conservative approach. Efforts to formulate internationally agreed standards started in the twentieth century with the 1931 Athens Charter (see Jokilehto 1999) (not to be confused with the other Athens Charter following the fourth congress on modern architecture in 1933). This advocated abandoning stylistic restoration and favoured conservation and maintenance of monuments that respected the styles of all periods. The successor to the Athens Charter was the 1964 Venice Charter (ICOMOS 1964), adopted by the newly formed International Council on Monuments and Sites and still a key document today. It is discussed further below. It was the first of many adopted by ICOMOS, designed to impose a certain 'way of seeing' and create an international convergence on a view of what constitutes acceptable action.

The next section discusses the relationship between conservation and modernity. The focus is on 'modern conservation', rather than stylistic restoration, as this became the dominant ideology, if not always the dominant practice, in the UK at least. However, although the discussion is concerned with conservation, stylistic restoration is no less modern a concept and a similar analysis would be possible. Bitter though the debates have been historically between opposing camps in the restoration versus conservation discourse, both are essentially operating within the same broad framework of modernity. Differences in the definition of the object, i.e. the architectural form of the building versus the historicity of the building embodied in its fabric, are at the root of the debate. However, there is no fundamental difference of opinion over which buildings are conceived to have historic value, or in the significance placed on heritage.

Conservation and modernity

For the purposes of this discussion we need to distinguish between a general process of modernism (defined here as 'modernity') and the specifically architectural Modern Movement. Modernity is taken to be a broad movement rooted in the Enlightenment period of eighteenth century Europe, drawing upon ideas of western thought from the earlier Renaissance, and the classical ideas that in turn informed that Renaissance. There was a broad social purpose of human emancipation, focused on the rights of individuals, and the enrichment of daily life. These goals would be achieved through the potential of an objective science and rational forms of organisation, underpinned by a universal morality (Harvey 1990; Healey 2006). The significance of scientific method is evident in the work of Johann Joachim Winckelmann. A Prussian, he became Chief Commissioner of Antiquities in Rome in 1763. The value he perceived in works of antiquity led him to develop a systematic survey method of all relevant objects, whether sculptures, paintings or architectural monuments. It also led him to distinguish new works from original fabric, an important principle for the conservative repair movement. Winckelmann has been called the 'father of archaeology' and he contributed to the development of modern art history (Jokilehto 1999).

Though the benefits were regarded as universal, in artistic terms this process came to be seen as led by avant-garde (Jencks 1996) or groups of elite experts. Art theory made artists into 'High Priests in a secularized society' (Pevsner 1960). It was a movement that was essentially secular and progressive, in the sense of seeking to break with history and tradition. It is this last characteristic of modernity that is most obviously in potential conflict with the process of conservation, although at the same time providing the stimulus for conservation thought and action. For example, while facilitating the industrial revolution, the Enlightenment (or 'Age of Reason') also contributed to other processes, including the development of a modern historical consciousness and the nation-state. The new relationships with culture and religion, with nature and environment, generated new conceptions of time. History came to be interpreted as a collective social experience which recognised that different cultures and places had different natures. Historicity, the belief that each period in history has its own beliefs and values, led to a consideration of works of art and of historic buildings as unique, and so worthy of conservation as an expression of a particular culture and a reflection of national identity (Jokilehto 1999). Furthermore, though the origins of the nation-state lie earlier, the concept crystallised in this period, aided by such traumatic events as the French Revolution. A more strongly defined nationalism, based around the territorial unit of the nation-state, demanded both a process of building identity and a common national heritage (Graham et al. 2000). Thus various European countries developed legal frameworks and heritage bureaucracies to protect national heritage, though Britain was a late entrant in this process. At the same time there was a developing view that cultural heritage might have a universal value to mankind.

Glendinning has argued that modernity has a double nature. Co-existing with open, dynamic modernity with its push for newness and change is 'traditionalism', which seeks to 'harness change and re-cement identity by appealing to the authority of traditions' (Glendinning 2000: 13). Heritage is integral to this. Though it may appear to be an anti-modern reaction it is just as modern an idea and, it is argued, lies in a symbiotic relationship with dynamic modernity. Traditionalism exists in the same discourse or narrative. It relies on concepts of historical change and human ability to control events in a way that is intrinsically modern. Along similar lines Brett argued that,

> it is no longer sufficient to describe the backward glance of
> nineteenth century culture as reactionary, escapist or anti-modern

> ... it is as integral to the experience of modernisation, (as) ... what appears to be its opposite. A modern culture ... is always Janus-faced, looking both backward and forward, never fully settled in the present.
>
> (Brett 1996: 26)

The painful process of primary industrialisation was accompanied by an idealisation of imagined pasts. 'This preoccupation could and did exist simultaneously with radical innovation, even in the same mind' (Brett 1996: 15). He linked this to the nineteenth century concern with 'national character' as part of the process of nation-building. The distant past was invoked and traditions were invented, such as royal pageants, as part of this construction of national heritages. Dellheim showed, in the context of Victorian England, how traditions were mobilised flexibly and selectively to support divergent points of view and how heritage was used to reinforce both local and national identity (Dellheim 1982).

Thus conservation is inherently 'modern' for two reasons. First, it is a reaction to the threat caused by progressive modernity and the change (whether aesthetic or social) that this implies. The impetus towards conservation and conscious selection and retention of buildings expands with each move to demolish or alter these buildings. It is bound into a complex dialectic with change, and used to affirm the continuity and stability necessary for nationhood. Second, conservationists are people of the modern age. Their concepts of history and cultural value and their methods of pursuing their goals are as intrinsically modern as those of the promoters of change. For example, from an early period they have relied on ideas of selection and classification, eventually expressed in state-defined and controlled lists, and on principles of conservation which, though morally based, can be rationally applied by a skilled elite.

Key figures, such as Ruskin, are bound into this framework of modernity. He was in many ways violently anti-modern in his critique of the consequences of the industrial revolution and industrial society (Wiener 1981) and medievalist in terms not only of his architectural preferences but also of those forms of societal organisation that he felt could address the ills of industrial society. However, these views stemmed from a well-developed modern historicity. It was Ruskin 'who equated visible history, social memory, tradition, the perennial, the timeless, with the great monuments of architecture. Architecture thus became the embodiment of the collective memory of a society, the living memory of a community persisting through generations' (Cianci 2001: 144). Critical, in his case, was the material truth of historic architecture, which has remained a fundamental precept of architectural conservation. This was the nation's heritage, not the modern replica. Both

Ruskin and subsequently William Morris, in their concern for preservation of particular structures, were expressing ideas about English identity. Both were medievalists. In addition to their well-known concern for ecclesiastical buildings they focused their attention on older, often relatively modest country houses, representative of a kind of yeoman England.

Conservation and the Modern Movement

The Modern Movement was essentially the architectural consequence of the broader process of modernity, albeit one that did not fully flower until the twentieth century. It gained prominence in the period following the First World War. Although it became the dominant idea in the architectural profession of what architecture should be, it was never the dominant building form. Modernist ideals and architecture were promoted through the *Congrès internationaux d'architecture moderne* (CIAM) and such talismanic figures as Le Corbusier. It can be characterised by its use of non-traditional materials, avoidance of ornamentation and, significantly for this discussion, its avoidance of historical associations. The Modern Movement, like the conservation movement, was highly moralistic. They share principles such as the stress on authenticity and honesty of expression, and truth to structure and materials.

Chroniclers of the Modern Movement have stressed the functional honesty of engineered structures from the era of the industrial revolution. Pevsner (1960) started his chronology of modern designers with Thomas Telford. Giedion, as part of the broad sweep of his modernist classic *Space, Time and Architecture* (1941), emphasised the profound impact of industrialisation. For him an important development in the second half of the nineteenth century was the reaction against architectural eclecticism and the search for a true building form of the time. For Gideon this was a demand for morality in architecture, and one of the key developments in this regard was the commissioning from Philip Webb in 1859 of the Red House by William Morris.

A historical perspective meant that historic architecture could be valued as part of the historical story leading to the present: historic buildings should be selectively retained as demonstrations of previous artistic achievement along the march of progress. In the UK Pevsner and Summerson, notable architectural historians and conservationists, were also firm advocates of modernism. Historic buildings were especially valued when seen to have qualities that accorded with contemporary values. Thus, as British modernism evolved in the 1930s, it did so in parallel with a growing appreciation of Georgian building, valued for its urbaneness and relative simplicity. Membership of the Modern Architectural Research (MARS) Group overlapped significantly with the Georgian Group.

The fracture between modernists and conservationists only really became a major schism in the mid 1960s: amongst the leading opponents of the demolition of the Euston Arch (a landmark of conservationist history) in the early 1960s were the modernist architects the Smithsons (Smithson and Smithson 1968). It was the shift from a conservation focus on iconic monuments to wider development struggles that opened the gap. Wright has argued that this led in turn to a conservation revivalist fable whereby all the manifestations of post-war Britain and the Welfare State, including its architecture, were vilified, and to the creation of a reactionary classicism as an alternative (Wright 1992). While this is undoubtedly an oversimplification of the rise of the conservation movement, subsequent validation as heritage through the 'listing' of such buildings as the massive deck-access housing scheme of Park Hill in Sheffield and of 1960s commercial buildings such as the Rotunda in Birmingham (see Figure 2.2), initially created tensions and challenged the internal dynamics of the conservation movement.

2.2
The listing of the Modern Movement: the Rotunda, Birmingham.
Source: author.

Architectural conservation principles today

Ideas about the nature of architectural conservation crystallised by Ruskin, Morris and SPAB have an enduring relevance today. Though these ideas have evolved and been codified in various ways they bear a strong relation to early formulations and show a direct ancestry of development. Emphasis is placed upon the authenticity of material fabric and also upon its aesthetic qualities; much less attention is given to historic association. The moral precepts relating to notions such as honesty and authenticity endure.

Ruskin and Morris were not professionals engaged in architectural conservation. However, throughout the twentieth century the practice of architectural conservation became more professionalised, codified and self-conscious about the benefits of scientific method. It also became more distinct as a specific sphere of professional expertise. A. R. Powys was a significant British figure in this process. Secretary of SPAB, his *Repair of Ancient Buildings* (Powys 1929, reprinted 1995) was considered for many decades to be the definitive manual for conservation practice. Based on SPAB principles it emphasised the importance of both systematic processes such as condition surveys and the specialised nature of skills required by conservation repair work. He was also a modernist, reinforcing the idea that interventions should be 'of their time' and writing about how tradition should inform recognisably modern architecture.

Codification can be traced clearly through a series of key international and British statements on conservation, starting with the Athens Charter for the Restoration of Historic Monuments in 1931 (Jokilehto 1999). A particularly significant benchmark in this respect was the 1964 Venice Charter (ICOMOS 1964), formulated at the International Congress of Architects and Technicians of Historic Monuments and adopted at its founding by the International Council on Monuments and Sites, an international grouping of conservation professionals. This charter emphasised the material authenticity of historic monuments. Though it allowed for a degree of restoration, it forbade conjectural restoration and stressed that valid contributions from all periods of building should be respected. It also reinforced the need for a systematic and scientific approach. In the UK, English Heritage's *Principles of Repair* (English Heritage 1991) presented similar principles, as does the more recent British Standard (British Standards Institution 1998). This latter document made reference to benefits to the wider community of the conservation of historic buildings and to the Burra Charter, adopted by ICOMOS in Australia in 1979, which introduced a significant shift in the evaluation of values in conservation. This is discussed in Chapter 10.

The idea of authenticity is central to the ideology of conservation described above. The importance of the concept led to a specific ICOMOS charter (ICOMOS 1994) arising from an international conference at Nara, Japan (Larsen 1995). The Nara Document spells out some fundamental considerations:

> Conservation of cultural heritage in all its forms and historical periods is rooted in the values attributed to heritage. Our ability to understand these values depends, in part, on the degree to which information sources about these values may be understood as credible or truthful
>
> (Paragraph 9)

and

> Authenticity . . . appears as the essential qualifying factor concerning values.
>
> (Paragraph 10)

Assi explicitly placed the idea of authenticity in a modern context, contrasting it with the concept of continuing reproduction in traditional societies (Assi 2000). Furthermore, 'To be authentic does not give value per se; rather it should be understood as the condition of an object or a monument in relation to its specific qualities. . . . Authenticity cannot be added to the subject; it can be revealed only in so far as it exists.' (Assi 2000: 60–1).

However, though emphasis on authenticity of material fabric is strong within the Western tradition this is not the only interpretation of the concept. It is perhaps no coincidence that the Nara Document was drawn up in Japan, where a quite different tradition exists. Regular demolition and rebuilding of key national monuments, particularly Shinto shrines, occurs in some cases. Authenticity rests not in the material fabric but in the continuation of the building tradition and techniques and in sustaining the continuing use (Larkham 1996). For example, at the main Shinto shrine, Ise Jingu, the house of God Amaterasu is rebuilt as part of a ceremony called *shikinen sengu*, a practice that has continued for 1300 years (see Figure 2.3). The new environment is held to purify the mind. Conservation is carried out through the ceremony (including destroying old and building new) in which the old generation pass on their roles to young ones (Anonymous 2007). Even in the West, quite different practices have been accepted. The rebuilding of Warsaw along historic lines after the Second World War ultimately led to its inscription as a World Heritage Site in 1980 for its expression of the national identity of the Polish people (Jankowski 1990; Jokilehto 1999).

The development of the discipline as a distinct canon of professional knowledge and values has also been advanced by individual writings. For

2.3
A detail of the Shinto shrine at Ise, Japan. The main shrine is rebuilt every twenty years.
Source: Mark Shucksmith.

example, the British conservator Sir Bernard Feilden, a former director of the International Centre for the Study of the Preservation and the Restoration of Cultural Property (ICCROM), in *Conservation of Historic Buildings* outlined a series of 'ethics' of conservation (Feilden 1994; 2003). These were based partly around technical practices, such as the proper surveying and recording of buildings prior to intervention, and partly on the principles justifying intervention, such as minimum interference and the reversibility of interventions made. The expert role of architectural conservators was stressed, not purely for technical skills but because, it was argued, of their more refined intellectual skills, aesthetic appreciation and judgement. This influences both what we conserve and how we go about it. Many relatively recent sources could be cited; two examples are given here.

Warren (1996) explored the principles of architectural conservation. He regarded decision-making as a complex but rational analytical process requiring skilful judgement: 'The subtlety and complexity of these interactions demand that conservation is treated, taught and understood as an art on which the application of intellectual endeavour imposes refinement in providing its rationale' (Warren 1996: 40).

Judgement is needed over ethical matters (equated with the intellect) and aesthetic matters (equated with the emotions). Thus, it was argued, a conservation project may be aesthetically pleasing but deceitful, or vice versa. For Warren, both ethics and aesthetics are important, but ultimately ethics (and the intellect) predominate. The most important criterion for conservation work is that it must be truthful and have integrity.

Earl (2003) covered similar ground. He discursively expounded a philosophy of conservative repair and emphasis on authenticity. He stated that,

> Very few really new issues are being discussed in the first decade of the twenty first century which were not being agonised over in the nineteenth century by the Scrape and Anti-Scrape factions, by Viollet-le-Duc, Ruskin, Scott, Morris and Lubbock and their contemporaries.
>
> (Earl 2003: xii)

2.4
A conservatively repaired Roman column, next to York Minster, with new work undertaken in brick.
Source: author.

Though Earl regarded legitimacy for conservation as stemming from public support, decision-making was seen as the preserve of experts. For example, he discussed the practice of façadism, of retaining the front or exterior walls of a building while reconstructing the interior. He made a distinction between professionals who specialise in the practice and 'genuine conservation experts', i.e. those professionals who share his values. In discussing more broadly the form that interventions in historic fabric should take, he stated that, 'The ideal repair/replacement, in my view, is one which the expert can detect fairly quickly and the inexpert will see when attention has been drawn to it' (Earl 2003: 82, 110).

The traditional architect Robert Adam has attacked conservation orthodoxy for the modernist ideology that underpins conservation principles such as outlined in the charters discussed above (Adam 1998; 2003). He has criticised the emphasis placed upon material authenticity or archaeological evidence, the anti-restoration position that tends to follow and the preoccupation with academic values and 'experts'. Perhaps above all he dislikes a principle that unites modern conservation and the Modern Movement: that interventions at either the scale of the individual building or the urban scale, in order to be authentic expressions 'of their time', have somehow to be separate from historical precedent. Thus, referring to the sort of post-war reconstruction discussed in Chapter 3 he contrasted the 'dishonest' restoration of St Malo favourably with the modernist reconstruction of Plymouth. This can perhaps be summarised as a lament at the fracture of connection with living tradition, which he seeks to sustain in his own architectural work.

Contemporary conservation practice is heavily 'modernist' in nature. A major part of its rationale derives from modernist concepts of historicity and its links to national identity. Our rationale for conserving remains underpinned by a Ruskinian morality of regarding fabric as a material testament to the continuity of the nation (Glendinning 2001a). Expert judgement identifies what to protect against supposedly rational criteria and consequently produces codified lists and schedules. The criteria for selection are organised around progressive concepts of society and built form, for example by listing the principal buildings of the principal architects, or by placing weight on 'first of type', now embracing the architectural Modern Movement too. Furthermore, as we can see from the above examples, architectural conservation action is underpinned by a set of values derived from a distinctly modern morality. Finally, the development of conservation is also a response to the impetus for change arising from other strands of modernity.

One note of qualification we need to introduce at this point is that conservation is not a homogenous activity; neither are its promoters a homogeneous group. For example, the interest in the 1930s in protecting urban Georgian buildings from metropolitan modernists started as a grouping within

SPAB (before breaking away to form the Georgian Group), which at the time was mostly characterised by a rather tweedy and nostalgic focus on the countryside. The conservation movement is a coalition containing quite disparate views (Hobson 2004) and has undergone a number of evolutions and shifts in focus, something discussed further in Chapter 7.

The conservation of place

The 'conservative repair' approach has dominated, and continues to dominate, architectural conservation for over a hundred years. However, the principles that have been discussed were developed primarily with either the individual building or monument in mind, retained for its artistic merit and archaeological worth. As town planning activity extended across the historic city in the post-war period, intensified during the 1960s and reordered to a much more conservation-based approach following the rejection of architectural modernism, conservation objectives increasingly had to be articulated at very different scales – at the level of a city, town, village or smaller area within these. Internationally, very different responses occurred in addressing this issue. For example, some major reconstructions of historic cities followed modernist principles of reordering urban space, and the implementation of these approaches in the 1960s was one of the reasons for the loss of faith in architectural modernism. There have also been variations of approach that seek to recreate historic forms. This includes the different approaches taken at Warsaw and St Malo, as mentioned above. It has also included more recent examples: the rebuilding or 'retroversion' of the historic Polish town of Elblag following historic plot lines but using post-modern architectural forms (Johnson 2000); the painstaking replica of historic buildings in Hildesheim, Germany, replacing 1950s functional buildings that had been built on the site of previous historic buildings (Jokilehto 1999); and the replacement of unpopular post-war buildings in Canterbury, England, with buildings of historic appearance but not following any specific historic precedent (Jagger 1998).

Emphasis on methods of conservation at the urban scale developed in the post-war period, and this is discussed in greater detail in the next chapter. It became a major issue in the 1960s, partly in response to the degree of transformation that was being wrought on towns and cities throughout the western world. In addition to responses within individual countries, such as the legislation enabling the designation of conservation areas in the UK (the Civic Amenities Act 1967), international bodies began to focus their concern and efforts on the issue. Two important international declarations were made in the mid 1970s: one by the Council of Europe, the Amsterdam Declaration (Council of Europe 1975); the other by UNESCO from its meeting in Nairobi

(UNESCO 1976). Subsequently, a counterpart to the Venice Charter was adopted for historic areas by ICOMOS in 1987, the far less well-known Washington Charter (ICOMOS 1987). All three statements echoed established 'scientific' principles, emphasising the importance of research and of sustaining authenticity. However, they extended discussion into areas beyond the traditional concerns of architectural conservation debate. In part this related to the object of conservation: for example, the Washington Charter emphasised the significance of urban morphology. However, of at least equal significance was a concern with process issues and the wider social relevance of conservation as an activity. All emphasised the importance of the integration between conservation and town planning at the urban scale, the significance of public opinion and support, and the need for works of conservation to be socially progressive. For example, the Nairobi statement was concerned that conservation works should not lead to displacement through gentrification and the Washington Charter stated baldly, 'The improvement of housing should be one of the basic objectives of conservation' (paragraph 9).

From a 'modern conservation' perspective, one of the difficulties of conservation at the urban scale is the translation of the notion of authenticity to this spatial scale. In seeking to conserve an ever-changing city, authenticity cannot just rest on the integrity of individual buildings and monuments. This was acknowledged during the discussions on the Nara Document, which recognised the need for urban areas to evolve and experience sociocultural change (Assi 2000). Conservation becomes not so much the protection of architectural fabric but a key element in the processes of urban management. Different commentators have struggled with this issue. Zancheti and Jokilehto (1997: 39) concluded that the objective of conservation now extends beyond material authenticity to include 'the maintenance of the historical integrity of cultures within a given urban structure'. Jiven and Larkham stated that: 'the overall 'character and appearance' . . . could be more important, to more people, than authenticity of original materials' (Jiven and Larkham 2003: 77).

Thus the issue of authenticity at an urban scale remains problematic for modern conservation, not least because of the fundamental need from this perspective to embrace change, even if the extent and form of this change remains difficult to define. The alternative is described by terms such as 'museumification' or 'Disneyfication'. These are pejorative terms for approaches that either resist all change or only accommodate change that involves reproduction of historic forms and styles. The historical perspective at the heart of orthodox conservation denies that urban management or change in this way is the authentic expression of contemporary culture. This is the very form of ideology that Robert Adam has challenged (see above). I now move to look briefly at two forms of method that have been applied to the conservation of places: townscape and urban morphology.

Townscape

The authenticity of fabric has been the principal ideological construct of conservation thinking in Britain for the last century and more. Aesthetic factors and picturesque composition have also been significant, however, and these are recurrent themes in English architecture and town planning in particular. The significance of the picturesque and visual to English design and architecture has been noted by writers across the generations (Pevsner 1956; Bandini 1992; Esher 1981). These broader disciplines have been important in the management of the historic environment, especially where the scale of consideration shifted from the architectural object to wider ensembles of buildings and to 'places'.

The emphasis in Britain on the appreciation of the informal, often accidental, aesthetic qualities of compositions of groups of buildings is again frequently linked with the Enlightenment period and traced back to eighteenth-century English landscape design. This encompasses, for example, the concepts of the 'picturesque' and the 'sublime', terms taken from painting composition. It is both present and embodied within the aesthetic sensibilities of Ruskin and Morris, with, for example, Ruskin's emphasis on 'sweetness of line', the asymmetries of medieval architecture and interest in the vernacular traditions of rural England. The significance of visual qualities is also evident, for example, in the countryside preservation battles of the 1930s, including the struggles to protect the settings of iconic archaeological monuments (Sheail 1981b).

This emphasis on informal visual effect is evident also in the development of ideas about town planning. For example, Raymond Unwin's influential book, *Town Planning in Practice: An Introduction to the Art of Designing Cities and Suburbs* (Unwin 1909, reprinted 1971) emphasised three-dimensional composition and a love of the picturesque and the vernacular. Unwin was influenced by practice in the German-speaking world. Particularly significant was the Austrian town planner Camillo Sitte and his key text, *City Planning According to Artistic Fundamentals* (Sitte 1889 (1945)), albeit Unwin's appreciation of Sitte's work was apparently limited as a full translation into English did not occur until the 1940s (Collins and Collins 1986). Though Sitte proposed guidelines for building new urban areas, this guidance was rooted in the study, analysis and appreciation of historic towns. He conceived of the city as a work of architecture and town planning and as a three-dimensional activity, and in the picturesque effects of the medieval city he discerned a conscious planning and creation of artistic effect. He had a preference for limited panoramas, rather than grand Baroque display. Cities were organised around space, with the major architectural works, such as churches, built-in rather than separated out as isolated monuments. He had a particular fascination for plazas and a preference for linked chains of dissimilar shaped spaces. His extensive use of historical precedent was geared towards an understanding of the creation of picturesque effect; it was not the systematic study of an urban morphologist (see below). He also had an interest in the preservation of the places he studied (Collins and Collins 1986). Sitte had a significant influence on the Townscape Movement in British practice, although Thomas Sharp, one of its originators, was unkind in his evaluation of Sitte (Sharp 1932).

Though the term townscape had existed in broadly its modern definition since the 1880s (Whistler and Reed 1994), Sharp was the first writer or planner of his generation to use the term in his plan for Oxford (Sharp 1948). Previously, in *The Anatomy of the Village* (Sharp 1946a), he set out principles of development and neighbourliness for creating new villages and new parts of villages using a townscape approach, considering such issues as arrangement of buildings, plan forms of settlements and architectural character. Sharp, and to some degree other planners of his generation, also deployed townscape ideas in the 'reconstruction plans' for British cities discussed in the next chapter.

Ideas about townscape are often also associated with a series of articles published in the *Architectural Review*, from the late 1940s onwards. This initiated with contributions written by the owner H. de C. Hastings and influenced by Pevsner (Erten 2002). This led from 1949 to Gordon Cullen's Townscape Notebook and culminated in his book *Townscape* (Cullen 1961). In rationalising the visual environment, Sharp, Cullen and others sought to take an intrinsically modern and rational approach to the evolution of place. Though historical examples were used in these analyses of townscape character, the

2.5
Harmony in diversity: Stamford, Lincolnshire (from Sharp 1968).
© Edwin Smith/RIBA Library Photographs Collection.

analyses themselves were in essence manifestos for urban design for architects and others involved in the creation and modification of urban environments, and not for the conservation of historic places.

Cullen's seminal text was followed in the 1960s by two other influential books that extended ideas of townscape more indirectly into conservation practice. Sharp's *Town and Townscape* (1968) was not a book with an especially militant conservation position; preservation was advocated only where it was seen to be highly important in historic or aesthetic terms. However, the idea of 'character' of place was important for Sharp. The character of places should be conserved, even where the material fabric was not. Character was a concept that Sharp and other planners had been using in their plans since the 1940s. It was conceived principally in terms of sensory experience, not only in visual terms but also, for example, in experiencing places free from excessive traffic. The concept of character was vague and remains so, and is perhaps part of the attraction to planners who can mobilise it to suit their own particular purposes. It helped in the development of the idea of conservation as the management of change: change could be justified if character was sustained.

It was only with Worskett's *The Character of Towns* (Worskett 1969) that townscape methodologies were systematically and extensively applied to conservation issues. Worskett separated townscape conservation from preservation, and though both were regarded as important and legitimate activities, it is with the former that he concerned himself. The semantic distinction between conservation and preservation, established in the 1960s, has become an important element of British practice. Preservation was presented as a static concept applicable to a limited monumental heritage, 'preservation as found', whereas conservation was held to be both a broader and more dynamic concept, a process of managing change while sustaining the essential qualities of place.

Worksett (1969: 7) argued that conservation was 'much more than simply preserving historic buildings'; for him it encompassed the whole quality of the environment, including the insertion of new buildings. Fundamental to townscape conservation was the management of change integrated with a comprehensive planning approach. The principles to be employed in managing urban areas, such as maintaining enclosure, were clearly derived from the townscape tradition. Again it was an analytical approach that privileged visual composition: the significance of factors such as a town's plan was mentioned but principally in terms of their effect on visual appearance. Stress was placed upon understanding the particularities of place, or local distinctiveness. It was the job of the expert, and principally the architect, to undertake these analyses.

Thus, though townscape is a set of principles and techniques principally to aid the creation of form, there are some clear resonances with notions of conservation, not least because conservation at the urban scale involves accommodating change and new design in some form. Baumann's analysis of townscape principles included, for example, 'significant differentiation' (place distinctiveness), 'character', 'sense of place' and 'context', all of which chime quite happily with usual ideas about urban conservation (Baumann 1997).

Townscape as an urban design methodology has been much criticised for its superficialness and over-emphasis on visual composition (Hillier and Hanson 1984; Punter and Carmona 1997; Ley 1989) Similarly, Baumann argued that, despite the complementarities, it is in itself a problematic tool for deployment in the practice of modern conservation. Key to this, he argued, is a lack of emphasis on what might be termed a 'scientific approach'. For example, no great stress is placed upon either research, documentation or, crucially, on authenticity. Its originators sought to give principles and method to underpin a better quality of urban development. Though much of what they espoused would seem compatible with conventional ideas about what makes a good historic townscape, in itself townscape advances no particular view on matters of architectural design or, more importantly on the balance between preservation and change. Originators, such as Sharp, never advocated the retention of relatively commonplace buildings in historic areas and would have been appalled by its use to legitimate the reproduction of historic styles of architecture. Baumann's view was that townscape provides a more robust method to aid modern conservation when synthesised with urban morphology.

Urban morphology

Analysis of urban morphology, or urban form, has had much less impact on British conservation practice than the visual analysis emphasised in townscape approaches. The study of urban morphology is a branch of historical geography. Its key origins are again Germanic and early twentieth century, though this time academic, through scholars such Schlüter (Larkham 1996). The key figure in introducing and furthering the study of urban morphology in Britain was M. R. G. Conzen, an émigré from the Nazis in the 1930s. He was known principally for his work on towns with a medieval plan, such as Alnwick (Conzen 1960), though the systematic study of the evolution of urban form is an approach that in principle could be applied to any settlement. Conzen was also interested in the application of his work to conservation (Conzen 1975). His conservation principles show remarkable coincidence with the ideas being espoused by such as Worskett. His understanding of the continuing change and evolution of urban form made him emphasise the management of change rather than preservation and the importance of the whole of a settlement rather than isolated buildings

2.6
Elements of the town plan (Newcastle upon Tyne) by MRG Conzen (from Whitehand 1981).
Reproduced from the Ordnance Survey map with the permission of the Controller of Her Majesty's Stationery Office, Crown copyright reserved.

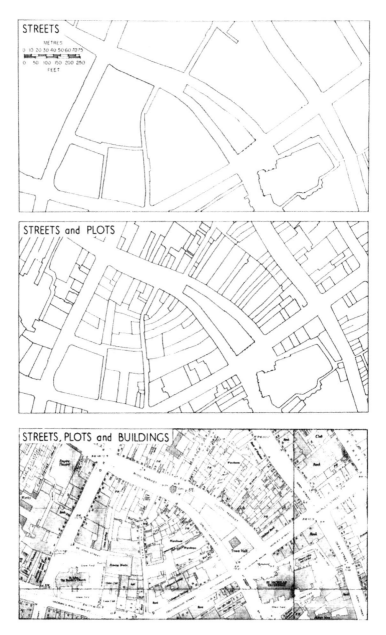

of special merit. In his prescriptions for Alnwick, he advocated preserving existing street spaces and continuous street fronts, removing traffic by constructing a bypass and finding alternative uses for buildings. However, unlike the work of the promoters of townscape, the work of Conzen remained largely unknown until 'rediscovered' and promoted by a number of geographers such as Whitehand (1981).

Mageean divided the geographic academic study of urban morphology, and its analytical approach, from those who use it as a tool in changing and creating fabric in a process of urban design, as indeed formulated by Conzen (Mageean 1998). Later in the 1980s the influence of urban morphological factors in defining conservation policies and values began to be seen. For example, English Heritage and local authorities introduced policies that specifically identified both the town plan and some of its components, such as burgage plots, as possessing a value worthy of protection: an extremely detailed morphological study apparently underpins recent design guidance in Stratford-upon-Avon (English Heritage 1988; Jiven and Larkham 2003; Stratford-upon-Avon District Council 2001).

It has been argued that urban morphology is a suitable platform on which to build a practical theory of conservation and management of historic areas (Larkham and Chapman 1996; Mageean 1998). Larkham argued it to be conceptually useful in three key ways. First, it emphasises the need for some continuity in built form. Second, it addresses the historic evolution of place, although Larkham acknowledged that the very detailed and intensive studies which are characteristic of academic urban morphology are unlikely to be practical for everyday planning use. Third, it provides an analytical framework – the division of the urban landscape into a hierarchy of streets, plots and buildings – which could be useful in understanding and monitoring change as part of the decision-making process. It is the rigour and historical grounding of urban morphology that make Baumann consider it a suitable basis for urban conservation when synthesised with the visual analysis of townscape (Baumann 1997).

Modern conservation

This chapter has briefly described the evolution of the practice of urban conservation and its extension from objects to areas. It has discussed how it developed as, and remains, very much a modern process, despite its frequent characterisation as anti-modern. Very specific sets of principles have evolved to deal with the definition of appropriate conservation at the level of the individual building or monument, but these have struggled to translate adequately to wider urban areas. The translation of conservation into an established and integral part of urban planning came with the loss of faith in modernist transformation in the late 1960s and early 1970s. Although generally lauded as a triumph for the conservation movement, this shift introduced some fissures with its modernist heritage and some weakening in terms of an overall sense of purpose given the startling diversity of protected heritage evident today. Chapter 4 and Chapter 9 return to the ways modernist conservation both adapted to changing circumstances and became subject to post modern influences and pressures.

Conservation has become a diverse practice, and conservationists are now a diverse group of people. Conservation has broadened such that Worskett could write, as long ago as 1982, 'Conservation is in as much danger from itself as it is from the old enemies of speculation, inhuman planning and insensitive architecture' (Worskett 1982: 151).

The varied motivations for advocating a policy of conservation and the benefits held to accrue as a result are something to which I return throughout the book. However, in the meantime, the next chapter looks more closely at the evolution of the relationship between conservation and planning between the 1920s and the 1960s.

Chapter 3

Policies and plans
The development of state intervention

Introduction

The emphasis in this chapter is upon the emerging relationship between conservation and town planning from the 1920s to the 1960s; from a period when an agitation for a comprehensive and effective conservation system developed, to the introduction of conservation areas through the 1967 Civic Amenities Act. The role of the state was transformed in this period from being a bystander to becoming a provider and implementer of a comprehensive conservation system.

There is a particular focus upon how ideas about the historic city translated to local level. What we encounter is a series of master plans, prepared by planners with their expert-knows-best certainties, seeking to balance the pressures of the twentieth century with the historic nature of the cities in which they were working. The balance between continuity and change, and the form that necessary changes should take, evolved over the period and began ultimately to point to an adapted modern conservation that more fully flowered in the 1970s.

Inter-war concerns

Progressive conservation

The inter-war period between 1919 and 1939 saw a significant development in the demand for conservation and pressure for this to be achieved through effective state legislation. There were both rural and urban strands to this activity. The Council for the Preservation of Rural England, a coalition of amenity groups, was formed in 1926 prompted by Patrick Abercrombie, the most well-known town planner of his generation. Concern for the conservation of rural England encompassed the preservation of historic buildings in the countryside but was more focused upon the impact of sprawling suburban and ribbon development and the trappings of rising levels of car ownership and bus travel, such as petrol stations and outdoor advertising. The countryside was being urbanised and suburbanised. Some of the major preservation battles fought at this time were not over the loss of historic monuments or buildings, but rather the loss of their 'natural' settings (Saint 1996; Sheail 1981b; 1981a). The principal means by which an agenda of countryside protection was promoted was through lobbying for more effective state legislation and planning controls as part of a vision of a modern ordered countryside (Matless 1998; Abercrombie 1943; Williams-Ellis 1978).

Thus, in terms of national campaigning, countryside protection was a major focus of energy in the inter-war period for the small proto-conservation movement. However, in the 1930s a more urban-orientated preservationist lobby began to develop. This had a metropolitan focus through the London Society and, from 1937, the Georgian Group, initially a wing of the Society for the Protection of Ancient Buildings. Preservation battles were fought unsuc-cessfully over, for example, various Georgian London squares, the Adelphi by the Adams brothers and Waterloo Bridge. Campaigns on city churches and Carlton House Terrace were more successful.

The embracement of Georgian architecture represented a rejection of both Victorian architecture and also bourgeois suburbia, as well as revulsion at the horrors of the nineteenth-century industrial city. Georgian was now regarded as representative of elegance and civility, and the urbane simplicity of much Georgian architecture could be linked to the values of the emerging Modern Movement in architecture. In the early years of the Georgian Group there was a significant overlap of membership with the radical MARS Group, which had been founded in 1933 (Stamp 1996). The modernist architect Ernö Goldfinger later remarked,

> The great contribution of England is Georgian. But hardly had I time to look at it and they were pulling it down. . . . My first office in London was in No. 7 Bedford Square, on the east side which belonged to the British Museum. You know they wanted to pull it down . . . Ignorant vandals – unbelievable!
>
> (Goldfinger 1981–82, cited in Stamp 1996: 84)

The conservation lobby in the 1920s and 1930s developed into a coalition rather than a unified grouping. Thus, while a preservation impulse related to the nineteenth century and the Arts and Craft Movement continued, the inter-war period saw a shift in the nature of preservation activity. New thinking linked the conservation cause more explicitly with a progressive modernism that was seeking major physical and social changes to the fabric of British society. However, preservationists across the spectrum increasingly viewed state intervention, through town planning, as the means to achieve conservation goals. It was the means both to protect beauty and heritage and to facilitate future development in an orderly and sympathetic manner. An argument was also developing that conservation should be viewed as a broadly based activity. For example, in Walter Godfrey's text *Our Building Inheritance* (Godfrey 1944), he argued for the conservation of modest historic buildings based upon an undervalued utility. He was particularly critical of an approach to appraising housing conditions that was overly concerned with standards that old buildings could inevitably not meet and which were therefore condemned to demolition (see Figures 3.1a and 3.1b).

3.1a
Walter Godfrey (1944) argued for rehabilitation of old cottages. No. 44 Midhurst, Sussex.
© English, Heritage, NMR.

3.1b
Sketch plans of
reconditioned
cottage.
Source: Hobson
family.
By permission of
Walter H. Godfrey's
family.

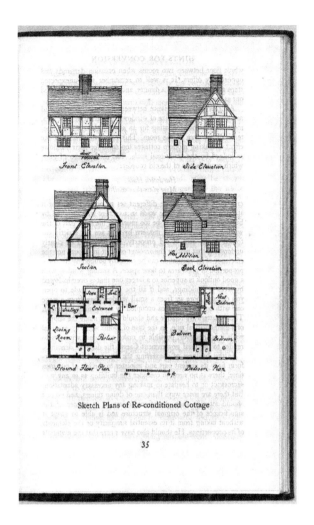

Sketch Plans of Re-conditioned Cottage

35

Inter-war legislation and an early plan

The first legislation that linked conservation with town planning occurred in the Housing, Town Planning Etc. Act 1909. In practice the planning legislation itself was weak and led to no conservation action (Delafons 1997a). Further references occurred in the 1923 Housing Etc. Act. Interestingly, this legislation authorised the Minister to make a town planning scheme to preserve the existing character and to protect the existing features of a locality where the 'special architectural, historic or artistic interest' warranted it (cited in Delafons 1997a: 38). Such a scheme might prescribe the space around buildings, or limit the number of buildings to be erected, or prescribe the height or character of buildings. This potentially allowed the way for conservation area-based legislation some forty-four years before the Civic Amenities Act in 1967. The origins of the clause in the Bill have been linked with concerns about the preservation of Oxford, and it was apparently inserted at the initiative of Oxford-graduate Civil Service lawyers (Sheail 1981b; Cocks 1998).

Concerns in Oxford were not unique. Lobbying for action also came from the newly formed Stratford-upon-Avon Preservation Committee, formed in response to a potentially damaging factory proposal. It commissioned a report from Abercrombie on the future planning of Stratford to present to the Corporation (Abercrombie and Abercrombie 1923). Conservation issues formed a major part of the report. Abercrombie justified this focus on the basis of the associations of Stratford with Shakespeare, still visible in the building stock, and more generally because of the antiquity and beauty of the town itself. 'Explicit and complete control' (1923: 15) was said to be required over development in the old part of the town, including over the architectural style of new construction. Abercrombie's report demonstrated an awareness of conservative repair principles but allowed for deviations from this orthodoxy, advocating restoration through the uncovering of historic fabric and condoning conjectural restoration and the incorporation of imported old fabric into new buildings in some circumstances. Though there was a modernist wish to avoid 'a sense of artificial and promoted antiquity' (1923: 8) in new construction, building in timber framing and in seventeenth-century styles was not ruled out. The report also expressed a concern for some of the more modest historic buildings in the centre of Stratford:

> humble brick buildings of no very certain date; some with casements and leaded lights, others with sash windows; for the most part buildings of long low proportions, roofed with brown tiles. These buildings are not merely inoffensive, any large destruction of them would leave Stratford decidedly poorer than it is now.
>
> (Abercrombie and Abercrombie 1923: 7)

As a town planning report for a historic city, the Stratford report was an important precursor of the reconstruction reports discussed below, not least as its principal author was Patrick Abercrombie, responsible for a number of key reconstruction plans. It was strongly pro-preservation and it was careful to stress the wider significance of Stratford 'for English- speaking culture' (Preface), to mobilise opinion away from focusing too narrowly on local concerns. Later preoccupations with suburban sprawl and the consequences of traffic growth were not yet evident.

The Stratford report was an early example of concerted action by a local group on preservation issues. While the national focus was on the countryside and Georgian London, pressure for development and change was occurring in historic cities up and down the country. Although local amenity groups had existed since the nineteenth century, this period saw groups arise in some of the most significant historic cities. Preservation groups were formed in Oxford in 1925, in Cambridge in 1928 and in Bath in 1934 (in this last case growing out of an earlier society formed in 1909). A number of historic cities also gained local acts of legislation giving a degree of control over such matters as the aesthetics of new buildings and demolition. Bath had the Bath Corporation Acts of 1925 and 1937; the latter brought in some controls over the façades of 1251 buildings. Many college buildings in Oxford were scheduled as ancient monuments. York had an architectural panel reviewing the design quality of proposals. Nineteen local authorities apparently obtained powers under local acts to draw up statutory schemes for their centres between 1926 and 1932 (Sheail 1981b).

The Town and Country Planning Act 1932 contained further enabling provisions on historic buildings. However, this led to an almost total lack of action, though, as Saint (1996) has pointed out, some at the time saw this as a prelude for a national survey of historic buildings. As with the wider town planning system, the landmark legislative breakthrough for the protection of historic buildings was to be the 1944 and 1947 Planning Acts. Thus prior to the Second World War, though conservation planning legislation existed, it did not lead to systematic national action. However, at local level a variety of preservation groups and local authorities used what means they could to influence development in their towns and cities.

War-time action and after

The listing of buildings

The stimulus to start what became the post-war 'listing' process developed from twin efforts: first, identification of important buildings to be kept if possible amongst the bomb-damaged buildings and, second, the foundation of the National Buildings Record to record threatened buildings. War tends to throw into sharp relief the role of historic buildings as part of national heritage and identity. This led in the Second World War to the systematic destruction of enemy heritage by both Allied and Axis Powers (Glendinning 2001b). It also led to policies to protect the architectural heritage of countries during invasion and occupation (Saint 1996); and individual combatants sometimes made extraordinary efforts to avoid the destruction of historic places, such as the voluntary German withdrawal from the historic city of Orvieto, near Rome (Hooper 2004).

An emphasis on ensemble and place was evident in the 1944 debates, which led to listing, the major initiative in the historic conservation sphere in the post-war period (though strong, effective controls over listed buildings had to wait until 1968) (Saint 1996). A key purpose for post-war listing was the identification of potential constraints to be included in or worked around in post-war reconstruction. Post-war development was to be led by the public sector. Thus lists of buildings were not a means of resisting rapacious developers, but guides to informed rational decision-making by municipal planners. At various stages the devolution of listing to local authorities and the desirability of consultation with owners were mooted. However, the principle of listing by experts on defined academic criteria was firmly established; the test of the importance and desirability of retention would come through the planning process. At the time it was generally accepted that many buildings so listed would be sacrificed in the higher interests of planning.

When listing began in earnest, tensions developed over the extensiveness and also over the speed of the process, as the lists were intended to be incorporated in first-generation development plans. In describing a clash between John Summerson and Walter Godfrey, with the former pushing for listing to be more selective and the latter for it to be more extensive, Saint divined, 'a division between the modern, discriminating art-history and pro-planning philosophy of the more progressive Georgians and the easier-going, inclusive antiquarian and vernacular-orientated approach of the SPAB' (Saint 1996: 130).

Summerson's view was emblematic of how conservation could be perceived as part of a modern, rational planning process. An architectural historian, who had written seminal books on Georgian London in the 1930s, he was a strong advocate of modern architecture and remained so despite the disappointments of the 1960s (Mandler 1994). In *The Past in the Future* he explicitly linked the development of preservation to that of objective scientific thought. Preservation should be selective:

> and one of the things I would stress is that preservation in general is only valuable where it is co-ordinated and related to a plan of positive development. The planned survival of old structures can enrich a town enormously. An unplanned development will result in pathetic patchworks of obsolescence.
>
> (Summerson 1949: 223)

Advocating the moving of historic buildings where necessary, using the case of Ford's Hospital in Coventry, he stated 'we cannot, surely, perpetuate an obsolete town-plan for the sake of one ancient and rather beautiful building' (Summerson 1949: 223).

Reconstruction: plans by Thomas Sharp and Patrick Abercrombie

The latter stages of the Second World War and the immediate aftermath saw a tremendous enthusiasm for planning, potentially entailing the radical rebuilding and re-planning of familiar towns and cities. Many towns and cities produced or commissioned plans for their future development, often focusing on the redevelopment of central areas. These ranged from modestly produced working documents to well-produced plans by a number of key national consultants. Two consultants, Patrick Abercrombie and Thomas Sharp, dominated commissions for historic cities. Abercrombie, at the pinnacle of the planning profession, represented the sophisticated mainstream of planning thought at the time. His commissions included Bath (Abercrombie *et al.* 1945), Edinburgh (Abercrombie and Plumstead 1949) and Warwick (Abercrombie and Nickson 1949), often in collaboration with others, as well as the most famous plan of the period, for Greater London (Abercrombie 1945). Sharp was some-what out of the mainstream and had a distinct and highly regarded approach. He was very influential in articulating the qualities of historic cities and developing approaches of 'townscape'. Commissions included Durham (Sharp 1945), Oxford (Sharp 1948), Exeter (Sharp 1946b), Salisbury (Sharp 1949b) and Chichester (Sharp 1949a). Together, the reports of Abercrombie and Sharp exemplify sophisticated and historically sensitive planning in the period. Their work provides the main focus of the discussion below (see also Pendlebury 2003b; 2003a; 2005).

In some places bomb-damage was the obvious stimulus to activity, but many of the towns and cities commissioning plans, including many historic towns, were unaffected by this. Historic cities that had evolved slowly over hundreds of years commissioned plans that, if implemented, would have led to rapid, large-scale transformation; major changes to urban form were considered to be inevitable. The root cause behind this activity was a crisis in the response to forces of modernity and to pressures that had been building up for some time, in particular the impact of the motor car and the political imperative of addressing slum housing. Underpinning these plans was an ideology that change should be addressed through comprehensive planning, rather than unregulated development and the muddled and unsatisfactory attempts at planning that had occurred up until that time. Planners with responsibility for studies of historic cities were faced with a particular problem: the need to reconcile functional modernity with the historic qualities of place. Just as the demand for comprehensive planning had developed in the inter-war period, so had an awareness of historic character and desire to plan for it. Character was conceived primarily as a sensory experience, particularly in terms of visual qualities but also in terms of enjoying places free from, for example, excessive traffic.

Character remained, however, a vague concept, and in part it was this vagueness that made it so useful to planners who could mobilise it to suit their own particular purposes. Preservation activity up until this time had been based mainly around campaigning for the survival of individual buildings. The concept of character helped in the development of the idea of conservation as management of change in a place. Change could be justified if character was sustained. Historic character was regarded as the experience of historic buildings and places in the present. The contemporary nature and experience of character was especially evident in Sharp's plans. Sharp was no antiquarian; he was interested in how the legacy of historical buildings contributed to contemporary form and visual effect. He was acutely conscious of the visual benefits of enclosure and usually opposed to the 'opening out' of major monuments proposed in other plans, such as those for York (Adshead *et al.* 1948) and Chester (Greenwood 1945). Sharp's Durham plan had an extensive discussion of the visual qualities of the castle and the cathedral. The domestic scale of the surrounding buildings in giving scale and controlling views of the principal monuments was held to be vital in this regard.

Neither Abercrombie nor Sharp showed the same interest in, or sensitivity to, historic urban form that they gave to the visual qualities of place, for example placing little significance on historically and morphologically significant extramural areas. For example, Sharp was adamant that there should be no recreation of the street plan of bomb-damaged areas in his Exeter plan. Both Abercrombie and Sharp displayed sensitivity towards modest historic fabric in contributing to the historic nature of place, but this did not mean that all such fabric could or should be preserved; many of these buildings were considered 'outworn' and in need of replacement. Historic character would be sustained through the careful management of change or 'the balanced approach'. In achieving twentieth-century functionality, roads loomed large. Sharp had a distinct approach to road provision, advocating 'substitute roads' (Buchanan 1958) and a rather romantic conception of the positive contribution they could make to place. Although other authors acknowledged the destructive impact of new roads, it was automatically assumed that cars should be provided for.

Sharp was the author of the period clearest at discussing the responsibility, and potential problems, of making large-scale interventions into the fabric of historic cities. Though elements of the historic city were sometimes presented as important planned effects, such as the approach to the cathedral from Owengate in Durham (see Figure 3.2) that he emphasised at length (Sharp 1945), there was a wider recognition that it was difficult to achieve the picturesque qualities of the old city through extensive new planned development. In all his plans, though, he explicitly advocated that new buildings should be clearly contemporary in style.

In advocating the retention of historic character and the preservation of significant numbers of buildings, consultant planners such as Abercrombie and Sharp were often acutely conscious that this emphasis might conflict with other local objectives, such as the desire to expand the industrial and economic

3.2

The view to Durham Cathedral up Owengate; the foil of domestic scale buildings and the partial concealment they give of the cathedral is a vital part of the experience of approach (from Sharp 1945).
Source: Edis Ltd.

base of the area. Therefore national (or international) significance was asserted to make conservation of historic character a higher-order objective than more parochial concerns (as regarded by Sharp and Abercrombie). Establishing the correct functional role of the town or city and limiting the size of settlement were regarded as key in this process.

In practice, few plans were realised to any great degree, victims of various circumstances including, crucially, a level of post-war austerity and a political retreat from comprehensive planning that made proposals hopelessly ambitious (Hasegawa 1999). Also, there was significant resistance from established commercial interests. Hague has shown how Abercrombie's plan for Edinburgh was politically side-lined owing, amongst other reasons, to its cost and potential disturbance to established interests (Hague 1984). This included the impact on the historic character of the city, of great concern to at least part of Edinburgh's bourgeoisie.

However, despite this one can discern important enduring legacies for historic cities. For the first time there was a body of planning documents that specifically recognised the significance of the historic city as a whole, albeit utilising a narrow definition of what it was important to preserve. The emphasis on character has proved to be extremely enduring and indeed formed the cornerstone of the national designation of protection of historic areas, conservation areas, introduced by the Civic Amenities Act, 1967. It was Thomas Sharp who articulated and developed these ideas most clearly. His Durham and Exeter plans were important stepping stones, but it was Sharp's plan for Oxford that showed a maturing of these ideas in his outlining of the concept of 'kinetic townscape', and this plan remains a classic townscape study, together with his later publication *Oxford Observed* (Sharp 1952).

Reconstruction planning elsewhere in Europe

The consequence of war-time destruction was clearly not restricted to Britain, and nor was the enthusiasm for the opportunity presented for modern planning (Diefendorf 1990). This was often pursued using conservative architectural styles, either traditional, regional or explicitly historicist, in a way generally rejected in Britain. In some places this was linked to an objective to recreate whole sections of destroyed historic cities. However, in all cases this conservatism and desire to recreate the historic city were tempered by modernity and the needs and desire to respond to modern conditions. For example, Middelburg, a major historic city in the Netherlands, was badly damaged by bombing in 1940. In the plans for reconstruction produced by the Dutch authorities during the German Occupation the desire for modern improvements, for example of traffic circulation, was balanced with recreating an identifiably historic Dutch character. The tensions that this created were resolved by seeking a 'Middelburg atmosphere' rather than great historical authenticity (Bosma 1990). In Hildesheim, West Germany, the destroyed city was rebuilt maintaining the historic street pattern and scale but using modern forms in the new buildings. The central square was subsequently rebuilt in the 1980s as a pre-war replica (Jokilehto 1998). Most famous of all the post-war programmes of reconstruction was the rebuilding of Warsaw as the Polish capital. The almost total destruction by German forces of historic Warsaw included a very specific targeting of culturally significant sites (Ciborowski and Jankowski 1962). The Nazis were particularly fierce in their destruction of anything that represented Polish history and culture. Out of the 957 buildings classified as historical monuments, 782 were totally destroyed and 141 partially destroyed. The historic centre was rebuilt, visually as close to a facsimile of the buildings that had been lost as it was possible to achieve. The outstanding efforts that were made in Warsaw were recognised by UNESCO World Heritage Site status in 1980. However, in Warsaw these reconstructions took

**Heritage rebuilt:
Warsaw, Poland.**
Source: Robbie
McDowall.

place within the framework of a modern plan for the city, with major modi-fications to the broader urban structure (Jankowski 1990).

To modernity and beyond

After the startling ambition of post-war reconstruction plans, the first generation plans produced under the terms of the 1947 Town and Country Planning Act seem very timid and dull, without any of the *argument* found in the earlier documents. Economic realities meant that the level of intervention proposed was generally far less than proposed in the earlier reconstruction plans. Conservation or preservation rarely appeared as an explicit issue. The plan prepared for Warwick (Warwickshire County Council 1951) was unusual in identifying areas of the city that should be protected as a whole.

However, towards the end of the 1950s and in the 1960s the momentum in favour of redevelopment of central areas grew rapidly, and the period of post-war austerity that had prevented implementation of most reconstruction plans was finally left behind. The number of comprehensive development areas being considered by the Ministry of Housing and Local Government rose from fifteen in 1959 to seventy in 1963 (though not all these were central schemes) (Ward 1994). This period also saw an architectural shift from the often conservatively styled buildings of the 1950s to bolder statements (Esher 1981).

Hand-in-hand with the objective of redeveloping city centres went a continuing preoccupation with the growth in traffic; indeed this remained a strong driver in the perceived need for redevelopment. This was exemplified by the government-commissioned Buchanan Report (Buchanan *et al.* 1963). Buchanan was then generally considered a sceptic on roads, although his report is now remembered as pro-road (Ward 1994). A strong theme in the report was the separation of vehicular and pedestrian traffic, including through vertical segregation, and the creation of environmental areas without through vehicular movement. The scale proposed for primary urban roads was acknowledged to be 'somewhat frightening' (Buchanan *et al.* 1963: 196). Buchanan acknowledged that a different emphasis was required in significant historic cities (a case study was made of Norwich; see Figure 3.4). The emphasis shifted to limiting accessibility, for:

> it is not a question of retaining a few old buildings, but of conserving, in the face of the onslaught of motor traffic, a major part of the heritage of the English-speaking world, of which this country is the guardian.
>
> (Buchanan *et al.* 1963: 197)

Generally, though, conservation was not central to land-use planning in the early 1960s. A key planning text of the period considered that the preservation of buildings 'is a subject on the edge of land Planning proper' (Keeble 1964: 315), and this was evident in many of the planning documents of the period. However, as the consequences of redevelopment in city centres became apparent, so opposition to the demolition of buildings grew; the exemplars of this in the early 1960s were the Euston Arch and the Coal Exchange, both in London.

Furthermore, as the decade developed so did a concern for area conservation. Government decisions to place Building Preservation Orders on listed buildings to prevent their demolition became increasingly influenced by group value (i.e. building ensembles), and in 1962 and 1963 government guidance placed stress on conserving the character of towns (Delafons 1997a). A disparate series of study groups began working on planning and historic areas, such as the the Historic Cities and Towns Project, which led to a conference and publication (Ward 1968). From 1963 the Council of Europe was pressing member countries for greater action (Council of Europe 1963) and this led to a conference in Bath in 1966 that urged the protection of historic areas, integrated with development planning (Civic Trust c. 1966).

In government Richard Crossman, Secretary of State from 1964, supported by junior minister Lord Kennet from 1966, was instrumental in putting the conservation of historic areas on the agenda, despite civil service

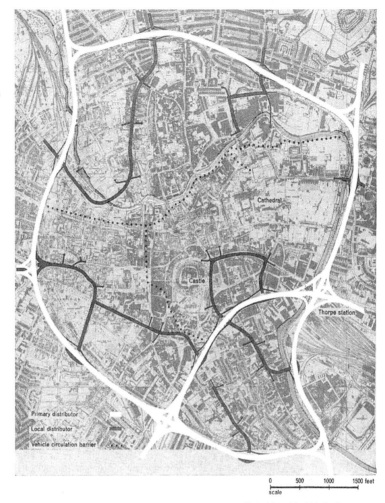

The breakdown of the old city into four main
areas or 'rooms'. There would be freedom for
pedestrians and cyclists and some bus services to move
from area to area, but for other traffic the approach to
the areas would be via the primary network. In
practice the siting of the 'barriers' would require much
detailed consideration.

resistance. This culminated initially in the 1967 Civic Amenities Act, which
created the system of conservation areas. Though the Act started as a Private
Member's Bill, introduced by Duncan Sandys, its scope and form were
influenced by discussions with Crossman (Delafons 1997a). The 1968 Town
and Country Planning Act then introduced for the first time comprehensive
controls over works to listed buildings. Coterminous with this legislation was
the commissioning in 1966 of the four well-known studies of historic cities,
Bath (Colin Buchanan & Partners 1968), Chester (Donald Insall and Associates
1968), Chichester (Burrows 1968) and York (Esher 1968). It is notable that York

was, initially at least, a reluctant participant, and a fifth town, King's Lynn, declined to meet its part of the cost of a study (Kennet 1972). Two of the resultant reports are discussed further below. In the subsequent development of policy Kennet was keen to shift the idea of conservation areas away from the setting of important buildings to a more broadly based conception and to encourage local authorities to designate rapidly and extensively (Delafons 1997a). This growing emphasis on area conservation is now considered in relation to three historic cities.

Newcastle upon Tyne: Brasilia of the North

The planning ambitions of Newcastle changed dramatically from 1958 under the political leadership of T. Dan Smith and a new Labour administration. Smith created one of the country's first free-standing planning departments and appointed the city's first Chief Planning Officer, Wilfred Burns. It was a period associated with redevelopment, and especially with the famous Development Plan of 1963 (City and County of Newcastle upon Tyne 1963).

At the end of the 1950s, the centre of the city in terms of its basic form had changed little since the mid nineteenth century. In the 1830s it had been given a remarkable late-Georgian commercial centre by a speculative developer, Richard Grainger. This had overlaid, rather than replaced, the medieval street plan. The architectural and historic qualities of the city, and especially the Grainger developments, had received increasing recognition by the 1960s (Pevsner and Richmond 1957; Nairn 1960; Sharp 1937). These qualities were recognised in the planning documents produced by Burns. The city centre was to be modernised and its role as a regional capital strengthened. To implement this vision major road development was held to be needed, including urban motorways close to the centre. Traffic and pedestrians were to be segregated, partly through multilevel circulation. The road system was intended to frame three major precincts in the city centre that would be pedestrianised as far as possible. At the same time the city was regarded as having a distinct character in need of preservation. No inherent conflict was perceived between these objectives; indeed they were seen as complementary, and part of the rationale for the road proposals was the removal of traffic from the historic core.

The proposed means of implementing these objectives involved removing much modest historic building stock. This seemed to be generally accepted, virtually without comment. However, the plan also proposed the removal of some key historic buildings that were subject to more debate. Most controversial of all was the proposal to demolish the three-sided Eldon Square, one of Grainger's principal developments, to make way for the modern shopping centre that now bears the name. Conscious of the sensitivity of this the City was at pains to justify its actions (City and County of Newcastle upon

Tyne c. 1964). There was actually little opposition to demolition at the time of the public inquiry on the issue in 1963; but subsequently considerable controversy developed owing to delays in the implementation of the scheme (Royal Fine Art Commission 1967; Sharp 1968; Delafons 1997a). Ultimately two sides of the square were demolished and one was retained, as the Secretary of State refused to sanction the demolition of a non-conformist chapel lying to the rear of the terrace.

However, in addition to proposing the modernisation of the city, the 1963 plan also established historic preservation as an important part of the planning strategy. Indeed, in March 1962 preservation was the subject of a specific report, *A Plan for the Preservation of Buildings of Architectural or Historic Interest* (Newcastle City Planning Department 1962). Four preservation areas were subsequently defined in the 1963 plan. All these areas contained buildings unlisted at that time but considered worthy of preservation. These areas were seen as areas of 'positive' preservation, with policies for enhancement, but also with restrictive development control policies. The focus was on visual qualities, and the Grainger developed streets were considered to be a major example of nineteenth-century picturesque town planning. For example, there was a policy of introducing a canopy on Grainger Street (part of the Grainger development and a principal shopping street), in an effort to restore an architectural unity that had been fragmented by the introduction of contemporary shopfronts and signage (see Figure 3.5). With the introduction of the Civic Amenities Act in 1967, Newcastle was very quick to use the defined preservation areas as the basis for designating two larger conservation areas.

Newcastle sought both to modernise and preserve (see Pendlebury 2001 for a fuller analysis of Newcastle in this period). The replanning of the city centre was intended to be undertaken on comprehensive planning principles, and though there were major elements of clean-sweep planning proposed, this was intended to be surgical and respectful of the character of Newcastle. Modernism in post-war Britain was influenced by enduring visual cultural traditions that stressed the combination of space, rather than the formal harmony of the individual building (Bandini 1992). This picturesque tradition was evident in the Newcastle planning documents of the early 1960s, with their emphasis on melding the best of the old with the new. However, by today's standard this was based upon a narrow view of what constituted the best of the old. It had broadened from key architectural monuments to include areas within the city, but these were highly selective and principally based around architectural composition. Other historic factors were not considered to be important. For example, the Bigg Market area of the city, which best demonstrated the medieval morphology of Newcastle, was not designated as a conservation area until 1970, and there was an explicit policy of introducing service roads in morphologically rich areas behind principal streets.

3.5
Part of the Grainger Street canopy, Newcastle upon Tyne, introduced in the 1960s to unify shopfronts and provide cover for shoppers. The canopy was subsequently totally removed in the 1990s with substantial grant assistance.
Source: author.

The approach to the planning of the historic city adopted in Newcastle in the 1960s has some parallels with the approach taken in Bath, which is now discussed.

The 1968 plans for Bath and York: sea-change or evolution?

Bath and York had both commissioned reconstruction plans in the 1940s (Abercrombie *et al.* 1945; Adshead *et al.* 1948) and as the pressure for post-war development grew conservation issues were significant in both cities. As Hargreaves (1964) and Nuttgens (1976) described, and as Esher (1968) audited, there were many conflicts over individual buildings and streets in York, some resolved with a favourable outcome from a conservation perspective, some not. Esher detailed the rate of attrition of listed buildings between the completion of the first list in 1954 and his study period. In thirteen years, thirty-one buildings had been added to the list, but sixty-three were demolished, with the total thus dropping from 652 to 620. In Bath Betjeman's remarkable 1962 film lampooned an imagined philistine, money-grabbing London developer wishing to demolish 'Georg-ee-an' buildings and was scathingly satirical about new buildings in the city. The imagined developer commented upon the then new technical college and its projecting lecture theatre:

> Today, building must express itself honestly and sincerely, as for instance in this feature, which might be termed 'the vital buttocks' of the construction. As you can see, it expresses its purpose, whatever that may be, sincerely, and this causes it to blend harmoniously and naturally with the Georg-ee-an on the left there. Each age should express itself as it really feels and you can see how this age feels about Georg-ee-an.
>
> (Stedall 1962) (see also Tewdwr-Jones 2005)

These last comments were both ironic and bitter: the camera-work made clear that there was no relationship at all.

Buchanan's 1968 report was a culmination of his work in the city and sits alongside his other work in Bath and in particular his *A Planning and Transport Study* (Colin Buchanan & Partners 1965). Traffic was the central preoccupation of the 1965 report. There was seen to be a terrible dilemma between relieving the city and its heritage of traffic, and finding routes to achieve this that did not adversely impact upon that heritage, and the plan contained proposals for a highly controversial east-west tunnel. The key elements of the historic environment were defined highly selectively. Broadly the focus was upon the medieval city core and the show-piece elements of the Georgian town, including the Circus and Royal Crescent. Otherwise, extensive comprehensive redevelopment was proposed, or at least accepted, for most of the city centre to the south and west of the historic core and for more limited areas elsewhere. Vertical segregation of traffic and pedestrians was regarded as desirable for the larger redevelopment areas.

The subsequent 1968 conservation study (Colin Buchanan & Partners 1968) was limited in that it only dealt with the part of the city that had been occupied by the medieval town. Thus, it did not include the Georgian expansion for which Bath is principally famous. The 1968 plans were demonstration studies of the practicality of reconciling preservation objectives with modern functionality, and in the case of Bath the complexity of the central area was considered more representative of such problems than the Georgian set pieces. Greatest stress was placed upon the city's visual qualities, for 'in Bath as a whole the façades are very much more important than the interiors' (p. 13). The study area was divided into four and ranked as highest, secondary and little importance and in need of large-scale renewal. With the first category preservation was held to be imperative. With the secondary areas the aim was to keep the best buildings and to conserve the general character, though large-scale renewal was not ruled out. In the other areas it was argued that there must be the acceptance of change. Areas one and two covered approximately sixty per cent of the area. Thus Buchanan was advocating major change to at least forty per cent of the historic core, and possibly more.

A key element of the proposals in the study of York undertaken by Lord Esher was to make the walled city liveable (Esher 1968). At the time of the study the residential population was 3500, a figure representing a long decline as commercial and industrial development had displaced people from the centre from the nineteenth century onwards. The target was to increase this to 6000. Measures proposed to achieve this included removal of some (but by no means all) industry from the walled city, with a focus on relocating industrial uses that both generated significant traffic and made a noxious neighbour. Some comprehensive redevelopment was envisaged, but focused on low-grade industrial use and was very modest and surgical when set beside Bath or Newcastle. The potential for re-use of vacant upper floors was also emphasised; there was a study of the Petergate area specifically on this issue.

Another key theme for making the city more liveable was the management of traffic; this included some pedestrianisation, although greater emphasis was laid upon restricting vehicular access to the historic core through the use of permits. Esher's terms of reference precluded him from considering traffic proposals for the city as a whole. However, he was very sceptical about the proposed inner ring road immediately outside his study area, and just beyond the medieval walls. His objections were made on both amenity and functional grounds. It was considered that such a road and its associated works, such as roundabouts and junctions, would dwarf the city walls and 'above all the Bars, whose impressiveness is dependant on the contrasting scale of the small buildings in their vicinity' (Esher 1968: 53).

The four 1960s conservation studies have often been considered one of the key defining moments in a sea-change approach to conservation and redevelopment in the late 1960s and early 1970s (e.g. Delafons 1997a). However, studies such as those for Bath and York represented degrees of evolution of an approach to historic cites, for which important antecedents can be found in earlier plans of the 1940s. The 1968 plans and their predecessors were all master plans grappling with problems of reconciling the historic city with modernity. All advocated a balance between the conservation of historic character and the continuing evolution of the living city, albeit the balance suggested varied significantly amongst the various plans. Provision for traffic was a major issue in both the 1940s and 1960s, as was the need for pedestrians to be able to enjoy historic areas free of excessive numbers of vehicles. The necessity for cities to be functioning modern places and the need to rationalise land use to some degree were common issues, but at the same time, though the emphasis varied between plans, there was recognition of the richness of mixing different uses, particularly those considered to be compatible neighbours. The need to find new uses for historic buildings whose original or existing uses were obsolescent was another recurrent theme (see Pendlebury (2005; 2006) for a fuller account and analysis of the 1968 plans for Bath and York).

Contemporary reviews of the 1968 plans tended to see a similar civic design focus between the four studies (Hall 1969) and focused on government inertia in implementing the plans' recommendations (Architectural Review 1970). However, with hindsight it is possible to see that the Buchanan and Esher plans had some profound differences in their approach to managing the historic city, although they shared some similarities of outlook. For example, there was the same rhetoric about the need for progressive planning and the same distaste for pastiche or historicist architecture. Modish 1960s solutions were evident in both. Buchanan advocated vertical segregation in Bath, and the Esher plan contained brutal multi-storey car-parks. However, there was selectivity in defining the historic city in Bath reminiscent of the 1940s plans, whereas in York it was conceived more inclusively and extensively and as a more intricate series of intimate visual relationships. Approaches to dealing with traffic were also quite different between the two plans. Buchanan saw the need to contain the use of road traffic but also the need for extensive new urban roads, and it was this balancing act between management and provision he sought to achieve in his work in Bath, seeking to minimise and mitigate the impact of what would inevitably be a major intervention in the urban environment. The City of York also proposed major new urban roads, but Esher challenged this in terms of both the aesthetic impact of a ring road as well as its functional logic. He signalled an approach with a greater emphasis on the management and containment of traffic.

The Buchanan studies of Bath did not represent a significantly more pro-conservation approach than Abercrombie's 1940s precursor; indeed, in some respects, such as the idea of vertical segregation, and the scale of roads and brutalist architecture proposed, their intended interventions were more drastic. However, with Esher's study of York one can see a distinct step change, most obviously through the relatively small level of proposed redevelopment, the particular emphasis on intensifying residential use and a changed emphasis on the relationship with the car and provision for its use. This latter issue became the key environmental battleground of urban areas in the 1970s and was of great significance in both the cities considered here; in both cases, ambitious road proposals were ultimately abandoned. The Bath study continued a focus on architectural selection as part of rational planning process, whereas the York study had more of the feeling of a discussion of an inhabited, cherished place (see Figure 3.6).

The Esher plan was to prove particularly influential: nearly forty years later Esher is still considered a major benchmark in conservation planning in York, whereas in Bath it is the reaction to modernist planning, *The Sack of Bath* (Fergusson 1973), that is the touchstone. Esher was part of a wave of activity that helped people evolve a new way of seeing the historic city which advocated drastically reducing the level of proposed planned intervention. What is remarkable looking at the Esher study today is how fresh and contemporary it feels in most respects, with its focus on creating a liveable city. As Gold (2004: 98) has written, 'It was the spirit of urban sustainability without the contemporary lexicon.'

Modernity and master plans

The future of historic towns and cities became an issue of concern and some local initiatives in the inter-war period. It was clear that modernity brought pressure and demand for change. Places not greatly physically affected by Victorian industrialisation and urbanisation were not left similarly unaffected by, for example, the desire to rationalise land use, the impact of chain store architecture or the demand for better housing conditions. Top of the list of issues facing the centre of historic cities was the growth of motor traffic: barely mentioned in the early 1920s, growing during the 1930s, a significant concern in the 1940s and a major headache by the 1960s. However, it was only the advent of the Second World War and its galvanising impact on British society that produced the firm beginnings of a national response to managing these issues in terms of support for comprehensive planning and, as part of this, the introduction of the system of listing buildings.

This desire to plan for the future during the war and its aftermath led many historic cities to commission or produce their own plans. Despite these being the result of local initiatives, consultants such as Sharp and Abercrombie were keen to emphasise the national and international importance of these particular places. They also often promoted an awareness that the significance of such cities related not just to a limited number of key monuments but to their more modest heritage. In addition, they were also developing techniques of management, such as townscape and the concept of character, that were to be of enduring importance, with 'character' becoming a cornerstone of the system of conservation areas.

Across the period covered by this chapter there was belief and confidence in the professions: experts planned for the good of all and were untroubled by later, post-modern uncertainties. The best means of reconciling the historic city with modernity was through comprehensive planning. Key to this was the balanced approach. A balance was advocated between the conservation of historic character and the continuing evolution of the living city, albeit the balance suggested varied significantly between plans. Modest historic buildings could not be preserved if they stood in the way of 'essential' planning improvements; this view was still very evident in the Buchanan proposals for Bath and even, albeit to a more limited degree, in Esher's plan for York. Traffic had to be both managed and provided for, usually at the cost of massive road schemes on the periphery of the historic core. As well as managing the impact of the twentieth century on historic cities, plans also had to reflect the need for new contributions to the development and architecture of the city, and most plans contained an explicit ideology that new buildings be clearly contemporary in style.

The plans of the 1940s were an important first major wave of plans to consider how the demands of the twentieth century might be reconciled in historic cities. The approach taken in Newcastle in the 1960s sought a similar balancing act, albeit with a newer, brasher modernity. The plans subsequently co-commissioned by the government for historic cities represent a further evolution of approach, rather than the radical sea-change that is now often assumed. However, there is no doubt that they were commissioned at the cusp of a period of great changes in attitudes towards places, planning and conservation and the role of people (and traffic) in each of these. Furthermore, although the emphasis in this chapter has been on conservation planning, the excerpt from the Betjeman film on Bath is a reminder that there were earlier critiques both of what was happening to historic cities and of developers and 'planner-experts' themselves.

The shifts in attitude of the 1960s were not very evident in the Bath report, which seems now to represent the old technocratic era of high intervention, an approach that was effectively to collapse in Bath in 1973 under a storm of national and local criticism. At York, though, Esher produced a report where the balance swung firmly to a more inclusive and embracing conservation of place and that is still considered a major benchmark for the city nearly forty years later. Both in the Esher report and in parallel work of the time, such as Worskett's *The Character of Towns* (Worskett 1969) discussed in the previous chapter, we can see that new approaches emerged in conservation planning. Though in essence still modernist, modern conservation and its role in the planning of towns and cities evolved and changed. It was partly, but not merely, a case of a more inclusive approach to protection. Although the plans of Abercrombie and especially Sharp were often inclusive and sensitive to historic character, in the late 1960s a more fundamental inversion started to appear. Conservation ceased to be a backdrop to a process of modern planning; rather it began to assume the foreground and become the starting point. It started to encompass the whole quality of the environment, including the insertion of new buildings. It gradually became the driver in the management of change.

Chapter 4

The 1970s
Shifting ground

Introduction

As discussed in the previous chapter, some sensibility about the importance of historic cities and conservation developed during the 1940s, 1950s and 1960s and was institutionalised through legislation and government financial assistance, albeit in what might now be considered a very rudimentary form. Different places and different people displayed different degrees of sensitivity to these historic qualities, but there was broad consensus that conservation should take its place in the wider activity of rational and comprehensive town planning. This fundamental construct came under sustained pressure during the 1970s owing to a series of circumstances; these encompassed a new economic austerity and a rise in popular challenge, leading to a loss of faith in the omniscient wisdom of experts and the collapse of the modernist project.

The idea that conservation should take its place in the foreground grew in importance and, gradually, became generally accepted. In June 1970 the Civic Trust announced the 1000th conservation area (Civic Trust 1970), and already the nature of conservation areas varied considerably, including within them historic streets, squares, village greens, town and city centres. The number of conservation areas reached 3000 by the mid 1970s. The legislation of the late 1960s, introducing conservation areas and listed building control, developed and extended further in 1972 to include the power to control the demolition of unlisted buildings in conservation areas; new forms of grant and additional monies were made available also. New legislation was accompanied by a welter of additional policy guidance (Delafons 1997a).

It is possible now to see the 1970s as part of an upsurge or rising tide of interest and emphasis on conservation that was reinforced in subsequent decades, as described in the next chapter. However, this was by no means clear at the time. One of the evocative legacies of the 1970s was the emergence of a rash of protest books, which positioned themselves at the centre of a heroic contest against the forces of philistinism, and which effectively formed a strategic part of the development struggles described below. Books addressing the country as a whole included *Goodbye Britain?* (Aldous 1975), *The Rape of Britain* (Amery and Cruikshank 1975), *Heritage in Danger* (Cormack 1976) and *The Erosion of History* (Heighway 1972) and those bemoaning the fate of individual towns and cities numbered such as *The Sack of Bath* and *Vanishing Bath* (Fergusson 1973; Coard and Coard 1973) or the *Erosion of Oxford* (Curl 1977).

In practice it was clear that different local authorities embraced the rise of conservation with varying degrees of enthusiasm and were often

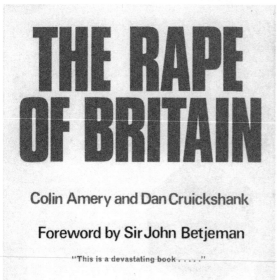

4.1
The 1970s produced many emotive texts arguing for conservation: the cover of *The Rape of Britain* (Amery and Cruickshank 1975).
© Elek Books Ltd.

perceived as the enemy. The reluctance of the City Corporation in Edinburgh to designate conservation areas and give maintenance grants was suggested to be due to having so much potentially preservable stock that the City authority saw it as an unbearable burden on the City's resources (Dennier 1976). A conference organised by the Civic Trust in 1970 effectively embarrassed the Secretary of State for Scotland into promising the necessary financial help and was instrumental in founding the Edinburgh New Town Conservation committee to vet grant applications for conservation work (Scottish Civic Trust 1970). However, by 1975, European Architectural Heritage Year, Edinburgh continued to be highlighted as much for its failures as its successes. Real progress had been made in the New Town, but the Old Town area was still largely neglected. At this point it was not even designated as a conservation area, despite its status since the 1990s as a World Heritage Site, in conjunction with the New Town (Cormack 1976).

Again with the benefit of hindsight, the 1975 European Architectural Heritage Year can be seen as an important cusp. The tide had truly turned at this point, and this Council of Europe initiative is discussed later in the chapter. When looking at the annual reports of the Historic Buildings Council (the government advisory body), there was a marked change in tone around 1975–6; the 'Unsuccessful Cases' section, which named outstanding buildings lost to the stock, disappeared, and the reports became much more focused on success. However, by the end of the decade concerns arose that the conservation movement's successes were to be all too transitory and that the tide was turning again.

A shifting context

Economy

Much of the credit for the rise of conservation as a social and political force in the 1970s has rightly been given to political struggles; sometimes as direct campaigns for the historic environment and sometimes as part of wider development struggles involving environmental and social justice issues, but which arose from comprehensive redevelopment. Another very powerful factor was the economic circumstances of the 1970s, exemplified by the three-day week of the 1973 Conservative government (with the attendant property-market crash), or the decision by the Labour government in 1976 to call in the International Monetary Fund. Though campaigners were able to claim the battle honours as development schemes were dropped all around the country, the reality was that this was often as much to do with collapsed property markets and slashed government budgets as with vociferous objections.

Social challenge

Unfavourable economic conditions combined with a growing swell of resistance towards the implementation of radical schemes of comprehensive planning. In many instances opposition was mobilised specifically by conservation causes; by buildings under threat and by the realisation of the environmental impact of proposed development schemes. This was evident in each of the three cities discussed in the last chapter. In Newcastle, York and Bath the keenest fights were over proposed new roads. In Newcastle the emergent pressure group, SOCEM (Save Our City from Environmental Mess), was ultimately unsuccessful in preventing the construction of the Central Motorway East, though most of the rest of the urban motorways programme in the city was ultimately dropped. In York, despite Esher's disapproval, the Council pushed ahead with an inner ring road proposal that was bitterly contested. New amenity groups were formed that were prepared to challenge the authorities more directly, and the road proposals were ultimately defeated at public inquiry (Lichfield and Proudlove 1976; York 2000 1972; Cummin 1973; Palliser 1974).

In Bath, more than in any other British city, there was a fierce backlash in the early 1970s over the planning and management of the historic city. Bath featured prominently in the polemics referred to above (Aldous 1975; Amery and Cruikshank 1975). It also generated both its own scathing comment on planning in the city (Coard and Coard 1973; Fergusson 1973) and extensive comment in the professional press (e.g. Architectural Review 1973). Central to the critiques was the idea that the more modest Georgian heritage, 'artisan Bath', had been undervalued. 'Every attack on a minor Georgian building is an attack on the architectural unity of Bath' (Architectural Review 1973: 280). Artisan Georgian buildings were argued as important to the story of Georgian Bath, because of their spatial role in linking the grand compositions and as high-quality, serviceable buildings. The significance of Bath was believed to lie in its totality as an artefact, principally of the eighteenth and nineteenth centuries, rather than in the architectural set-pieces as such. This lament at the loss of artisan Bath was compounded by replacement modern constructions that were indifferent at best. The tunnel proposal was particularly opposed (the Bath Corporation scheme was even more brutal than the Buchanan one) and it was finally abandoned in 1976, though probably as much for economic reasons as any other.

However, in addition to the campaigns that related specifically to the conservation cause, there was a wider resistance to redevelopment in many locations across the country: broader struggles over ideology, and the power and rights of politicians, professional bureaucrats and property speculators to impose their visions on communities. Castells's analysis of urban social movements across the globe in this period defined them as focused upon demands for better living conditions, the affirmation of local cultural identity, the conquest of local political autonomy and on citizen participation (Castells 2004). In this context the conservation of the historic environment was often a useful tool that could be mobilised rather than the primary focus of struggle.

London, with the large financial gains anticipated from redevelopment, was the inevitable location for a concentration of such contests. Conservation issues barely featured in some of the more celebrated cases, despite involving areas that would now be recognised as architecturally rich. Wates (1976) detailed the conflict between a local community and the nexus, all too common at the time, of a local authority and property developer, in an area in Camden just to the west of Euston Station. In his description of events there was a focus on the retention of buildings as part of a rich and diverse community, as part of the ideas that had grown momentum since Jane Jacobs' famous *The Death and Life of Great American Cities* (Jacobs 1961), but there was very little mention of historic merit.

Conservation issues were slightly more to the fore in nearby Bloomsbury. In 1970 conservationists were shocked at the proposed destruction of Woburn Square by the University of London – by this time the climate strongly favoured the retention of Georgian London – but protests against plans approved ten years previously were in vain (Aldous 1972). But the battle for Bloomsbury was not over, as illustrated by the struggle over the siting of the British Library. The proposal was to build the new library complex on a site held to be 'the last genuinely residential community in Bloomsbury' (London Borough of Camden 1974: 7). This was successfully opposed by Camden Council as involving 'the demolition of a long-settled London neighbourhood' and, but almost as an afterthought, 'part of the Bloomsbury Conservation Area' (London Borough of Camden 1974: 7).

Wright (1992) described the resistance in the Mapledene area of Hackney to the council's housing proposals involving compulsory purchase and redevelopment. The Mapledene Residents Advisory Committee was formed to defend a very different vision of the area, based partly around the social vision of a mixed community and partly around arguments about historic importance and architectural merit. The Hackney Society insisted that the area was an example of Victorian town planning at its best and stressed the high-quality architectural detail of the houses. The 1971 compulsory purchase order was rejected by the Secretary of State for the Environment, but Hackney Council came back in 1975 with a proposal to build upon the long gardens of the properties, with access provided by the demolition of a small number of houses, including a listed building. Again the proposals were resisted, with the residents being supported by the Hackney Society and the Victorian Society. Again, they were successful.

The most famous conservation–development struggle of all in this period was the battle over plans for the Covent Garden area. The possibilities for major development in the area became apparent with the decision in the mid 1960s to relocate the fruit and vegetable market, eventually executed in 1974. From its creation in 1965, the Greater London Council (GLC) formulated ambitious proposals for comprehensive redevelopment, involving demolition of two-thirds of the buildings in the area (see Figure 4.2). In the early 1970s, the heterogeneous communities of residents, small traders and so on in the area mobilised to oppose the GLC plan. Opposition at this stage was not focused on conservation issues but on a lack of consultation and on the intended displacement of the residential population. The ultimate outcome of a planning inquiry in 1973 into the GLC's proposals effectively killed comprehensive redevelopment, combined as it was with the listing of 245 buildings in the area, while at the same time essentially confirming the role of the GLC as the appropriate body to undertake a comprehensive approach to the planning of the area. The Covent Garden Conservation Area was designated in 1972 and extended in 1974; the Seven Dials Conservation Area immediately to the north was also designated. The subsequent Action Plan of 1978 (GLC 1978) was of a very different character, encompassing a much more sensitive attitude to both place and process.

The story of Covent Garden in the 1970s is often understandably lauded as one of the great successes of the conservation movement: a rich, complex area was physically saved from modernist expurgation and transformation (Home and Loew 1987; Anderson and Green 1992; Delafons 1997a). Yet for some of those involved in the struggle, this was ultimately a tale of defeat and bitterness. Anson (1981) argued that from the outset there was an inherent, though sublimated, conflict in the alliance to stop the 1960s GLC

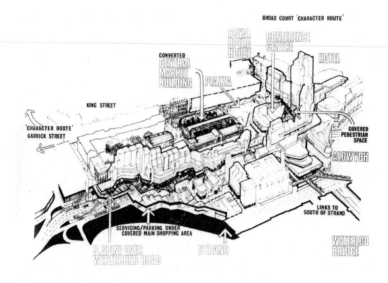

4.2
The GLC's proposed modernist construction of Covent Garden.
© City of London, London Metropolitan Archives.

plans; the working-class residents of the area fought to sustain their place and community and the middle class were preoccupied with the physical character of the area. The prevention of redevelopment did not impinge on the attractiveness of the area to the real-estate market. The ensuing process of gentrification led to the dispersal of working-class residents, which was as inevitable, if perhaps more attritional, as if the area had actually been flattened. This pyrrhic success for community-based conservation activism, before longer-term displacement by capital, is a story replicated around the world, with, for example, the Rocks area of Sydney exhibiting close parallels to the Covent Garden case (Wirth and Freestone 2003).

The fall of modernism

The cases described above all form part of the crumbling edifice of modernist approaches to city planning and architecture, as detailed at the end of the 1970s by Ravetz (1980) and Esher (1981). Increasingly the wider public challenged the authority of the state to physically reconstruct their lives, and, in turn, the professionals charged with implementing these visions began to lose faith in the visions of the 1960s. Again, the era has left a legacy of seminal polemics on the problems of bureaucratic comprehensive planning, such as *People and Planning* (Dennis 1970) and *The Evangelistic Bureaucrat* (Davies 1972) or, in the case of the USA, Goodman's *After the Planners* (Goodman 1972).

Responding to the changed climate some planners began to embrace this new environment, both in terms of support for greater public participation in the planning process and of a sympathetic view towards conservation, as well as seeking to change methods of designing new environments. For example, the Essex Design Guide was a famous attempt to create new housing areas that were less dominated by the car and highway standards and more responsive to local vernacular traditions (Essex County Council 1973). The fall of modernism is discussed further in Chapter 9.

Civic engagement

As the machinery of conservation planning evolved, it became evident that in many places local civic groups were active in securing its implementation. In significant measure this was the result both of encouragement from a government, anxious about the powers it had devolved to local authorities, such as conservation area designation, and of a wider discourse of extending public participation within the planning process. The 1969 Skeffington Report (Great Britain. Committee on Public Participation in Planning 1969), which heralded statutory participation rights in the preparation of development plans, was a landmark in this respect, although it is questionable how much this represented any real sea-change in attitude (Ravetz 1980).

More specifically in terms of conservation processes, in 1968 central government introduced the concept of Conservation Area Advisory Committees (CAACs). The intention was that:

> local planning authorities should establish conservation area advisory committees, including persons not members of the authority, and refer to them for advice applications which would, in the opinion of the authority, affect the character or appearance of the conservation area ... The work of these advisory committees need not be confined to questions arising on applications for planning permission or listed building consent. They could also play a useful part in the general care and maintenance of conservation areas and in making positive proposals for their enhancement.
>
> (MHLG Circular 61/68 cited in Jordan *et al.* 1975)

Though local groups were often included on the committee, typically member-ship also comprised representatives from national amenity groups and professional bodies, as well as local authority members.

Research on the Chester CAAC, apparently the first such committee created in 1970, emphasised that early committees were often engaged in formative work within their area; few if any conservation areas might have been designated, and thus committees were sometimes influential in setting the agenda for a particular locality. What was also clear was that the principal purpose of committees was to bring technical conservation expertise to local authorities, often at the time not in possession of these skills, rather than broaden participation per se (Jordan *et al.* 1975).

Beyond such formal mechanisms as CAACs, it was evident that many local groups were engaged with local authorities in supporting the development of conservation policy formulation and action as part of a 'responsible' style of action (Lowe and Goyder 1983). Many local societies interested in the built environment affiliated themselves to the national Civic Trust formed in 1957, hence the specific term 'civic societies'. In 1960 approximately 300 societies were registered with the Trust; by 1967 this was 600, reaching a peak of around 1300 in the late 1970s (Andreae 1996; Larkham 1996). Smith (1974) detailed examples from Greenwich, Carshalton, Bedford, Tonbridge and Exeter of local groups preparing reports on issues such as potential conservation areas. Local amenity bodies are discussed at greater length in Chapter 7.

New agendas

Thus the conservation movement in the 1970s was emerging in a rather different form than its previous incarnations. New, more broadly based groups were springing up, prepared to be more confrontational than some of the older established civic groups. Conservation was increasingly linked to wider social processes and the broader environment rather than being exclusively an issue to do with architectural merit or historic importance. This extension of the conservation value-system underpinning justifications for conservation activity, to include explicit contemporary economic and social gains, has proved of enduring importance.

In the 1980s it was the economic utility of heritage that rose to prominence, an argument used to appeal to the Thatcher governments and discussed in Chapters 5 and 6. In the 1970s, though, the emphasis was more on the social purpose and role of conservation, and this is the focus of the discussion in subsequent sections below. In his review of conservation in Europe, Appleyard talked in terms of 'social conservation, the maintenance of [the] neighbourhood [for] the existing population' having equal prominence with 'physical conservation', 'the preservation or restoration of the urban fabric for aesthetic or historical and touristic reasons' (Appleyard 1979: 33).

At the same time it should be noted that conservationists were subject to accusations of elitism: there has been an enduring perception of conservation as a middle-class activity, and conservationists were lambasted for imposing their tastes on society at the expense of social progress. Drawing from his experiences working as a planner for the Greater London Council, Eversley viewed conservation as very a much minority interest:

> What society suffers from . . . are the extraordinary tastes of that small group of people who constitute, for instance the Historic Building Council. . . . It is these people who dictate what is good and beautiful, according to aesthetic standards known only to themselves, but which are supposed to have absolute values. That is to say, no price is too high to pay for the community to conserve these buildings.
>
> (Eversley 1973: 270)

The Labour politician Anthony Crosland, while acknowledging conservation concerns, argued in 1971 that economic growth and social redistribution must take priority and criticised conservationists for what he saw as their indifference to the needs of ordinary people (Smith 1974). The urban sociologist Ray Pahl was alive to the potential distributional consequences of a policy of conservation, recognising in 1970 that it might lead to displacement through gentrification-type processes (Smith 1974). This last point was prescient, and the theme of gentrification is revisited below. Furthermore, local groups were, and continue to be, characterised as middle-class in composition, lacking representativeness of the communities they spring from and redolent of self-interest and 'not-in-my-backyard' (NIMBY) attitudes (Rydin 2003).

Pronouncements

Preservation and Change, published by the Ministry of Housing and Local Government in 1967, defined the importance of the historic environment in relation to beauty and visible history (Ministry of Housing and Local Government 1967). However, by the turn of the decade more sweeping statements about the value of historic places became commonplace. For example, Duncan Sandys, initiator of the Civic Trust while a Minister in 1957 and promoter of the Civic Amenities Act, which led to the creation of conservation areas, stated in a speech to the Civic Trust in 1971 that conservation touched 'basic values within the nation'; it provided a link to the very 'root of national identity', set against a sense of loss of direction in the post-war period (Civic Trust 1972). This was representative of a growing trend to provide psychological justifications for conservation work. Further evidence that the concept of conservation was perceived as broadening out to include communities and individuals came later in Department of the Environment circular 46/73 entitled *Conservation and Preservation*; this contained the extraordinary quote from Lord Stamford which suggested that a broad view of conservation should 'have care for the conservation of existing communities and social fabric, wherever public opinion points clearly towards it' (Department of the Environment 1973).

Thus, historical justifications for protecting and conserving old buildings on the basis of art-historical criteria, which suggested a high degree of selectivity, shifted to much more inclusive arguments more firmly based on the character of whole settlements. Furthermore, there was a perception of a broader social and psychological purpose in sustaining places, implying the need to conserve much more ordinary environments for the benefit of local communities, in contrast to the rather narrow preoccupations traditionally held by the conservation movement.

Redefining the heritage

In parallel with statements indicating or arguing for a wider social purpose in a policy of conservation, definitions of what was worthy of being labelled as heritage were being pushed ever wider to encompass more modest elements of the built environment. The decade saw, for example, the establishment of industrial archaeology and vernacular architecture as worthy of serious study and protection, in both cases from a position where interest had been gradually developing in the post-war period. The development of industrial archaeology as a discipline was probably in part related to a realisation that Britain was rapidly de-industrialising, though Samuel (1994) seemed to view its development as essentially an extension of male hobbies concerning mills, canals and so on. However, it can also be seen as having a class dimension. Hitherto, the material artistic fruits of industrialisation, such as country houses, had been recognised as of value. Now it was time to recognise the processes of production that, through wealth accumulation, had allowed the construction of such buildings. An early success was perhaps the upgrading of Albert Dock in Liverpool to Grade I status in 1968 (Samuel 1994); by the end of the 1970s, industrial heritage was firmly established as a conservationist cause and was, for example, the subject of a major SAVE report and exhibition, *Satanic Mills* (SAVE Britain's Heritage 1979). Allied to the growth of industrial archaeology was the development of open-air museums linked to industrialism, with major sites at Ironbridge in Shropshire and Beamish in County Durham. Although later caricatured as part of Hewison's *Heritage Industry* (1987), at their inception in

4.3
In the 1970s, appreciation developed for industrial heritage. Historic mill buildings in the Lower Ouseburn Valley, Newcastle upon Tyne, now converted into the National Centre for the Children's Book, a theatre, artists' studios and a bar.
Source: author.

the 1960s they were seen as being at the radical end of museum practice, emulating earlier Scandinavian examples and bringing access to this heritage to a broader spectrum of society.

The study of vernacular architecture had also been slowly developing in the post-war period. 1971 saw the publication of Brunskill's seminal *Illustrated Handbook of Vernacular Architecture* (Brunskill 1971). Oliver's *English Cottages and Small Farmhouses* (Oliver 1975) included a polemical plea for the importance of vernacular building and its conservation, whereas an article by Tarn (1976), based on the Derbyshire Peak District, was an argument for the conservation of ordinary vernacular, while recognising the need to sustain the vitality of communities.

European Architectural Heritage Year 1975

One of the defining events of heritage protection in the 1970s was European Architectural Heritage Year (EAHY), designated by the Council of Europe. In retrospect EAHY can be seen as an event that mobilised very different discourses about the state of the conservation movement. In official programmes EAHY was a celebration of the achievements of conservation planning over the preceding few years. For example, the document produced for Bath (Bath City Council 1975) made no mention of the conservation controversies that had raged in that city, as exemplified by *The Sack of Bath* (Fergusson 1973). However, for more radical elements of the conservation movement, it was an opportunity to publicise ongoing failings in heritage protection. Thus it was in 1975 that SAVE Britain's Heritage was formed, following the exhibition the previous year at the Victoria and Albert Museum, *The Destruction of the Country House*. The first press release early in 1975 announced that, in EAHY, applications to demolish 334 listed buildings and a further 163 in conservation areas had already been received (Binney 2005). However, in the British context overall, there seems to have been a determination to engage at a grass-roots level. Conservation activity was now seen to encompass modest acts of environmental improvement, and it has been said that EAHY 'had something of the character of the village fete' (Delafons 1997a: 110).

Internationally, the main contribution of the year was a programme of pilot projects (fifty projects in seventeen different countries) demonstrating a variety of conservation problems and possible solutions. The four principal aims of EAHY were: to awaken the interest of the European peoples in their common architectural heritage; to protect and enhance buildings and areas of architectural or historic interest; to conserve the character of old towns and villages; to assure for ancient buildings a living role in contemporary society (Council of Europe 1973). The aims of EAHY in the UK were defined as: practical enhancement projects in conservation areas, such as building renovations and re-use, pedestrianisation schemes and removal of street 'clutter'; the

4.4
Building preservation trust activity celebrated during EAHY: a before and after from Norwich (Dartmouth 1975).
Source: Norwich Preservation Trust.

inauguration of a campaign for environmental education; and the establishment of a national revolving fund for architectural heritage works (the Architectural Heritage Fund so created provides finance for building preservation trusts to this day).

There was a concerted effort within EAHY to be non-elitist. For example, in *What is Our Heritage?* (Dartmouth 1975), the relatively common-place, such as Monkwearmouth Station in Sunderland or small regency terraces in Cheltenham, received as much attention as the architecturally grand; albeit with hindsight these attempts at a more inclusionary discourse, with the text by the Countess of Dartmouth and the foreword by the Duke of Edinburgh, can seem hilariously patrician (for example, 'A few months ago, some friends from the Argentine came to stay with us in the country' (p. 86) or 'Prince Philip has suggested that people whose hobbies are related to conservation, might extend their activities into weekend or part-time work' (p. 20)). There was also a sense of looking to Europe to acquire experience and inspiration. Elements of European city management were studied. The cleaning of historic buildings, for example, was seen as a 'European' thing. Paris had gone though a comprehensive process of cleaning and this was seen to inspire British cities to do likewise. There was a real sense that EAHY would bring European countries closer together in recognition of their shared past, even when this was embroiled with conflict and war. EAHY led to the Council of Europe's Amsterdam Declaration, which emphasised the necessity of integrating physical and social conservation (Appleyard 1979). The promotion of the concept of 'integrated conservation', the embedding of conservation activity firmly in a wider process of land-use planning, was considered key, and this idea was entrenched in subsequent Council of Europe Conventions, the 1985 Granada Convention, concerned with architectural heritage, and the 1992 Malta Convention, concerned with archaeology.

The review of the heritage year by SAVE in *The Architects' Journal* (SAVE Britain's Heritage 1975) remained as unimpressed with EAHY as its initial press release, noting that listed buildings were being demolished at the rate of one a day. It suggested that the public funds had been wasted on super-ficialities and that the campaign should have concentrated on legal sanctions, fiscal reforms and encouraging owners to maintain their buildings. Local authority officials were still regarded as 'philistines'. Overall, though, EAHY was judged a success (e.g. Delafons 1997a). Viewed another way, it can be seen as a high point of the decade, with the gains achieved threatened by lack of political support and renewed economic austerity towards the end of the decade. I return to this below.

Whose homes? Whose conservation?

As part of a book celebrating EAHY, Worskett (1975) discussed progress in British conservation. He distinguished between areas where a combination of legislative measures and the market had made conservation a comfortably established reality, and those areas that needed public intervention to resolve physical and economic problems. Even here though, at the height of EAHY, there was a note of disquiet about the operation of the market and its propensity simply to move social problems somewhere else. Nor was he alone in these concerns. In the same volume, describing the parlous state of New Lanark (now a World Heritage Site), Jeffrey (1975: 70) opined that 'the village must not be allowed to become a dormitory for commuters', and in an editorial insert between chapters it was stated that,

> Conservation in its true sense will be seen to have failed if they [attractive villages] end up as dormitories to the large cities, with their housing 'gentrified' and their industrial buildings either demolished or turned into museums.
>
> (Cantacuzino 1975a: 60)

Bailly was another who, in one of the official EAHY publications, devoted considerable space to the social consequences of conservation actions, including the effect of speculators and 'the capitalistic transformation of the town [which] profoundly affects its historic value and function' (Bailly 1975: 84). Bailly also discussed the case of Bologna. Bologna then and subsequently was held up as a model of successful conservation policy in achieving the rehabilitation of buildings while sustaining and reinforcing the existing community (Bandarin 1979). In Bologna conservation policy was integrated within wider planning and housing policies that had been evolving since the late 1950s. Traditionally run by a Communist local government, policies were formed to oppose speculative property market gains, improve the housing conditions of the working class and protect the heritage of the urban centre. Integrated into this process was the partial decentralisation of power to neighbourhood councils. At a conference in 1966, the eminent architect Leonardo Benevolo, who was engaged on studies from 1962, produced a methodology and system of regulation for maintaining architectural typologies; this was not just a focus on appearance and the façade. The master plan for the historic centre was adopted in 1969. It defined typologies and indicated allowable uses for each typology and the kind of renovation allowable for each typology.

Central to the debate was discussion about who should benefit from this conservation process, and there was an explicit objective of resistance to large-scale gentrification. Thus, a key conservation principle evolved: conservation goals were not to be directed exclusively towards building fabric, but were also to include 'cultural conservation', sustaining the existing population and culture, rather than seeing historic buildings as neutral containers for the highest value economic activities. In the early 1970s the administration of the city developed the 'Public Housing Programme for the Historic Centre' to provide public housing through the renovation of historic buildings. As stated at the time by propaganda for the scheme, 'Conservation signifies the social reappropriation of the city. In this case "Conservation is Revolution"' (reproduced in Bandarin 1979: 187).

Restoration plans for one
quarter. From Accame

4.5
**Restoration plans
in Bologna (from
*Conoscenza e
coscienza della
citta : una politica
per il centro
storico di
Bologna*).**
© Giovanni M.
Accame.

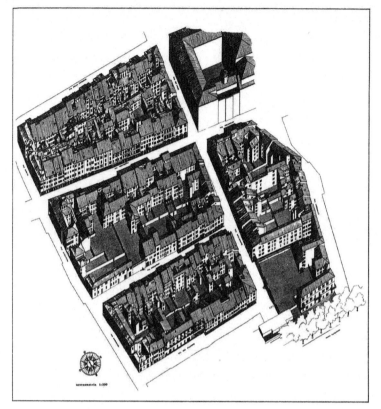

The policies in Bologna provided inspiration for other cities in the
Emilia-Romagna region at least. However, such integration between physical
conservation and social sustainability was not evident in much of the western
world and specifically not in the United Kingdom. Though gentrification was
often discussed as a problem, little was done to prevent it, and indeed public
policy often contributed to its acceleration. Not surprisingly, gentrification was
particularly evident in London. Raban, in *Soft City* (1974), famously caricatured
the aggressive gentrification of a square in Islington, kick-started by conservation area status. Here and elsewhere this status seemed to fuel rapidly
escalating property prices. Furthermore, it was clear that new, middle-class
residents used conservation status in battles over urban space. For example,
in the Barnsbury area in Islington, middle-class amenity groups, using conservation justifications, sought to prevent the compulsory purchase and demolition
of property for council redevelopment that was supported at public inquiry
by working-class residents (Ferris 1972 cited by Lowe 1977), and to push

through-traffic out of the area into surrounding working-class neighbourhoods (Croot 1985). National shifts in housing policy towards rehabilitation, with refurbishment grants available to owners, tended to benefit colonisation by middle-class owner-occupiers with access to matching capital, rather than assisting existing tenants (Appleyard 1979).

Spitalfields in East London is one location involving many who subsequently formed the conservation 'great and the good', where the ultimate effective gentrification of an area has been portrayed as one of the heroic victories of the conservation movement. The beginnings of the Spitalfields conservation story were very 1970s in flavour, combining elements of both aristocratic patronage and militant action by an upper-middle-class cultural cabal. The historic qualities of the area had been recognised since the 1950s, both by some of those who then participated in the 1970s action (Blain 1989) and more officially by the Survey of London, and in 1969 the local authority designated three conservation areas in the locality (Jacobs 1992). A particular characteristic of the area were the houses built by French Huguenots, with studio mansards built for their weaving businesses. However, despite official recognition of heritage significance, buildings were disappearing fast: by 1977 only 140 of the 230 eighteenth-century buildings remained of those identified by the Survey of London as having architectural value. The decision to form the Spitalfields Historic Building Trust was apparently taken at a country-house weekend in Northern Ireland hosted by the Marchioness of Dufferin and Ava. Thus, this was not a grassroots organisation from within an existing local community; indeed the Trust asserted that this was effectively an empty area in the city (Blain 1989). It consciously sought influential people to further its objectives, and some of the participants, such as Mark Girouard, Dan Cruickshank and Raphael Samuel went on to become well known in architectural and conservation arenas.

At its outset, at least some members of the Trust had a social as well as architectural purpose to their mission. Girouard was the founding Chairman of the Trust. In 1979 he outlined his vision for the area in *Country Life* (!). What Girouard sought to create, evoking the spirit of the eighteenth century, was a mixed community of different ethnic groups and classes rather than the segregated enclaves that had typified London from the nineteenth century (Wright 1992). So, for example, he was very positive about the influence of the Bangladeshi community in the area; many of the occupied buildings in the area were used by Bangladeshis for small-scale garment manufacturing. However, alongside this progressive interpretation of the eighteenth-century spirit, the 'New Georgians' in the 1980s celebrated the coexistence of affluence with extreme poverty in the area as part of a picaresque tableau, also harking back to the eighteenth century (Wright 1992).

In order to break out of the cycle of active and passive building neglect in the area, the Trust used direct-action tactics. In 1977, 5–7 Elder Street was squatted, as were other buildings subsequently. These were 'top-persons' squats: a photo in the Trust's tenth anniversary book shows Sir John Betjeman coming to visit, dodging scaffolding, plastic cup in hand (Girouard *et al.* 1989)(see Figure 4.6). To ensure the appropriate conservation of buildings, the key modus operandi of the Trust was to acquire them: by the tenth anniversary they had recycled seventeen buildings. In selling them on they sought new owners whom they considered sympathetic (Blain 1989). With opaque means of buyer selection and with rising property values in the 1980s, there arose the spectre of public money (projects often attracted grant-aid) being used to create personal fortunes (Wright 1992). I return to the Spitalfields story, charges of gentrification and the pursuit of a particular and inauthentic aesthetic vision in Chapter 6.

4.6
Conservation activism: Sir John Betjeman is escorted by Dan Cruikshank past No.9 Elder Street, Spitalfields, during its occupation in 1977.
Source: The Architectural Press.

The end of the decade

If EAHY was a high point of the period for the conservation movement, the low point came towards the end of the decade when the hard won gains of the 1970s appeared to be in danger; some sense of this uncertainty is conveyed in the conclusion to Dobby's book of the time where he expressed the view that 1975 might have been a peak for conservation in Britain (Dobby 1978). Within a country in economic crisis, heritage issues were not high on the political agenda and the lack of resources was particularly acute. Though it was not in the conservation-planning arena, the case that embodied the period was the 1977 sale of Mentmore Towers, a large country house in Buckinghamshire. This was the subject of a big conservation campaign, including a SAVE report, but the government failed to take up its option of a £2 million sale price for the house and contents, even though it was clear that this was a fraction of the true monetary value (Booker 1980; Binney 2005).

In the planning arena, Delafons (1997a) and Saunders (1996) noted how Labour ministers were hinting that too many marginal buildings had been listed. There was discussion on removing controls from some listed buildings, the numbers of listing inspectors were reduced to an all time low, and budgets were tightened. However, and perhaps remarkably given the complexion of the incoming government, this was all to swing back round in favour of conservation objectives in the 1980s, as discussed in the next chapter. What disappeared from sight in the 1980s and 1990s was the idea that the conservation of the historic environment had a wider social purpose. Instead, the economic utility of heritage came to the fore, though SAVE had blazed this trail with *Preservation Pays: Tourism and the Economic Benefits of Conserving Historic Building* in 1978 (SAVE Britain's Heritage 1978).

An adapted modernity

The role of conservation in planning was transformed during the latter part of the 1960s and the 1970s. The number of listed buildings grew, listing status acquired effective controls, the system of conservation areas was created, and control over demolition was added subsequently. Above all, policy presumptions shifted, and the wider attitudes of society changed. Rather than the retention of isolated historic buildings within city-centre redevelopments, it became the norm, even if still often contested, that redevelopment should work around a much more broadly defined historic city. What it was felt important to protect became less selectively defined and employed less patrician criteria. The position of conservation in city management moved from the periphery to the centre ground.

In part this change resulted from local development struggles up and down the country, as immortalised in some of the evocative polemics of the period. In part, it was a consequence of local groups using 'responsible styles' of action to engage with local authorities and persuade them of a more conservation-sensitive approach. In part, it was the result of economic circumstances that made large schemes of road or property development unrealistic. While such successes for the conservation movement meant that many historic buildings and areas were spared from the bulldozer, there was also a strong consciousness that a policy of conservation carried social consequences that needed to be integral to a process of conservation planning. Much is made of the role of the collapse of modernist architecture and planning in this shift. But perhaps it would be truer to say that the collapse, and the schism between modernism and conservation, related to a particular *version* of modernism. Certainly, the grandiloquent schemes, brutally forced onto historic cities, that had too often characterised the 1960s and early 1970s were generally vanquished. And figures who had been in the vanguard of the conservation movement while being keen advocates of large-scale redevelopment, such as Sir John Summerson, seemed peripheral and anachronistic in the new climate.

Conservation, though, continued as a modern practice, in the terms set out in Chapter 2. The pendulum swung to be more oppositional to many of the manifestations of modernism, but conservation remained closely bound into the modern planning system nevertheless. It used the same mechanisms: the listing of buildings derived for 1940s re-planning remained the cornerstone of the protection system. It was listing that killed the GLC's scheme for the redevelopment of Covent Garden. Furthermore, the GLC remained responsible for implementing a comprehensive planning scheme, albeit to a very different vision. Expert knowledge was still to the forefront, and it was in this period that a conservation profession began to develop at a local level. Critical key precepts, such as authenticity, continued in importance. There remained a dominant view amongst conservationists that new buildings should be 'of their time', i.e. clearly contemporary and not reproductions of historic styles, albeit they should be more sympathetic to historic form than some of the monsters of the preceding period. Influential concepts from the 1940s, such as townscape, were adapted to conservation practice, initially by Worskett (1969) but subsequently by others (for example Burke 1976). The association of historic places with community identity that was developing was predicated upon modern ideas of historicity. Indeed, the social concern over the consequences of conservation actions indicated that there was an ongoing belief in the progressive role and potential of conservation planning. This was not a break with modernity, but an adaptation of it.

Chapter 5

Conservation, Conservatives and consensus

Introduction

The British Conservative governments between 1979 and 1997 are usually associated with a strident agenda of economic liberalism, combined with a centralisation of political power, which affected land-use planning along with other policy spheres. However, not only did the conservation of the historic environment escape these forces, but its policy significance actually strengthened during this period. In a time associated with the breakdown of post-war political consensus, conservation policy goals achieved a virtually unchallenged consensus for the first time. There are a few exceptions to this success story of the conservation movement: for example, physical relics of the coal industry were generally removed with unseemly haste following the pit closures in the wake of the miners' strike of 1984–5. However, in the main the period was characterised by a consolidation and strengthening of conservation policy at a previously unprecedented level.

Parallel to this strengthening of conservation policy, during the 1980s there was a growth of public interest in a more broadly defined idea of heritage, expressed not only through interest in historic buildings, but also through such media as fashion and lifestyle. The antiques business boomed, lifestyle magazines focusing on historic styles proliferated and so on (Wright 1985). This taste for heritage provides an important backdrop for understanding the growing emphasis on conservation-supportive policies. I return to the public popularity of heritage and conservation in Chapter 7. Linked to the apparent attraction of the public to heritage is its commodification, and this is the theme of Chapter 6.

The main focus in this chapter is on the conservation-planning system of this period. In order to demonstrate the shifts in favour of conservation policies, the chapter examines the protection regime and its evolution during the lifetime of Conservative administrations (a fuller account can be found in Pendlebury 2000). Subsequently, the discussion shifts to a more local level: how was a policy, apparently sympathetic to conservation, implemented on the ground? In particular I consider the issue of change in commercial centres, where tensions inevitably exist between rich historic environments and the commercial desire for change. Again, by and large, a policy of conservation proved enormously popular with local planning authorities. There was a shift from the 1970s debate about *whether* historic buildings should be retained to one of *how* they should be retained. Total demolition of listed buildings became rarer and rarer, but permission was given for the transformation, almost beyond recognition, of many historic buildings through such drastic processes as façadism. Finally, and briefly, the issue of new design within historic centres is considered, focusing in particular on the 'style wars' of the 1980s between modernists and traditionalists, the latter exemplified by the Prince of Wales.

Conservatives and planning

Analyses of planning in the UK during this era generally divide the period of Conservative power into two parts: first, the period of Margaret Thatcher's prime ministership, or 'Thatcherism' (1979–1990) and, second, the post-Thatcher governments of John Major (1990–1997), characterised not only by a change of leadership, but also by a reconfiguration of the government's approach to the planning system.

There has been general consensus over the nature of the political agenda during the Thatcher period (reviewed by Allmendinger and Thomas (1998)). This has tended to be described in terms of the breakdown of a post-war planning consensus, based on the need physically to reconstruct the fabric of cities, and its replacement with a neo-liberal agenda aimed at giving the market greater freedom to develop in ways of its own choosing. To facilitate this, there was both a centralisation of control and a limitation on the discretion available to local planning authorities. In practice, in order to achieve regeneration objectives and overcome resistance from vested interests, there was a fragmentation of the system. This was characterised by Thornley (1991) at various levels: first, the general case, where the market was given greater freedom, and local authority development control powers were weakened;

second, where more extreme liberalisation was introduced, sometimes together with other measures such as changed governance, to achieve urban regeneration/transformation (for example, Enterprise Zones and Urban Development Corporations); third, the protection of vested interests in defined areas of restraint, such as areas of countryside protection, the green belt and areas of cultural heritage.

There has been less of a clear consensus over the precise Conservative political agenda for planning in the 1990s. However, the basic agenda can be seen as one of modified continuity, with the emphasis still firmly on the dominance of the market and the exertion of central control to enable that market to operate freely (Thornley 1998). In order to achieve policy objectives there was, however, a shift from interference in day-to-day decisions via the appeals process, to an emphasis on a tighter policy framework. Central prescription occurred through a series of Planning Policy Guidance Notes (PPGs), which in turn formed a key framework for locally produced development plans that themselves gained new emphasis with the Planning and Compensation Act 1991 and its reference to the 'plan-led system'.

Conservation and Conservatives

Protection

In the period immediately before 1979 the Labour government seemed at best lukewarm to certain elements of conservation policy. Proposals were mooted to remove statutory controls from some listed buildings, and the number of inspectors identifying buildings for listing had sunk to an all-time low (Saunders 1996). However, a very different pattern emerged in the 1980s and 1990s. In this and following sections, central government's approach towards conservation over the eighteen-year Conservative administration is audited and examined. The main focus of discussion is on the degree of protection afforded to cultural heritage, though organisational and resource issues are also briefly considered.

The basic procedural town planning framework as set out in primary legislation was not fundamentally altered in this period. Changes were generally effected through modifications to secondary legislation/statutory instruments and policy guidance (Thornley 1998). This was also largely true in the conservation arena, though legislation did lead to the creation of new protected categories (for example, the Register of Parks and Gardens of Special Historic Interest), and some organisational change (for example, the creation of English Heritage). Few efforts at deregulation were evident in the legislation or statutory instruments relating to conservation.

While the overarching framework of legislation remained stable, quite dramatic changes occurred in the amount of the historic environment that was protected and the policy framework that was applied to it. As Table 5.1 shows, the number of listed buildings increased massively during the period of Conservative governments. The first listing programme ran from 1947 to 1968. When the Conservatives came to power in 1979 a second programme was proceeding, though very slowly. This was dramatically accelerated in 1982 by the allocation of substantially increased resources, and the second programme was completed by 1989. In the late 1970s there were four inspectors working on the resurvey, but at the height of activity in the mid 1980s this rose to a peak of 110 (Robertson 1993a). Much of the credit for this enormous expansion in resources has been given to the personal support of the then Secretary of State for the Environment, Michael Heseltine. For many, the case that defined the

Table 5.1 **Growth in numbers of listed buildings and conservation areas in England 1977–1997**

	Number of listed building entries	Increase	Applications to demolish (no. of buildings)	Consent for demolition	% of listed buildings where consent given for demolition	Conservation areas	Increase
1997	451 287	936	233	58	0.013	8724	132
1996	450 351	1516	225	61	0.014	8592	157
1995	448 835	2056	198	51	0.011	8435	120
1994	446 779	3309	219	92	0.021	8315	343
1993	443 470	2795	284	64	0.014	7972	368
1992	440 675	1627	263	68	0.015	7604	46
1991	439 048	2008	363	84	0.019	7558	401
1990	437 040	3386	401	110	0.025	7157	442
1989	433 654	3094	397	97	0.022	6679	382
1988	430 560	25 174	585	156	0.038	6297	226
1987	405 386	10 009	606	170	0.042	6071	138
1986	395 377	27 657	511	157	0.040	5933	146
1985	367 720	29 641	490	180	0.049	5787	178
1984	338 079	29 614	418	216	0.064	5609	213
1983	308 465	20 721	445	171	0.055	5396	120
1982	287 744	7549	523	161	0.056	5276	116
1981	280 195	6877	471	147	0.052	5160	346
1980	273 318	6633	542	276	0.101	4814	189
1979	266 685	6815	654	301	0.113	4625	192
1978	259 870	8300	770	n/a	n/a	4433	251
1977	251 570		703	306	0.122	4182	343

Note: Data in this table were taken from the annual publication, *English Heritage Monitor* (Hanna, annual from 1978–98). Owing to changes in data production in the period there are likely to be some inconsistencies in the data, but these are minor and do not alter the overall trends evident.
Source: author 2006

zeitgeist for the period was the demolition, during the August Bank Holiday in 1980, of the Firestone Factory (a 1930s Art Deco building in London), while it was under consideration for listing. This seems to have been an important spur and appeared to have incensed Heseltine (Stamp 1996; Larkham and Barrett 1998). Numerically, much of the expansion of listing during this period consisted of vernacular buildings in rural areas. For example, the number of listed buildings in Cheshire rose from 2070 to 6450, with the biggest increase being in rural areas (Bott 1987). However, as the list grew in size, it also accommodated a greater diversity of building types, including for example significant numbers of industrial buildings. Indeed, following the rural resurvey, more limited resources were devoted to enhancing some lists in urban-industrial areas. This led, for example, to the doubling of the number of listings in Hull (Cherry 1996). Subsequently, the focus shifted to thematic work, including textile mills and post-1945 buildings (Saunders 1996; Cherry 1996). Remarkably, given the political complexion of the government, this included the listing of welfare-state housing, such as Alexandra Road in Camden (see Figure 5.1) and Keeling House in Bethnal Green (see Figure 9.6). Again, this has been credited to a sympathetic minister, in this case Peter Brook (Harwood 2005).

Though conservation areas are designated by local authorities, they are relevant to this discussion of central government policy. They are analogous to green belts, in so far as they are a policy device with substantial legislative and policy weight endorsed from the centre, but identified locally. However, unlike green-belt boundaries, which are defined and enforced by development plans that are subject to central government scrutiny, conservation areas are created on a resolution by a local authority, with no central government check. It is notable that Conservative central governments did not make any serious

5.1
**Alexandra Road,
Camden, London,
listed in 1993.**
Source: author.

attempt to limit the administrative discretion of local planning authorities to designate new areas, despite the growth in designations and in critical commentaries on local authority use of these powers (Jones and Larkham 1993; Morton 1991). Table 5.1 shows how the number of conservation areas increased steadily throughout the period of Conservative administration. Furthermore, many other conservation areas were extended. The growth in the number of conservation areas is discussed further below.

There were three key central government policy statements of relevance in the period under consideration. When the Conservatives came to power in 1979, policy was set out in Department of the Environment *Circular 23/77: Historic Buildings and Conservation Areas – Policy and Procedure* (Department of the Environment 1977). This was superseded in 1987 by *Circular 8/87* (Department of the Environment 1987), bearing the same title, and in 1994 by *Planning Policy Guidance Note 15: Planning and the Historic Environment* (Department of the Environment and Department of National Heritage 1994). Table 5.2 summarises the policy set out in these documents on a number of key issues. In comparing 23/77 and 8/87, no radical changes are evident, though there were some significant shifts in emphasis. For example, in the early 1980s (and confirmed in 8/87) Michael Heseltine emphasised the need for adequate efforts to be made to reuse listed buildings before allowing their demolition (Andreae 1996). The Circular was regarded as strengthening conservation policy (Arnold 1987). PPG 15 involved a fundamental redraft of previous guidance. As such there were subtle nuances and shifts, but again the overall sense is of policy continuity. So, for example, a presumption in favour of the preservation of listed buildings was retained. Generally the orientation of changes seemed to be towards, first, a strengthening of conservation policy (for example, with an antagonistic attitude towards façadism) and, second, an increase in the amount of policy advice to local authorities (for example, on conservation area designation) and exhortations to more firmly attach conservation to other processes (for example, development plans and public consultation). The PPG was seen as a greater assertion of conservation interests than ever before (Mynors 1994; Delafons 1997a).

All applications for the total demolition of listed buildings have to be referred to central government, as do any requests to delist buildings. Table 5.1 shows a trajectory for these categories as remarkable as the growth in the number of listed buildings. In both cases the general pattern was a decrease in the number of buildings granted consent for demolition or withdrawn from the list. Given the increase in number of listed buildings, the proportion of listed buildings authorised for demolition fell markedly from 1979. More debatable, during the 1980s especially, was the government's influence through the planning appeal process on the degree of intervention permissible on listed buildings. This is discussed below.

Table 5.2 **Summary of Circulars 23/77 and 8/87 and PPG15 on key policy issues**

	Circular 23/77: Historic Buildings and Conservation Areas – Policy and Procedure	*Circular 8/87: Historic Buildings and Conservation Areas – Policy and Procedure*	*PPG 15: Planning and the Historic Environment*
Historic Buildings			
Demolition of listed buildings	'the presumption should be in favour of preservation' 64 Specific criteria for proposals to demolish: the condition of the building; 'the importance of any alternative use for the site and, in particular whether the use of the site for some public purpose would make it possible to enhance the environment and especially other listed buildings in the area; or whether in a run-down area, a limited redevelopment might bring new life and make the other listed buildings more economically viable.' 63(d)	'the presumption should be in favour of preservation' 91 Specific criteria for proposals to demolish: the condition of the building; the adequacy of efforts made to retain the building in use; 'the importance of any alternative use for the site and, in particular whether the use of the site for some public purpose would make it possible to enhance the environment and especially other listed buildings in the area; or whether in a run-down area, a limited redevelopment might bring new life and make the other listed buildings more economically viable.' 90 (d)	'There should be a general presumption in favour of the preservation of listed buildings . . .' 3.3 Specific criteria for proposals to demolish: the condition of the building; the adequacy of efforts made to retain the building in use; 'the merits of alternative proposals for the site. . . . Subjective claims for the architectural merits of proposed replacement buildings should not in themselves be held to justify the demolition of any listed building. There may very exceptionally be cases where the proposed works would bring substantial benefits for the community . . .' 3.19 iii
Façadism	No specific mention, though should consider the importance of the building and merit including e.g. design, plan materials. Guidance on interiors in Appendix.	No specific mention, though should consider the importance of the building and merit including e.g. design, plan materials. Guidance on interiors in Appendix.	'The preservation of façades alone, and the gutting and reconstruction of interiors, is not normally an acceptable approach to the re-use of buildings: it can destroy much of a building's special interest and create problems for the long-term stability of the structure.' 3.15
Justification for proposals	Nothing	Nothing	'Applicants for listed building consent must be able to justify their proposals.' 3.4

Table 5.2 continued

	Circular 23/77: Historic Buildings and Conservation Areas – Policy and Procedure	Circular 8/87: Historic Buildings and Conservation Areas – Policy and Procedure	PPG 15: Planning and the Historic Environment
Relationship with other elements of the planning system			
Economic function of conservation	No mention	'Conservation makes good economic sense. Neglect of buildings will involve bigger bills in the future; an empty building is a wasted asset. Conservation schemes revitalise run down areas, and create a better environment, good homes and opportunity for employment.' 153	'... conservation and sustainable economic growth are complementary objectives and should not generally be seen as in opposition to one another.' 1.4 'Conservation can itself play a key part in promoting economic prosperity by ensuring that an area offers attractive living and working conditions which will encourage inward investment – environmental quality is increasingly a key factor in many commercial decisions. The historic environment is of particular importance for tourism and leisure . . .' 1.5
Urban regeneration	No reference	'In the areas of Urban Development Corporations and in Enterprise Zones and Simplified Planning Zones, normal listed building control applies, but in these areas and any others where economic regeneration is vital or if it is a question of finding a new use for an individual building, the aim should be to demonstrate that conservation can be successfully incorporated into the revitalisation proposals and not be regarded as an obstacle to their implementation.' 5	No specific reference.
Development plans	No reference	Few references. Authorities urged to review conservation area designation programme when plans prepared, as a means of publicising proposals.	Whole section, including, e.g.: 'Structure, local, and unitary development plans are the main vehicle for ensuring that conservation policies are co-ordinated and integrated with other planning policies affecting the historic environment.' 2.2

Source: author 2006

Conservation governance and resources

A major organisational change in dealing with conservation during the period
of Conservative government was the creation of English Heritage. This new
body, which became fully effective in 1984, assumed various responsibilities
from the Department of the Environment (DoE) and from various other advisory
bodies existing at the time. It became advisor to the government on
conservation planning matters, with ultimate administrative responsibility
remaining with the Secretary of State. Though some saw English Heritage,
especially in its early years, as comparatively ineffective (Andreae 1996), a more
common view was that with the creation of a staffed independent advisor, the
government developed 'a new and powerful voice for conservation' (Delafons
1997a: 142). So, for example, English Heritage has frequently appeared at public
inquiries to put forward a conservation case, something that could not have
happened when powers resided with government alone. In creating English
Heritage, Michael Heseltine explicitly seemed to want to give a clear and visible
voice for conservation (Kennett 1991 cited in Larkham and Barrett 1998).

Analysis of the resources available to conservation through this
period is extremely complicated. Overall it seems that public resources were
not as constrained as in many other policy areas. On the one hand, it is stated
that English Heritage resources fell in real terms, and that, as a discretionary
activity, conservation was hit by restrictions in local government expenditure
(Larkham and Barrett 1998). On the other hand, an alternative analysis indicated
that greater sums in real terms were available to English Heritage compared
with its predecessor, the Historic Buildings Council (Saunders 1996). The
additional resources that were directed at the listing programme have
been described above. Furthermore, in some locations, such as the Urban

Development Corporation areas, an emphasis on property-led regeneration, especially during the 1980s, enabled expensive and high-profile conservation projects to proceed. In the 1990s, major regeneration efforts occurred in city centres, such as the Grainger Town area of Newcastle upon Tyne, and again allowed substantial resources to be committed to conservation-related work. Finally, in the latter part of the Conservative administration, the creation of the Heritage Lottery Fund (HLF), as part of the National Lottery, allowed unprecedented sums to be directed towards public- and voluntary-sector conservation projects (Saunders 1996).

Conservative Party politics

It is very difficult to explain satisfactorily why conservation policy strengthened so markedly during this extended period of Conservative government and how much it related to immediate practical politics and how much to more structural explanations of the role of culture in society. In Chapter 9, there is a brief discussion both on the political function heritage might have embodied for the Conservatives and on dominant ideology theory, which sees cultural constructs such as heritage as reinforcing class and power relations. This section looks more specifically at different strands of thought within the Conservative Party before moving on to consider the significance of the conservation lobby.

Conservative Party politics can be considered at two levels: first, differences of policy approach and emphasis taken by successive Secretaries of State for the Environment and, second, broader tensions between the traditional Tory centre and the radical Right. Michael Heseltine, Secretary of State for the Environment between 1979 and 1983 (and again between 1990 and 1993), has often been characterised as a minister who took a close and supportive personal interest in conservation matters (Larkham and Barrett 1998). At the opposite end of the spectrum in this regard was Nicholas Ridley, Secretary of State between 1986 and 1989. In 1988, Ridley publicly attacked what he viewed as an over-emphasis on conservation, stating,

> I have a recurring nightmare, that sometime in the next century the entire country will be designated under some conservation order or another. The people actually living there will be smothered with bureaucratic instructions limiting their freedom. We will have created a sanitised, bureaucratised and ossified countryside out of something which has always been, and should always be, a product of the interaction of man and his environment as time goes by.
>
> (cited by Larkham and Barrett 1998: 57)

Differences between Ridley and Heseltine were illustrated by an exchange of correspondence between them in the professional planning press in 1988 (Thornley 1991).

Nevertheless, despite such political differences, conservation policy enjoyed continuity and remained unchallenged. For example, the accelerated resurvey programme, the initiative for which Heseltine is given greatest credit, was only agreed three weeks before his departure from office (Robertson 1993a). Its implementation occurred over a seven-year period until 1989 and was largely uninterrupted under a series of Secretaries of State considered to take a more libertarian approach to planning (Hall 1997), including Ridley's tenure. Similarly Circular 8/87, with its policy continuity and strengthening, was produced during Ridley's time in office.

Support from some Conservatives for a policy of conservation was to be expected (see, for example, Cormack 1976); what is more surprising was the lack of a sustained right-wing critique. Thornley (1991) reviewed a number of right-wing treatises on the planning system produced in the 1970s and 1980s, and by and large conservation protection was exempted from these critiques and calls for deregulation. Official investigations into conservation, such as a Select Committee in 1986 and the Public Accounts Committee in 1992, barely bothered questioning the essential basis of the conservation system (Delafons 1997a).

Right-wing Conservative MP Teresa Gorman's libertarian attack on conservation controls, in the wake of her own prosecution for unauthorised works to her listed house, was notable for its iconoclasm (Hirst 1996). The only other fundamental critiques of conservation in this period, apart from the occasional speech by Nicholas Ridley, come from outside the government and Conservative Party. For example, there were claims from the architectural profession and the development industry that the extent of protection had grown too large (Saunders 1996). This challenge was taken up by property interests and the right-wing think tank, the Centre for Policy Studies, when objecting to the City of London Local Plan in the mid 1980s, in the period leading up to 'the Big Bang' (Thornley 1991). In 1985 there was a brief campaign by the National Farmers' Union and the Country Landowners Association against the rural listing resurvey programme (Robertson 1993b). However, these attacks on conservation orthodoxy were few and, at the national level at least, almost entirely unsuccessful.

The conservation lobby

There are a number of external forces that might have inhibited successive Conservative governments from attempting to liberalise conservation controls and policy. Key amongst these is the political pressure exerted by a range of organisations that, collectively, can be considered as a conservation lobby; this included local authorities, many of which were Conservative.

Though political complexion is not a reliable indicator of a local authority's approach to, and emphasis on, conservation, it is a policy issue that is often of more significance to Conservative local authorities, and NIMBY lobbies may assume more political significance than elsewhere. Many of the better resourced conservation functions are to be found in traditionally Conservative shire areas. So, for example, Hampshire and Essex County Councils lobbied for the accelerated re-listing programme and were able to respond quickly to facilitate the programme when it proceeded (Richards 1993; Robertson 1993a). One grouping of local authorities, the English Historic Towns Forum, became a vocal advocate of strengthening the status of conservation areas by bringing minor changes, 'permitted development', within planning control to prevent the erosion of character through small-scale incremental change (English Historic Towns Forum 1992).

These local authorities can be considered as part of a distinctive conservation lobby or community. There are a number of significant, specific professional groupings. At a national level, the creation of English Heritage was a key factor. The civil service background of many of the original staff must also have helped to sustain an influence on, and links with, the DoE. Also during the 1980s, there emerged a lobby of conservation professionals working within local government, the Association of Conservation Officers, which subsequently transformed into the more broadly based Institute of Historic Building Conservation. This was part of the process of the professionalisation of local authority conservation, such that 'Conservation Officer' became a familiar and established term. However, in addition to this professional voice, a distinctive feature of conservation was the size and range of the associated conservation amenity movement. It was this movement that, since the nineteenth century, had been the driving force behind the pressure for developments in conservation legislation (Delafons 1997a). One measure of the significance of some of the national societies is their incorporation in legislation as statutory consultees on applications affecting historic buildings from the 1960s onwards. A range of commentators attest to the influence of these national groups from a variety of perspectives (e.g. Delafons 1997a; Saunders 1996; Larkham 1996; Stamp 1996). Though their precise influence during the period of Conservative government is difficult to establish, it is clear that individually and collectively they mounted well-orchestrated campaigns against perceived threats both to the conservation system and over individual cases. For example, Delafons (1997a) referred to the government's surprise at the strength of reaction from interested parties to a number of consultations during this period, and final versions of policy were generally more conservationist in tone than were the preliminary drafts. High-profile, and expensive, campaigns were also fought on key proposals. For example, when planning permission was given by the Secretary of State for a scheme at No. 1 Poultry in the City of London, which involved the demolition of listed buildings and unlisted buildings in a conservation area, SAVE Britain's Heritage pursued the case through to the

House of Lords, as discussed further below (Larkham 1996). However, particularly during the Thatcher period, it has often been considered that there was a decline in the influence of the 'great and the good' (Hewison 1995) as the government continually challenged the power of policy-influencing groups in many spheres (Richardson 1993).

Conservation at local level

This section considers how the national entrenchment of conservation within the planning system translated to the local level. Inevitably this is a complex picture, influenced in different localities by different political circumstances and different economic realities. There is no doubt, however, of the general willingness of local authorities to use those conservation policy mechanisms within their control. For example, as we have seen, new conservation area designations (and extensions) grew at a rapid rate. In the 1970s, the main focus of designation was on the historic core of settlements. In the 1980s, there was increasing emphasis on residential suburbs (including the once reviled 1930s 'Metroland'), together with more novel designations, such as areas of industrial archaeological interest, and transport corridors (Jones and Larkham 1993). The Association of Conservation Officers started as a grass-roots network of local authority conservation officers, which reflected the growing identity of these specialist posts within local authorities. Punter (1991), in his case study of Bristol, discussed further below, highlighted the significance of the appointment of a specialist conservation professional in mobilising conservation activity in that city in the late 1970s and early 1980s.

The reasons why the collective culture of local authorities shifted from being regarded as the developers' friend in the early 1970s to becoming the apparent advocate of conservation are also complex. In part, local authorities were responding to central government policy, which was consolidating the position of conservation. In part, however, it has been argued that local authorities were seeking to subvert central government policy. In particular, government Circular 22/80 (Department of the Environment 1980), reinforced by Circular 31/85 (Department of the Environment 1985), firmly indicated that local authorities should not, as a rule, intervene in design matters. This context, together with the control over demolition given by conservation area status, is thought to have given impetus to the designation of conservation areas in the 1980s, as design remained a more valid material consideration in such locations (Punter and Carmona 1997; Thornley 1991). Some local authorities were also acting opportunistically to attract external resources as part of early efforts to use conservation as a means of regeneration. Again, this was apparently the case in Bristol (Punter 1991).

However, beyond this immediate policy context, a range of broader factors may have contributed to this new-found enthusiasm for conservation. Officers and members of local authorities as individuals may have been caught up in the general popularisation of ideas of heritage described below. Given their professions and roles, they may have been particularly affected by a loss in faith in the modernist approaches to urban issues deployed during the 1960s and early 1970s. They will also have been affected by the changing role of local authorities in the 1980s. Conservative governments, hostile to local authorities, eroded their powers and resources in this period. Local authorities were no longer the powerful shapers of development interests that they had been prior to the economic collapses of the mid 1970s. Their role as controllers and managers of change was further weakened by liberal national planning policies. Conservation and conservation area designation was one sphere in which they could exert more influence than had previously been the case. The creation of a professional cadre of conservation officers may in itself have significantly helped to fuel local conservation activity as this emerging professional group sought to define its role.

The degree to which conservation agendas were prominent in the 1980s was, of course, highly variable. For a city such as Newcastle upon Tyne, experiencing massive social and economic stress in this period, conservation issues were not very prominent (Buswell 1984). Indeed, the city found it difficult to think strategically at all about the key locale of its heritage, the city centre, at this time (Healey 2002). In other cities, such as Leeds, attention given to the officially sanctioned heritage of listed building and conservation areas was accompanied by the ongoing clearance and destruction of the Victorian inner suburbs (Powell 1981). For a city such as Chester, however, conservation was emerging as never before as a key policy issue, integrated as part of a social, economic and environmental strategy (Mageean 1999). Conservation was seen as a tool for encouraging the development of commercial uses in under-used areas and increasing residential use in the city centre.

The expansion in the numbers of conservation areas did eventually prompt a counter response. Morton (1991) in particular was responsible for mounting an attack on the expanding number of designations. He was writing as a consultant, frustrated in his dealings with some local authorities, about the way in which he believed conservation powers were being used unreasonably to inhibit development through control over demolition, and about the extra leverage conservation area status gave over the form of new development. The quantity of conservation area designation was held to be excessive. He argued that designations were not meeting the statutory criterion of 'special architectural or historic interest'; furthermore, few local authorities could clearly articulate why their conservation areas were 'special' and therefore could not give adequate guidance about how they should evolve. Where there had been significant erosion of the character of areas, local authorities were unwilling to relinquish their additional powers and to de-designate conservation areas. Concerns about these issues were amplified by a series of case law decisions in the late 1980s and early 1990s that had emphasised the policy importance of conservation area status, though subsequent cases suggested a more permissive stance (Mynors 1999). No legislative changes resulted from this lobbying. However, this critique was influential as part of the shift from conservation as a campaigning movement to conservation as management of the historic environment. For example, PPG15 subsequently emphasised the importance of reference to locally defined criteria in local authority designation of conservation areas. It also stressed the importance of preparing character appraisals to assist both authorities in their management of areas, and those outside the authority in understanding the rationale for designation.

Further discussion of conservation in residential areas and of how conservation has increasingly become linked to issues of regeneration are discussed in Chapters 7 and 6, respectively. Below I briefly consider how conservation objectives were reconciled with economic interests in commercial localities during the mid 1980s property boom.

Conservation in commercial centres

One of the severest tests of the new-found emphasis on conservation policy objectives in the 1980s came from developers in economically buoyant commercial locations. This was perhaps particularly so in cities such as Newcastle upon Tyne, where this new-found buoyancy was a shift from generally more depressed prevailing market conditions and, consequently, where any investment opportunity was bound to be snatched at by local authorities. Larkham and Barrett (1998) provide a useful study contrasting the experiences of Birmingham and Bristol in this period. Both local planning authorities sought to strengthen and formalise their conservation policies, mainstreaming them into their planning activity. Both authorities increased the number of conservation areas in their respective cities, with the number in Birmingham rising from fifteen to twenty-five and that in Bristol from sixteen to twenty-nine during the 1980s. Both authorities also extended a number of existing conservation areas.

However, though there were similarities between the two authorities, there were also differences. In Birmingham, the development of conservation concerns happened later and was initially more tentative; the city only gradually moved away from its post-war planning doctrine of comprehensive redevelopment and functional efficiency. It did not have the crucial support enjoyed by Bristol of grants and enhancements financed by the Historic Buildings Council. Its legacy of nineteenth- and twentieth-century buildings was relatively lightly protected by listing. Thus, although Birmingham sought to reinforce its conservation policies by designating conservation areas and developing a local list of historically important buildings that were not covered by national listing, in practice it found itself in a relatively weak negotiating position. Its position was further undermined by key planning appeal decisions. Planning inspectors overturned local authority refusals of planning permission and listed building consent and allowed highly interventionist schemes of façadism, which retained only the external envelope of the historic building.

Punter (1991) considered the conservation programme in Bristol to be an unqualified success, both in achieving better results in the development control process than Larkham and Barratt (1998) found in Birmingham, and in capturing resources to help in the regeneration of inner areas from the late 1970s. The success of the latter programme helped sustain political support for the mediation of change through the planning process. Bristol became a 'Priority Town' for the Historic Buildings Council in 1977 and was thus provided with generous funding over a ten-year period. The use of detailed design briefs and the existence of a more extensive listed-building stock were also held to be contributory factors (Larkham and Barrett 1998). However, Punter acknowledged that criticisms were made during the period over the degree to which façadism was allowed and over the quality of conservation schemes. Furthermore, Larkham and Barrett showed that, though Bristol had a better record than Birmingham in achieving its objectives, it did not always succeed with detailed outcomes when these clashed with, for example, commercial desire for on-site car-parking.

Thus, though local authority-promoted central redevelopment schemes, sweeping aside large parts of historic cities, had largely stopped by the 1980s and a pro-conservation attitude prevailed, the management of commercial localities was still a significant arena of contestation. Conflict shifted from struggles over the total demolition of listed buildings to the degree of permissible intervention into historic fabric, as pressure for alterations became applied to historic interiors in particular. One common means of resolving the contradictory policy goals of the government, which emphasised both the importance of market liberalisation and the historic environment, was façadism – the retention of a historic façade or façades and the redevelopment of a building interior. Developers often promoted such schemes, playing lip-service to conservation objectives while achieving the commercial space they wanted. Even when local planning authorities sought to resist these pressures, they could find themselves undermined by the appeals process.

Such tensions in commercial areas are inevitable but were particularly marked in the booming economy of the 1980s. They continued in the economic downturn of the early 1990s, but not to such an extreme degree. The 1990s also saw significant regeneration projects in commercial areas when the government began to focus on the viability of town centres. I discuss this further in Chapter 6.

Design in the historic city: a prince among men

Ideas of 'townscape' as a means of thinking about new buildings in historic areas (and elsewhere) had been evolving, as previously discussed, as a strong thread of British practice since the 1940s. The prominence and popularity of such ideas were boosted in reaction to the fractures of large-scale redevelopment in the 1960s and 1970s. During the 1980s arguments over design reached a level of prominence not experienced in living memory, in large part owing to the high-profile interventions of the Prince of Wales. However, the nature of the argument had become rather different: it was no longer so much about *form* as *style*. That buildings should pay some regard to existing urban form was now broadly accepted, but what architectural dress should they assume? It was a battle between modernists, headed by the architectural profession establishment and traditionalists, led by the Prince of Wales.

One significant battle over the conservation of historic buildings, urban form and ultimately architectural style took place in the heart of the City of London. In May 1984 Prince Charles was invited, as part of the 150th anniversary celebrations of the RIBA, to present a Gold Medal to Indian architect Charles Correa. The Prince used the opportunity to launch a tirade against the arrogance of modernist architects and planners and to attack plans for a tower block at Mansion House Square, which he called a 'giant glass stump'. At Mansion House Square, in the heart of the City of London, the property developer Lord Palumbo had spent more than twenty years assembling a large site of mostly late-Victorian buildings, eight of which were listed, with the intention of redeveloping it with a Mies van der Rohes-designed thirty-storey skyscraper. The scheme was intended as a posthumous celebration of one of the twentieth century's most famous modernists and would have been Britain's only example of his work. Support came from many in the architectural establishment including, for example, Sir Richard Rogers and, interestingly, Sir John Summerson, prominent conservationist and architectural historian, representing an older emphasis of selective preservation of older buildings (Andreae 1996; Mandler 1994).

However, shortly after the Prince's speech the Secretary of State refused planning permission for the scheme. A subsequent proposal was drawn up by James Stirling, in accordance with advice from the Secretary of State who suggested that a less dominant scheme might be acceptable (Delafons 1997a). The massing was similar to the existing buildings, and Stirling stressed the 'contextual' nature of the scheme, although Prince Charles likened the design, unflatteringly, to a 1930s wireless set. Permission was finally granted, with the appeal inspector's report stressing the quality of what was proposed. This was despite a desperate rearguard action by conservation groups led by

SAVE Britain's Heritage (see Figure 5.3) that ended in the House of Lords, and the new building finally opened in 1996. Conservationists' great fear with this scheme was that it would set a precedent: listed buildings could be demolished as long as the replacement design was deemed to be of sufficient quality. This did not happen in practice, and from a conservation perspective it proved to be very much a one-off case. However, at another level it is a case very typical of the period, albeit one of high profile and prestige. A modernist replanning with skyscraper and plaza was rejected, whereas a city block, contextually designed, proved acceptable. New buildings were expected to pay at least lip-service to the existing grain of the city.

The Prince's interventions continued through the decade. In another speech at the Mansion House in 1987, the Prince was scathing about post-war development in London, and this was influential on the long debates over the redevelopment of Paternoster Square, the setting for St Paul's Cathedral. The post-war scheme was designed under the overview of Holford in the 1950s (although not completed until 1967) and was widely considered as a bleak and uninviting place. In a complicated series of events the Prince of Wales was influential in supporting a classical revival scheme by John Simpson in competition with the official scheme commissioned from Arup Associates. Simpson eventually displaced Arup as master-planner for the site, in partnership with Terry Farrell and Thomas Beeby. However, the scheme did not proceed, and the site was ultimately redeveloped following a master plan by William Whitfield, with most of the buildings following a restrained contextual modernism; they in their turn are perhaps typical of 1990s responses to historic locations and admired by some and loathed by others (Powell 2003; Glancey 2003).

5.3
SAVE Britain's Heritage campaign document against the demolition of the buildings at No.1 Poultry.
© SAVE Britain's Heritage.

If nothing else, the interventions of the Prince of Wales raised the profile of architectural design in public debate, and this in itself was welcomed by many design professionals (Punter 1990). He went on to produce principles of urban design (HRH Prince of Wales 1989), which led to the then president of the Royal Town Planning Institute producing his own ten commandments of urban design (Tibbalds 1992). In the Poundbury extension of Dorchester in Wiltshire, Prince Charles has sought to put his beliefs into practice (see Figure 5.4). Though some of the original, classical ideas in Leon Krier's master plan were diluted, classicism and historical revival more generally were to prove very popular in the 1980s and 1990s across the different sectors of building. This was particularly evident in commercial architecture in towns and cities. A well-known, extreme manifestation of this was Richmond Riverside, a large office scheme designed to appear as a group of neo-classical buildings by Quinlan Terry; albeit this was a skin of historicism, concealing modern open floor-plan offices (see Figure 5.5).

Larkham (1996) characterised the strategies used for new build in historic cities in four categories: deliberate contrast, use of local architectural idiom, disguise and 'revival' styles. With the first category he made a distinction between buildings that, although contrasting with their setting, do so in a

5.4
**Neo-traditional
building at
Poundbury.**
Source: author.

5.5
**Neo-classical
architecture,
Richmond
Riverside.**
Source: author.

considered way, rather than merely ignoring their surroundings as often occurred in the 1960s. Second, local architectural idiom encompassed the adoption of a style that relates in some way to local building styles, often in a very superficial use of 'features'. Third, disguise encompassed façadism and the pretence that large urban interventions are actually a series of smaller buildings, using different materials and architectural detailing for different elements of what is in reality one building. Finally, 'revival' styles included all the different adoptions of historical architectural design, with Richmond Riverside being a particularly overblown example. It is probably too early to come to any definitive conclusions about the impact of new buildings on historic areas in the 1980s and 1990s. However, though there are undoubtedly positive examples of each of the categories that Larkham identified, the feeling within much of the professional world at least is that much 'lowest common denominator' architecture took place, with buildings designed to achieve the least contentious route to planning permission rather than to grace our towns and cities in the decades to come. For example, the architectural journalist and conservationist Kenneth Powell wrote an article in 1989 about new development in Leeds entitled 'The Offence of the Inoffensive'. New buildings were characterised as being feeble and depressing parodies of Victorian Leeds buildings, following a bland 'Leeds look' imposed by the planning authority (Powell 1989). Every British city could provide examples of such debased design.

With the exception of schemes such as the Mies van der Rohes scheme at Mansion House, which was literally a throwback to a different era, designed as it was many years before, architecturally much of the contestation in the 1980s was about style. On the one hand, developers and architects

5.6
Lowest common denominator: weak pastiche: a hotel in Cambridge.
Source: author.

accepted that they had to respond to some degree to traditional street patterns and forms, albeit this might only be a disguise to shochorn in and conceal very large buildings. On the other hand, local authorities were frequently willing to accommodate, or unable to prevent, large-scale development in sensitive areas. This was achieved using what Pawley (1998) has termed 'stealth architecture', very large buildings that conceal themselves from the street by using basements, broken up façades, set-back attics and so on, and by façadism.

Though this tension between conservation and development has not disappeared, much of the heat has gone from the argument in recent years. In particular, the strident confrontations between modernists and traditionalists have died down, although the practice of both approaches continues. There is now perhaps more of a centre ground about suitable design in historic settings, using restrained contextual modernism, such as at Paternoster Square. It is an area where the relevant agencies, English Heritage and the Commission for Architecture and the Built Environment (CABE) have worked to promote consensus through such publications as *Building in Context* (Larkham 1996; English Heritage and CABE 2001). I return to this theme in Chapter 9.

Consensus?

In their review of planning under the Conservatives, Allmendinger and Thomas (1998: 240) stated that conservation remained 'virtually unscathed' during the era of Conservative government. The reality was rather different: not only was conservation not on the neo-liberal agenda but positive measures were actively taken in its favour. Conservation largely escaped even the rhetoric of liberalisation. Rather, the policy significance of conservation developed and strengthened during this period. Furthermore, the specific outcomes of listing large numbers of buildings and designating conservation areas often led to the protection of environments spatially removed from the natural, obvious, conservation-supporting constituencies of leafy suburbs and the countryside, and included, for example, inner urban areas and seemingly unpopular post-war buildings.

However, beneath the surface of this acceptance of conservation as a benign, consensual activity, significant issues were being played out. Conservation as an important activity was not overtly challenged, but how it should be undertaken – effectively, whether it should be skin-deep – was being negotiated via innumerable planning decisions up and down the country. As developers shifted from replacing old buildings to severely transforming them, some of the contestation was sublimated, but existed nevertheless. Indeed, conservation, from being part of a process of resistance to development through heroic struggles over the previous 100 years, was now promiscuously used by developers anxious to display rather fig-leaf-like conservation credentials as part of the legitimation of change. In turn this linked to changed ideas about the relationship between new and old buildings in the historic city, the culmination of a process of renegotiation that had started in the late 1960s. The old idea that historic buildings were exemplars in an ongoing progressive architectural continuum had largely died at this point. The primary role of buildings both old and new was perhaps now to give an ambience to place, as part of a process of 'heritagisation'.

Chapter 6

The commodification
of heritage

Introduction

As noted in Chapter 1, the benefits derived from sustaining built heritage, as officially asserted in government documents, have undergone a dramatic transformation from the modest claims of *Preservation and Change* (Ministry of Housing and Local Government 1967) to the sweeping pronouncements of *Force for Our Future* (Department for Culture, Media and Sport and Department of Transport Local Government and the Regions 2001a) in a manner that reflects the evolving discourse around heritage. In particular, there is a far greater tendency to perceive heritage as producing immediate and instrumental benefits, rather than conceptualising it as important for its own sake. Thus, as discussed in Chapter 10, attention is now given to the role of the historic environment in policies relating to social inclusion. However, the set of values most dramatically and assertively to the fore over recent decades has been the economic benefits that can accrue either from the material reality of the historic environment, or from the image of age and 'historicness' it conveys. The economic exploitation of culture and heritage is not a new phenomenon. Ousby amongst others has eloquently described the long history of profiting from visitors to historic sites (Ousby 1990). However, it is evident that the economic function of the historic environment has come more to the forefront in recent times.

This chapter discusses the phenomenon of 'the heritage industry' before returning to the theme of gentrification introduced in Chapter 4. The focus then shifts to the broader role of culture in economic restructuring, with particular reference to post-industrial cities. Finally, the focus shifts directly to the articulation of conservation as an agent of regeneration. This chapter only fleetingly touches upon the role of tourism in these processes; this is returned to in Chapter 8.

The past as valuable commodity: the heritage industry

As described in Chapters 4 and 5, conservation became established as a major objective of planning policy in the 1970s and 1980s. In part this was reaction against the 'shock of the new', especially when the new was shockingly awful, as all too frequently seemed to be the case. But the celebration of old buildings and historic places was also part of a wider shift away from the modernity of the 1960s and early 1970s (a period often now portrayed as rather kitsch) to a wider fashion for the old and reproduction, which embraced many things including clothes, furniture and interior design more generally. So, for example, in the 1960s the gentrifiers discussed below had been content to move into Georgian houses and substantially remodel them with the help of modern stores such as Habitat. By the 1980s, while the fundamental economic and cultural precepts of gentrification remained largely the same, the cultural signals were different: gentrifiers were now more likely to be found in architectural salvage yards looking for the 'correct' Victorian fireplace. Magazines focusing on 'the period home' and 'country house style' flourished. The inexorable rise in membership of the National Trust, and access to its historic houses, complete with unchallenging interpretation, tea and gift shop, continued apace. Heritage had become a major consumption activity.

For many cultural commentators and conservationists, reared in a modernist tradition that privileged authenticity and rather austere conceptions of protecting the 'true' cultural worth of the historic environment, the shameless and casual economic pillaging of history was all too much; so much so that 'heritage' became a problematic term. A defining articulation of this was Hewison's classic polemic *The Heritage Industry*, sub-titled *Britain in a Climate of Decline* (Hewison 1987). Hewison regarded the heritage industry as devaluing the cultural worth of cultural objects repackaged for mass consumption. He described how he was motivated to write the book by a broadly accurate statistic (which appalled him) that every week or so a new museum opened in Britain. The bland romanticisations of presentation in many of these museums, found also in National Trust properties, were the subject of Hewison's ire. The popularity of Laura Ashley shops, with period styling and the recreation of old fabrics was a symbol of the taste for all things past. Furthermore, the emphasis laid on marketing the past was evidence of a profound British cultural and economic malaise, a nostalgic fantasy and yearning for earlier times in an attempt to dispel a perception of decline.

Hewison was by no means alone in his distrust and distaste for the commodification of heritage: it was evident throughout the conservation movement. This antagonism to the notion of heritage led to what Samuel termed 'heritage-baiting' (Samuel 1994). Conservation professionals sought to distance themselves from what they regarded as the inappropriate and *inauthentic* exploitation of their preserve, the stewardship of cultural assets. The actions undertaken to sustain or generate economic use of the heritage, whether referential to its heritage status or not, if not undertaken in accord with prevailing principles might be denied as conservation and seen to be as bad as, or even worse than, the total removal of the heritage asset. In the domain of conservation planning Boyer discussed, in her term, 'the city as spectacle', a commodified location for consumption (Boyer 1996). Like many other commentators, she pointed out how 'heritage solutions' to the planning of the public realm (in terms of paving, street furniture and so on) often led to the erosion of a sense of place as standard catalogue solutions were imposed. As discussed in Chapter 5, architecturally vague revival styles became a dominant form, as did the practice of façadism in commercial centres. For Urry, the historic environment had become an integral part of conceptions of the consumer society, 'stage-sets within which consumption can take place' (Urry 1995: 21). These themes are returned to in Chapter 9.

The rise and rise of period houses

Chapter 4 briefly discussed how the symbolic value of old housing became combined with its economic potential in the 1960s and 1970s in the process of gentrification. Classic accounts of gentrification, such as Raban (1974) writing about Islington in the 1970s, talk of middle-class pioneers moving into working-class neighbourhoods and being the effective vanguard agents of the displacement of existing residential communities. It is this displacement that is at the heart of the critique of gentrification as a social and economic process. Atkinson (2003) defined the key components of gentrification as being the class-based colonisation of cheaper residential neighbourhoods and a reinvestment in the physical housing stock. Classic gentrification occurs through a series of individual actions, cumulatively having a collective effect (Butler 2005). Whether the displacement of an existing population is a necessary factor, or intrinsically socially regressive, is disputed (Butler 2003), though for some gentrification sits as part of a strategy of 'revanchism', involving the appropriation of urban space for the advantaged, combined with aggressive and oppressive policies of exclusion and control of low-income and marginalised groups (Smith and Williams 1986).

What draws gentrifiers to move into a neighbourhood is complex and disputed, and the nuances of gentrification can vary considerably between different locales, as Butler has described for different areas of London (Butler 2005). However, many writers have linked gentrification to the appeal, as well as the affordability, of attractive older houses, or 'the heritage aesthetic'; history becomes a commodity for middle-class self-expression whereby oldness and history are essential features of the process (see for example Butler 1997; Ley 1996; Wright 1985; Zukin 1987). In focusing on 'correct' restoration and the way an area should look, the incomers reinforce their own identity (Butler, 1997) and can further marginalise existing residents, especially those whose modernisations are out of step with the tastes of the gentrifiers (Zukin 1987).

Chapter 4 discussed the 'rediscovery' of Spitalfields in east London and its role as an example of 1970s activism, complete with the squatting of buildings to prevent their demolition. The story of Spitalfields in the 1980s became subject to critique, including by some of the original participants (Samuel 1989), as it was argued that it became a very particular story of gentri-fication, whether with the collusion of the Spitalfields Historic Buildings Trust or not. Samuel, in a critical address to the Trust's tenth anniversary conference (subsequently published as the *Saving of Spitalfields*) acknowledged the socially benign intentions of the Trust; however, by saving buildings and putting them to more valuable uses, the Trust altered the property market and unleashed economic forces that transformed the nature of the area – in his view for the worse. For Wright also, the success of the early projects in demonstrating the potential of the area was inevitably going to lead to gentrification. The role of a particular aesthetic in the regeneration of Spitalfields was also highlighted by both Wright and Samuel (Wright 1992). Samuel argued that houses had been restored to a 1980s aesthetic, created around a fantasy of Georgian Spitalfields. In the process, he argued, one of the key messages of conservation orthodoxy, respecting the contribution of all periods in understanding the history of a building or area, had been lost (Samuel 1989):

> It is the pathos of conservation, even where, as in Spitalfields, it is carried out under expert guidance, that it produces the opposite of its intended effect. Returning buildings to their original condition (or attempting to do so) robs them of the very quality for which they are prized – *oldness*, that 'pleasing decay'.

> (p. 164)

And,

> for all the insistence on authenticity, there is an inescapable element of artifice. The houses are designed not as living and working

6.1
**Restored houses
in Spitalfields,
London.**
Source: author.

environments, nor yet as family houses, but first and foremost as
period residences.

(p. 162–3; emphasis original)

Thus, for Samuel, the buildings become as much fashionable 1980s commodities as conserved historic houses. Spitalfields undoubtedly became a
more attractive location for the market, both for expensive residential property
but also increasingly for commercial development, sited as it is on the edge
of the commercial core of London. As developers moved into the area, the
conservation of Spitalfields for Jacobs (1996) had gone from being part of a
resistance to change in the 1970s to becoming part of a process legitimating
change. So for example, as Samuel described, Bengali sweat-shops were
encouraged to leave historic buildings, and empty sites were acquired for
neo-Georgian office developments. The counter-case was made by Blain, who

denied that gentrification had taken place, arguing that the area was effectively empty and therefore displacement could not take place, before concluding slightly quixotically that, 'If this is gentrification, and the thriving, mixed and above all viable community that (for all its shortcomings) is Spitalfields today is the result, then give me more of it' (Blain 1989: 19).

Spitalfields is a rarefied example owing to the quality of the buildings and the prominence of some of the people who have been active in the area. However, the role of conservation in effecting the transformation and colonisation of place has been posited for other less celebrated places. Butler (1997) described the gentrification of two areas in the London Borough of Hackney (De Beauvoir and North Defoe) and the key contribution of conservation to this process:

> The struggle to preserve [its] historical value has, in both areas, served to bring incomers together. . . . In both De Beauvoir and North Defoe there is a sense of history and historical authenticity which newcomers have struggled to save from the 'philistinism' and narrow self-interest of local authorities, local residents and profit-orientated developers.
>
> (p. 107)

These battles have taken different forms in the two areas. In De Beauvoir this included seeking conservation area designation and promoting buildings for listing, as well as the use of environmental measures such as traffic management. In North Defoe, Stoke Newington, the focus was more on fighting to protect open space. For Butler,

> The fight to maintain the status quo and an image for the future is therefore firmly rooted in the expropriation of the past. It is also often the means whereby a class of people with this 'cultural capital' can come together to protect 'historical authenticity' and, at the same time, fight for their future. In other words the fight for preservation is a focus for relatively isolated middle-class people to unite together to promote their individual and collective interests.
>
> (p. 109)

Furthermore, Butler saw part of the attraction of living in an old house in a gentrifying area as the opportunity to restore and improve the property in a way that appears altruistic, but conceals an acute awareness of economic self-interest. This stands in marked contrast to another view of Stoke Newington recorded by Wright (1985), of his conversation with a working class resident of nearby Hoxton:

> she comments approvingly on a house which from any culturally sanctioned perspective is a complete eyesore. Its bricks have recently been covered with fake stone cladding, the sash windows have been replaced with cheap louvers, and the whole place is painted up in gloss so that it shines like a birthday cake . . . Somebody owns this place and their renovation of it speaks of pride, self-determination and freedom to this woman who has live her whole life in council flats.
>
> (Wright 1985: 235)

Gentrification is thus a process whereby cultural capital is used as part of a process of place transformation and which creates economic value. It is able to do this because old housing has become an established feature of the middle-class housing market. Integral to this is an aesthetic about how such property should look. On the surface, with rhetoric about historical authenticity, this connects to orthodox conservation principles, but in reality the connection tends to be loose and imperfect. What is usually sought is something that 'looks right', rather than an application of the archaeological principles of 'conservative repair'. From a conservation perspective, though, the rehabilitation of neighbour-hoods and the recovery of some semblance of their architectural and spatial qualities are generally portrayed as positive activities. The term gentrification, with the negative connotations it conveys, has generally been absent from conservation discourse since the 1970s. In the UK in particular there has been blindness to the wider social context of conservation activity. Indeed, Hobson, in interviews with conservationists, found that gentrification was regarded as benign, as it may bring more conservation-sympathetic owners, and any social problems attendant on this were thought to be beyond the concerns and competence of the conservation sector (Hobson 2004).

Re-imagining the post-industrial city

From the mid 1970s onwards, the economies of many industrial towns and cities throughout the developed world faced crisis. The UK underwent dramatic restructuring, and many manufacturing jobs were lost in this period. De-industrialisation stripped away traditional industrial bases, and many cities were left with little option but to attempt a radical reinvention of themselves, often seeking to use heritage and culture more broadly as part of place marketing and the promotion of inward investment. Particularly badly affected were those towns and cities whose fortunes had been built on the rapid industrialisation of the nineteenth century.

Selling places

Industrial cities have a history of selling themselves from the mid nineteenth century onwards (Kearns and Philo 1993; Ashworth and Voogd 1990; Ward 1998). Though attempts were aimed traditionally at attracting new businesses and residents, exploiting the past of a place is not a new concept. Nor is the use of heritage in place promotion restricted to industrial cities (for example, see Cowen 1990 for a discussion of Cheltenham), although interestingly research in the Netherlands revealed towns with the most monuments and strongest existing heritage reputation used these least as part of their promotion, and vice versa (Graham *et al.* 2000).

The history of place promotion is, as Ward put it, 'local history . . . selectively plundered to demonstrate the inevitability of success'; thus images of industrial prowess would be juxtaposed with ones of historic buildings and symbols denoting past importance (Ward 1998: 163). Place marketing became increasingly significant in the 1980s at the time when former industrial cities were attempting to carve out a new role for themselves and place 'distinctiveness' was seen as a key way of giving one city the edge over another (Harvey 1989). Projects based around regenerating older, 'characterful' areas were a key element in promotional material. In the UK, for example, the Urban Development Corporations used place marketing to suggest a bright new future backed up by claims of a glorious past. Sheffield 'used to be the greatest steel-producing centre in the world' (Sadler 1993: 180), and similar recourse to past greatness was found in the marketing literature of many traditional industrial centres. Historic imagery might be inserted alongside other, non-related selling points: for example, Cambridge as a historic city in promoting hi-tech industries on its periphery (Ashworth and Voogd 1990).

A key element of this promotional activity is that only positive imagery is welcome, representations of a heritage that is well–maintained, pristine and restored. It is also highly selective in its symbolic intent. For example, nineteenth-century mill buildings become symbols of Victorian invention and enterprise rather than the misery and squalor of those who worked in them. This sanitisation process was evident in an example drawn from Hull (Atkinson *et al.* 2002). Place marketing has elided the city's history as a leading fishing port in the twentieth century in favour of an image based around pioneers, whether historical figures such as the slavery abolitionist William Wilberforce, or contemporary industries, to suggest the city remains a centre of initiative and progress. The proposed redevelopment of a former fishing dock led to contestation through a planning inquiry between developers promoting a bland, 'anywhere' maritime scheme and local groups and politicians arguing this was a key locale for a more tangible and appropriate site of memory and place of reference to Hull's more recent maritime history, including, for example, the thousands of trawlermen lost at sea. The proposals involved the demolition of what were argued to be some of the few remaining substantial buildings of the modern fishing industry. A planning application was refused, but the developers won their permission on appeal at public inquiry. A sanitised image of waterside development that can be marketed to consumers prevailed over the local attachment to an uncomfortable but very keenly felt local heritage.

Culture and regeneration

Efforts to change place image and the exploitation of locations such as waterfronts as part of the re-imaging of post-industrial cities have been wrapped up in a wider process of seeking to use culture, and so-called cultural industries, as part of a strategy of regeneration. Miles and Paddison commented that, 'Within the space of little more than two decades, the initiation of culture-driven urban (re)generation has come to occupy a pivotal position in the new urban entrepreneurialism' (Miles and Paddison 2005: 833).

This is a global phenomenon but more highly developed in economically advanced nations and, they feel, perhaps particularly highly developed in the UK. Certainly, as they point out, such strategies have been supported by government policy, with personal statements such as the former minister Chris Smith's *Creative Britain* (Smith 1998) and official statements such as *Culture at the Heart of Regeneration* (Department for Culture, Media and Sport 2004). The spatial manifestations of culture-based approaches, for example through the development of 'cultural quarters', often areas with an exploitable legacy of under-used old buildings, have been much written about (see, for example, Montgomery 2003; 2004). The Castlefield area in central Manchester was labelled an Urban Heritage Park in 1983, with the intention of using the area's largely derelict heritage to develop tourism, something that was extremely successful and acted as a catalyst for regeneration more generally in this part of Manchester (Tiesdell *et al.* 1996). An even better-known example is Temple Bar in Dublin, a tightly knit area of the city with many historic buildings. Regeneration was started by creative industries moving in while the area was under threat of redevelopment for a bus station, attracted by low rents and short leases. With the abandonment of redevelopment proposals, the promotion of the area as a cultural quarter was officially sanctioned, and it has become one of the best-known tourist destinations in the city (Tiesdell *et al.* 1996). However, although regeneration has taken place and created a vibrant part of the city, it has been critically appraised in terms of its impact on the historic qualities of the area. Though the overall grain and 'feel' have been sustained, historic buildings have been demolished, and others reduced to a façade, or otherwise unsympathetically altered (Negussie 2001).

At a more strategic scale, the benefits of achieving nomination as European Capital of Culture (ECOC) have been the focus of considerable

6.2
**Old and new in
Temple Bar,
Dublin.**
Source: author.

attention. Glasgow was ECOC in 1990, and this has often been taken as the
moment at which the potential to exploit this status as an agent of regeneration
was realised (Garcia 2005). Certainly, the competition was fierce for ECOC
status for 2008 between a series of British cities. The impact of such status
is hotly debated. In the case of Glasgow, Laurier (1993) suggested that the
subtext of the year was to hide a grim working-class history from tourists and
captains of industry, whereas, with a longer time perspective, Garcia detected
a long-term positive impact on local images and identities. Subsequently, the
city has sought to continue to utilise cultural promotion in regeneration and
promoted the 1992 Glasgow's Alive campaign and the 1999 Festival of
Architecture and Design and the City. The latter resulted directly in the
conversion of the Charles Rennie Macintosh Herald building into the Lighthouse
Architecture Centre. Thus, on this occasion, a key historic building achieved
re-use as part of a cultural event.

The heritage dividend

Thus heritage has often formed a key element of regeneration strategies based on culture. There has also been a strong tradition in recent years of arguing for the 'added value' brought by historic buildings to processes of property-led regeneration, not only in terms of the economic performance of such buildings, but also in terms of their wider impact and role in lending distinctiveness or character to area regeneration, to helping make 'place'.

The economic advantages that might derive from older property have been recognised for many years. Jane Jacobs (1961) argued for the importance of old buildings in the early 1960s, as they were flexible, low-rental and, as such, were useful to small businesses, promoted mixed use and enabled entrepreneurial risk-taking, though this was not a heritage-based argument as such. However, there has been a long tradition in the USA, where economic arguments are always powerful, of demonstrating the economic worth of the built heritage (see for example Rypkema 2001; 1992). Often this has been linked with post de-industrialising reinvention. In many industrial cities there were vast areas of built fabric that was un-reusable, such as relatively modern shipyards, docks and steel works. However, alongside this, many cities also displayed a fine architectural legacy from their industrial past as they began to realise this might be an exploitable economic asset. The 1970s saw schemes such as Quincy Market/Faneuil Hall in Boston, historic buildings developed as a 'festival marketplace' for tourism-leisure shopping, and Harborplace on the Baltimore waterfront, without the historic buildings of Boston, but a historic location nevertheless.

On a larger scale, Lowell, Massachusetts is an example of a manufacturing town that from the 1970s onwards sought to regenerate a declining economy through exploiting its industrial heritage; much of the associated buildings were empty and unused but, fortuitously, not demolished. Lowell had a legacy of great textile mills, similar to those that might be found in some of the cotton towns of Lancashire in England. A series of preservation initiatives in the city culminated in securing congressional approval in 1978 to make Lowell a new kind of national park, one based upon labour and industrial history (National Park Service 1992). This enabled the city to develop the sort of visitor attractions and supporting infrastructure around which an urban tourism industry could operate. In Lowell this seems to have worked, in both directly creating a new economic activity and in shifting perceptions of the city, such that new employers were attracted to relocate there (Tiesdell *et al.* 1996). This perceived success spawned a host of imitators in the north-east United States. However, the success of Lowell has not been easily replicated, especially without the key mechanism of National Park status (Ashworth and Tunbridge 1990).

6.3
**Lowell Mills,
Lowell,
Massachusetts,
converted into
apartments as
part of the city's
regeneration.**
Source: author.

The economic potential of heritage as a means of supporting and justifying conservation activities was perhaps seized upon a little later in the UK. SAVE Britain's Heritage produced *Preservation Pays* in 1978 (SAVE Britain's Heritage 1978), and one of the legacies of EAHY was the stimulus to create the building preservation trust movement that has often focused on demonstrating the economic potential of recycling historic buildings in marginal locations. Covent Garden became a festival marketplace-type shopping arena (see Figure 6.4), effectively almost accidentally, given its brush with redevelopment early in the 1970s. Saved from wholesale clearance by community

6.4
**Heritage
commodified:
shopping and
entertainment,
Covent Garden,
London.**
Source: author.

activism, the area was steadily gentrified, in the broader meaning of the term, as investors realised its potential. Perhaps the exemplar of the 1980s was the way in which the restoration and re-use of Albert Dock, a large complex of Grade 1-listed warehouses in Liverpool, became the regeneration flagship of the Merseyside Development Corporation. This combined the physical regeneration of superb-quality industrial buildings with a focus on culture as discussed above; Albert Dock hosts both a maritime museum and an outpost of the Tate gallery.

By the early 1990s significant parts of the conservation sector in the UK had fully embraced these more economically instrumental relationships. In part this had been driven by central government policy. One of the controversial government initiatives in the early days of the Thatcher government was an increased emphasis on making the management of historic properties, held in care by the government (and subsequently English Heritage), more business-like (Delafons 1997a; Wright 1985), and the economic role of conservation emerged in planning guidance in DoE Circular 8/87, which argued that conservation and regeneration are essentially complementary (Department of the Environment 1987).

English Heritage: regeneration agency

A key body in mediating and promoting this agenda has been English Heritage. Throughout the course of the 1990s, English Heritage became steadily more engaged with urban regeneration. For example, it reorientated its historic area funding regimes. Its grant schemes traditionally focused on the highest-quality historic environments, regardless of the economic conditions in an area. The introduction of Conservation Area Partnerships in 1994/95 represented a shift towards a more problem-solving targeted approach. The English Heritage area funding scheme, Heritage Economic Regeneration Schemes (HERS), launched in 1999, was explicitly targeted at the most deprived areas as defined by government indices. Only one of the five objectives for the programme was focused on English Heritage's traditional concern, the conservation of historic fabric. In 1999 it also introduced an Urban Panel to its governance structure, a specific reflection of the importance of urban regeneration to its activities (Beacham 2001).

English Heritage's focus on regeneration is, in some degree at least, part of a process of better positioning itself in relation to government policy. English Heritage, in its early years especially, often had an image of a patrician and obstructive London-based body. It has pursued a strategy of decentralising staff from London to regional offices, which partly stems from a perception of the new significance of regional levels of governance and of Regional Development Agencies in particular (English Heritage 1999). It has increasingly sought to link conservation with wider social and economic benefits: in particular, regeneration but also, for example, issues of sustainability and excellence in new architectural design (English Heritage 1997; English Heritage and CABE 2001). The need for such repositioning received new impetus with the shift from a Conservative to a modernising Labour government in 1997 and the perceived threats associated with this change. For example, in its *Prospectus*, the government-commissioned Urban Task Force (UTF) made reference to historic buildings being a restraint on regeneration (Urban Task Force 1998). This provoked an immediate and well-organised response from both English Heritage and other conservation groups (English Heritage 1998; SAVE Britain's Heritage 1998), and the final report of the UTF was noticeably more positive about the historic environment (Urban Task Force 1999). This also illustrates that the repositioning of the role of conservation has not been confined to English Heritage. There are many examples of local authorities and other agencies, such as amenity bodies and pressure groups, using the same rhetoric. So, for example, Birmingham City Council entitled its conservation strategy *Regeneration Through Conservation* (Birmingham City Council 1999).

A subsequent English Heritage publication, entitled *The Heritage Dividend* (English Heritage 1999), was the start of a continuing process of more thorough documentation of the economic impact of heritage-spending and the ability to present this in terms of those performance measures and indicators that might be recognised by evaluators of mainstream regeneration funding schemes. It was followed up with a second Heritage Dividend report (English Heritage 2002b), and there have been a number of other reports seeking to demonstrate the economic impact of heritage spending: for instance on waterways (ECOTEC 2003) and traditional farm buildings (English Heritage and DEFRA 2005) as well as on the economic contribution of cathedrals (ECOTEC 2004). The HLF has sought to document its contribution to regeneration (Heritage Lottery Fund 2004), and there have been further publications setting out principles and good practice of conservation and regeneration (for example Drivas Jonas c. 2006; English Heritage 2005c). In reflecting on the history of the Heritage Dividend initiative, a 2005 report noted that, 'The brand has played a key role in the promotion and repositioning of English Heritage as a pro-active, enabling organisation, fully engaged in regenerating some of the UK's most economically deprived and physically run-down communities' (English Heritage 2005a: 3), while also pointing out that the measures adopted have focused on positive by-products rather than the core purpose of the schemes. That is to say, what has been measured has been related to mainstream regeneration rather than to the success of schemes in terms of conservation measures and values.

Leading on from this, and beyond bodies such as English Heritage and the HLF acting in a very specific political context, not all in the conservation movement are persuaded about the easy compatibility of conservation and

regeneration objectives. Hobson (2004) found that, while his interviewees in the conservation sector understood the political importance of the regeneration agenda, this was accompanied by some suspicion, with some interviewees arguing that this imperative was being used to legitimate inappropriate development. The pragmatics of economic possibility were being used to override conservation concerns.

Industrial conservation areas

Alongside such well-resourced and high-profile schemes as Albert Dock from the 1970s and 1980s, a number of local authorities were pursuing more modest schemes using conservation to revitalise industrial areas. Typically, these were areas of great historical significance that had been spared redevelopment, but in which industrial uses had declined. Often, as well as the historic qualities suggested by the location, there was potential for new uses; for example, they might be somewhat cut off by large roads, but they were areas relatively proximate to the city centre and higher-value uses. Kelham Island in Sheffield, the Lace Market in Nottingham, the Jewellery Quarter in Birmingham and Little Germany in Bradford are all examples of such areas. Typically, the objective was to sustain remaining industrial uses while attracting new investment and to sustain historic buildings while introducing high-quality new design. The Lace Market, Nottingham, is an area adjacent to the city centre, historically used for manufacturing lace. Here city council policy for a long time was to resist introducing new uses, such as offices, to the area; the objective was functional as well as physical regeneration. This proved unsustainable, and in the late 1980s the council was forced to change its approach and accept the market-led restructuring of the economic base of the area (Tiesdell 1995; Tiesdell *et al.* 1996). With the uplift of the property market in the later 1990s, gentrification of the area proceeded apace, and it is now thought there is a danger that the creative industries, to which the Lace Market has been home, will be priced out and displaced (Hardill *et al.* 2003).

Such issues have been evident in the Jewellery Quarter in Birmingham, with arguments over branding the area as an urban village; some considered this an essential vehicle to achieve a vibrant, regenerated area (Warburton 2002), but others saw it as a vehicle to erode both physical and functional heritage (Haddleton 2003). The Jewellery Quarter is an area with a legacy of both eighteenth-century domestic architecture and subsequent, mostly small-scale, industrial buildings, used for manufacturing jewellery and other small metal goods. Until 2000 it was partly covered by three conservation areas, but with wide corridors between each. The urban village scheme was argued to be bringing poor-quality housing development into these corridors, displacing the historic manufacturing base and doing nothing to conserve the historic buildings of the area. It has been described as 'the biggest threat the Jewellery Quarter has ever had to face' (Haddleton 2003: 29) In this case, there has been something of a swing back to a greater focus on conservation, with the uniting of the conservation areas and a further 106 listings in the area made in 2004.

With both the Lace Market and the Jewellery Quarter, there has been a tension between functionally sustaining industrial uses and physically conserving buildings. The very attractiveness of the physical buildings has contributed to higher-value uses wanting to colonise the area and displace

6.6
Old and new in the Jewellery Quarter, Birmingham.
Source: Steve Tiesdell.

existing uses. Where local authorities have sought to protect uses as well as buildings, as in Nottingham, they have often found this impossible. Furthermore, within the regeneration efforts in these areas, there has often been a suspicion that what is sought is a superficial aura of 'historicness', rather than something grounded in an understanding of the area's history and its legacy of buildings. This was the case with the Jewellery Quarter, where as a local activist Marie Haddleton wrote 'I said that the Jewellery Quarter was heading towards becoming just a yuppie housing estate with a blue plaque on the wall declaring: "This was Birmingham's Jewellery Quarter" ' (Haddleton 2003: 29).

Grainger Town, Newcastle upon Tyne

Similar issues have been raised in the regeneration and conservation of the Grainger Town area of the city centre of Newcastle upon Tyne (Pendlebury 2002). The regeneration of Grainger Town between 1996 and 2003 by a specially created body, the Grainger Town Partnership, was a very high-profile project that featured very heavily in the sort of conservation and regeneration literature referred to above. The label Grainger Town was developed as part of an effort to revive and revitalise the area. Though the area is characterised by many very high-quality historic buildings, it was realised that this part of the city centre was facing major problems. The locational gravity of both retailing and leisure uses had pulled much of the investment to other parts of the city centre. Office uses had also drifted away from the centre to a variety of business parks. Thus a combination of the changing geography of the city, together with a decentralisation of functions from the city centre, had left large swathes of the middle section of the city suffering from problems such as high vacancy rates (especially of upper floors) and poor building condition.

A strategy prepared in 1996, *Grainger Town Regeneration Strategy* (EDAW 1996), served as a defining vision for those at the heart of the regeneration of Grainger Town. However, this vision, or the vision when practically implemented, was not shared by all the stakeholders in the area. Few denied that the area had a significant heritage worthy of retention, or that the area needed to function economically in contemporary terms, but the interpretations of what this meant varied dramatically. The key partners involved, such as the Partnership team, Newcastle City Council, English Heritage and English Partnerships, held to a broadly shared vision of a Grainger Town transformation that promoted major change in the area but was premised on this occurring in retained historic fabric. Some schemes had support from all sectors. One such was the re-use of a flamboyant nineteenth-century gentlemen's club, empty since the 1970s, by the Wetherspoons pub chain (see Figure 6.7). However, there were often tensions over the reconciliation of contrasting aspirations in the area. No clear consensus existed over degrees of acceptable intervention in order to achieve regeneration and conservation objectives. Sustaining the

6.7
Grainger Town, Newcastle upon Tyne, showing the Union Club restored as a pub and the now demolished 1970s Westgate House.
Source: author.

partnership required skill from the Partnership team and a degree of pragmatism and strategic compromise and sacrifice from partners.

By contrast, those less central to the Partnership felt less constrained in being openly critical. Conservationists were often disappointed with the detailed results achieved. This related partly to compromises that were argued as necessary to achieve economic uses for buildings, for example, the use of façadism. Partly, though, it related to a lack of attention to more detailed issues of authenticity. Examples included the joinery detailing of windows and shop-fronts. This was especially frustrating to conservationists. These sorts of conflicts occur in all such commercial locations, but the resources of the Partnership were seen as an additional opportunity to 'get things right'. Instead, Grainger Town became regarded by some as a marketing device, interested in achieving superficially acceptable results and disinterested in 'true' conservation.

Different sorts of issues are raised by the example of the Grainger Market. Part of the success of the Grainger Town project was considered to be the attraction back into this part of the city of high-value retailers. This has occurred principally in streets adjacent to a magnificent Grade I listed covered market, the Grainger Market, which has traditionally provided food shopping for low-income groups. The success of the regeneration programme has already displaced lower-income shoppers from the area; now it has brought pressure to 'upgrade' the nature of tenant in the market, a move, if it occurs, that will displace users who traditionally have had this outstanding building as a backdrop for their shopping. As the Grainger Market is clearly in need of substantial investment to its building fabric, this shift has been broadly welcomed by conservationists (notwithstanding the shift away from historic usage), providing the investment is spent 'correctly'.

The problems that conservationists have had with the Grainger Town process can be summarised by a semantic dispute that arose when Grainger Town hosted an international conference. Objections were made to the description of Grainger Town as a 'conservation-led' process, which dissipated when this was changed to 'heritage-led'. Annoyed by the lack of application of conservation principles in many cases, the objecting conservationists could live with the looser (though disliked) term, heritage, with its suggestions of commodification. At the same time, it was notable that the anxieties expressed were mostly concerned with the impact of the project on the fabric of the area rather than with any broader social and economic consequences.

Commodification, for good or ill

In the UK, conservation pressure groups such as SAVE Britain's Heritage have been articulating the economic case for conservation since the 1970s, following an even longer-established trend in the USA. The economic potential that might be constructed around heritage was demonstrated through high-profile projects such as Covent Garden in the UK or Quincy Market in the USA, and through the myriad actions of individual gentrifiers in areas of attractive older housing. In the 1980s, conservation and economic development became explicitly interlinked as part of government policy. This in turn was part of a broader attitude shift towards culture in public policy, whereby increasingly it has been viewed as part of the economy rather than separate from it. Thus, it is undoubtedly the case that heritage and its conservation have become more commodified in recent decades, but the question remains: should this be a fundamental concern for the heritage sector, or an advantageous legitimation? Critiques of the commodified role of heritage, played in the processes described above, can be divided broadly between those focused on the social and distributional consequences of such change, and those more narrowly concerned with conservation values.

Social critiques

The processes outlined in this chapter – gentrification and culture- or property-based regeneration, as well as the potentially all encompassing 'heritage industry' – all have their critics. Often the criticism is based upon the social and distributional consequences of these processes, whether this is seen as aggressive revanchism, as a collective consequence of individual actions, or a public regeneration policy that is inefficiently poor in dealing with systemically deep-rooted social and economic problems. Thus, if a public policy, such as the Urban Renaissance agenda, is considered to be problematic, as suggested by Lees (2003), on the basis that it is a 'gentrifiers' charter', the desire of a body such as English Heritage that wishes to be associated with this agenda must be considered equally problematic.

These, however, are not prominent critiques within the British conservation literature. At an international level, awareness of the social consequences of conservation actions was sustained in the 1980s by the ICOMOS Washington Charter (ICOMOS 1987, discussed in Chapter 2) and by oblique references to social issues in the Council of Europe's Granada Convention (ratified by the UK government) on architectural heritage (Council of Europe 1987). But in the UK, by and large, debates within the heritage profession between the 1970s and recent years steered away from such issues. This lack of reflexivity is a weakness of the movement and could be seen as evidence of earlier assertions about the intrinsically right-wing nature of heritage (Ascherson 1987), or at least of an inherent social and political conservatism within the sector. Alternatively, it may be a reflection of unwilling-ness in the sector to engage in critical debate, paralysed maybe by the political capital that could be made of this by its critics, such as they are. By contrast, at a pragmatic level, the conservation sector has displayed much more alacrity in attaching itself to any economic or social benefits that might be seen to be associated with heritage and its protection.

The challenge to authenticity

Thus the focus for those in the conservation sector has rarely been about the potentially socially regressive consequences of a commodified conservation, but mainly about some of the key tenets of modern conservation exemplified by the concept of authenticity. This can be understood as forming part of a wider modernist critique of the packing and selling of culture as a commodity (Boyer 1996) or, perhaps more contentiously, as part of a shift from exclusive 'high culture' to a mass-produced commodified culture (Graham *et al.* 2000). This can be read as a post-modern pressure on the process of modern conservation.

In practical terms, by placing economic goals at the forefront, critical concerns over honesty of intervention can be compromised. So, for example, the market may prefer a chimera of antiqueness to a conservatively repaired building with its transparent display of interventions. Market performance may mean, say, that developers push for effectively a new product, such as a new building behind a retained façade, which has a historic image but contemporary performance and functionality. Even if conflicts are not so explicit, economic drivers may simply mean that conservation goals take a back seat and are forgotten, as is maintained by some conservationists to have occurred in Grainger Town. While key heritage and conservation stakeholders, such as English Heritage, have been keen to emphasise the compatibility of the market and the historic environment, and indeed the positive role that heritage can play in regeneration, it is clear that there are some dissenting voices in the wider sector.

A fact of life

The historic environment in the UK is defined through legislation and its application diversely and extensively; it is a rich, heterogeneous mix of buildings, areas and landscapes, extending far beyond historical preoccupations with a limited number of monuments. If it is accepted that the heritage we seek to protect is defined in this broad way, then the inevitable reality is that most historic buildings, or buildings in historic areas, have an economic function, or rather *need* to have an economic function (as they always have had) to survive. It would be naïve in the extreme, therefore, to think that issues of conservation and heritage would not inevitably become bound up in issues of economy and in processes such as regeneration. Furthermore, the post-industrial focus on culture as an economic good is a global force of great power, and again it is inevitable that the historic environment, and the way that it is perceived and used, will be affected by this. In this context, railing against commodification per se would seem to be a futile activity.

The commodification of culture and heritage is a fact of contemporary life. In practice this has brought opportunities and problems to the sector, with possibly more of the former than the latter. Politically, the conservation sector has *had* to demonstrate its usefulness as part of a broader set of social and economic processes. In doing so, protection regimes have been sustained and new resources attracted, while at the same time there will always be local battles to be fought about particular buildings and places.

In practice, the processes of transformation, of which conservation is part, will sometimes be socially progressive, or benign, or sometimes socially regressive. What can be dispiriting is the unwillingness of the conservation sector to move beyond a magpie-like acquisition of the benefits of association with regeneration. The sector has steadfastly largely avoided more critical discourse over issues such as gentrification, with which it has, like it or not, a relationship.

Chapter 7

Conservation and the community

Introduction

One of the recurrent themes in this book is how, in recent decades, conservation became established as a rarely contested, major objective of planning policy. In part, this is held to relate to the wide public support that exists for conservation policies. There is certainly a massive popular interest in the western world in more broadly defined conceptions of general and personal heritage, as evidenced in the UK by a rash of history-related programmes on television and the large-scale pursuit of researching family trees.

However, the initial focus in this chapter is upon the 'conservation community'. It is a characteristic of the conservation world that, alongside the professional conservationists, planners, architects, surveyors and so on engaged in conservation planning issues, there is a well-established amenity movement of non-professionals. Together these make up a rather heterogeneous, wider conservation community or movement, very disparate in some ways, but yet capable of presenting a remarkably unified front to perceived external threats; what in other contexts has been termed a 'community of practice' defined by mutual engagement, joint enterprise and a shared repertoire (Wenger 1998).

The next section briefly sketches the historical development of the national amenity movement. One of the reasons this is important is because this history is influential in shaping the attitude and thinking of the conservation movement today. A powerful mythology has developed that emphasises the triumphs and heroic failures of the movement and serves to validate its importance, both historically and in contemporary society. To state that this is a mythologised history does not mean that it is untrue, or at least untrue in large part; what is important is the way these historical accounts contribute to the identity of the conservation movement. The discussion then shifts to a consideration of local amenity bodies, which, while having at least an equally long history as national groups, came to the fore in more recent decades, perhaps especially since the formation of the Civic Trust in 1957. Characteristics of the amenity movement include self-presentation as being representative of wider public opinion (though there is in reality an ambivalence about public opinion, as will be discussed), an assertion that it occupies the moral high ground and an emphasis on an emotional defence of heritage, stressing its role in national and local identities (Law 2004; Hobson 2004).

In the subsequent section, the focus shifts away from the conservation movement towards how the wider public relates to the historic environment, and the efforts of English Heritage to show the importance of this environment to the wider public. The idea is introduced that, insofar as this support can be demonstrated, the *way* in which the historic environment is valued is perhaps rather different from modern conservation principles, relying more upon a 'heritage aesthetic'. Next, the empirical evidence from the limited research that has been undertaken on the wider public and the conservation planning system is reviewed, touching upon issues of knowledge of conservation planning and engagement with processes. In so doing, the focus is primarily on the heritage that some people engage with most: that is the heritage of where they live. Although we are still concerned with officially sanctioned heritage, generally through conservation area designation, it involves a different qualitative and geographical focus from that in the preceding or following chapters. It is a shift of gaze towards the relatively ordinary and towards the residential. This is a long way from the concerns of the founding seers of the architectural conservation movement, moving away from archi-tectural monuments and towards the residential suburbs, despised by prevailing aesthetic and professional opinion for much of the twentieth century. Though these represent the humble part of protected heritage, we should remember that these areas are typically not *that* humble. Most people do not live in a conservation area, and most residential conservation areas cover areas of relatively expensive and architecturally 'superior' middle-class housing.

The community of conservation

There are many different amenity groups in the heritage sector, mostly with relatively small memberships and representing, at the national level, a constellation of particular interests and concerns. The temporal focus of some of the principal groups is apparent in the names of, for example, the Georgian Group, the Victorian Society and the Twentieth Century Society. A myriad of other groups exist around thematic interests, such as the Theatres Trust and the Garden History Society, along with a vast range of locally based groups.

Those at the heart of conservation activity have long seen the need to work together to provide an effective and coherent voice. So, for example, in the voluntary sector a still extant Joint Committee of the National Amenity Societies was formed in 1972. The formation of Heritage Link in 2001 extended this cooperation to over eighty bodies (at the time of writing) in the heritage sector, including such diverse organisations as the Architectural Heritage Fund, the Black Environment Network, the Cathedral Architects Association and, at a very different scale, the National Trust. The mission of Heritage Link is to bring 'people together who care about our heritage to formulate policy, influence opinion and achieve change on issues of common concern' (Heritage Link 2004).

There are, though, distinct emphases and nuances of principles and approach within the heart of this 'conservation family'. For example, the exacting principles associated with the William Morris-founded SPAB give quite a different emphasis from the pragmatic campaigning of a body such as SAVE Britain's Heritage.

A key part of the conservation movement today is an emergent conservation profession. Prior to the 1970s, this essentially consisted of a small and rather unfashionable grouping within the architecture profession. The institutionalisation of conservation objectives in planning law and policy helped create specialist positions in local authority planning departments from the late 1960s, and such positions began to grow through the 1970s. A factor that helped accelerate this trajectory towards the definition of a distinct conservation profession, in England at least, was the creation of English Heritage in 1984, detaching conservation at a national level from government and allowing distinct professional identities and career paths to develop. Another key stimulus was the coming together of the growing band of professionals, employed by local government to operate the conservation planning machinery, to form the Association of Conservation Officers in 1982. This group developed into the Institute of Historic Building Conservation (IHBC) in 1997. The employed officers who work for amenity bodies should also be considered conservation professionals.

The conservation community is a coalition of interested groups rather than a unified movement. One of the remarkable features of the ascendancy of conservation in the last twenty years is the ability of this broad church of conservation to suppress contradictions of approach and internal division and to present a united front to policymakers at key times. In recent years, it is notable how skilfully the conservation movement has responded to changing policy directions. So, for example, the sector was regarded as very effective at lobbying for its position in the formulation of planning policy guidance in the 1990s (Department of the Environment and Department of National Heritage 1994; Delafons 1993; Delafons 1997a), and amenity bodies were quick to respond alongside English Heritage to the potential threat posed by the early work of the government's UTF (Urban Task Force 1998; English Heritage 1998; SAVE Britain's Heritage 1998) and quick to embrace the regeneration agenda, as discussed in Chapter 6.

Conflicts within the sector do occasionally occur. Larkham has referred to a specific clash between SPAB and the York Archaeological Trust over the restoration of Barley Hall, a fourteenth- and fifteenth-century hall-house in York (see Figure 7.1). SPAB considered the extent of restoration undertaken by the Trust to have led to the effective destruction and loss of authenticity of the medieval structure (and indeed, the building's category of listing was subsequently downgraded), and to be 'reproduction heritage: meticulously researched and beautifully executed fakery, but fakery nonetheless' (SPAB, cited in Larkham 1996: 263).

7.1
Barley Hall, York, controversially restored by the York Archaeological Trust.
Source: author.

It is remarkable that such open conflict is relatively unusual. Bodies at the heart of the conservation movement will generally subscribe, in broad terms at least, to the principles of modern conservation outlined in Chapter 2. However, there is interpretive flexibility in the application of these principles. Hobson (2004) felt there to be a lack of a clearly defined consensus in the sector on a shared-value framework, but he also described a 'rolling consensus' (p. 121) between key opinion formers in the sector, which allows for a more discursive approach and helps minimise conflict. As I will discuss in Chapter 9, post-modern influences have also had an influence and, as I will also discuss, above all there is a pragmatism in the sector that can validate a range of practices and sublimate potential conflict.

It is clear that most of the groups in the conservation-amenity sector seek to be 'insider' rather than 'outsider' groups, pursuing a 'responsible style' of action (Lowe and Goyder 1983; Coxall 2001). They want to be seen as legitimate and recognised by both national and local government, and want to use this legitimacy to create the 'right' political agenda and to influence policy formation and implementation.

National amenity bodies and conservation mythology

Running through Chapters 2–5 are references to amenity bodies and their involvement in the political process of making the conservation system. Indeed, it is a key foundation myth of UK conservation that its origins lie in voluntary, non-professional activity (see, for example, Saunders (1996; 2002)), and volunteers are still said to be 'the lifeblood of the heritage sector' (Heritage Link 2003: 1). Neither John Ruskin nor William Morris were architects, but rather extraordinary polymaths and polemicists, capable of articulating a reaction both in opposing a countervailing and Establishment view (in the Church of England at least) on the appropriate treatment of the artistic religious heritage, and against the impact of nineteenth-century industrialisation and modernity more generally. By way of contrast, their French contemporary Eugène Emmanuel Viollet-le-Duc was a professional architect and very much a man of the Establishment. Similarly, the development of conservation from these early and limited origins into its current position of major policy significance is portrayed as a series of gains made through the heroic struggles of the voluntary amenity movement at both national and local levels, usually in the face of official indifference or active antipathy. For conservationists this is not a process that stops. There is always further ground to be won, and eternal vigilance is necessary to prevent the loss of ground already gained, a particular issue with a modernising Labour government thought to be indifferent to conservation issues (Venning 1999). These attitudes were evident in a bitter piece in *The Guardian* newspaper, celebrating the reopening of St Pancras Station in London for Eurostar trains, while decrying as hypocritical the attendance at the opening of figures such as the Mayor of London (Jenkins 2007). Since the 1970s in particular, amenity societies have sought to represent their views as evidence of a wider public mood and opinion.

The creation of SPAB in 1877 by Morris and others, and the enduring significance attached to its manifesto, were reviewed in Chapter 2. Subsequent to its foundation, the central narrative of the development of the national amenity movement has often focused on the idea of an evolving taste and valuing of architectural style, in advance of official attitudes and wider public taste. The conservation movement is presented as a vanguard defending a newly appreciated heritage, endangered by others such as government and developers. Thus the formation of the Georgian Group as a breakaway from SPAB, touched upon in Chapter 3, was the response of a new, largely Metropolitan-based, generation, re-evaluating the merits of Georgian architecture and often linking its relative simplicity and urbaneness with Modern Movement architecture. At the same time, Georgian London was being demolished at a rapid rate. By the 1950s the focus had shifted to Victorian architecture, with the Victorian Society being formed in 1958. Subsequently, the Thirties Society was formed in 1980, later rebranded as the Twentieth Century Society to encompass more recent buildings. Alongside this chrono-logically based trend has been the development of groups based around particular spheres of interest. The most venerable of these are the Ancient Monuments Society and the Council of British Archaeology. The Civic Trust and its founder, Duncan Sandys, were of undoubted importance in developing consciousness of, and tools to protect, wider conceptions of the historic environment, by pioneering environmental improvements in historic areas and promoting the concept of conservation areas. Many other groups exist, including the Garden History Society, SAVE Britain's Heritage, a UK branch of the international organisation, the Documentation and Conservation of the Modern Movement (DoCoMoMo), and relatively esoteric bodies such as the Tiles and Architectural Ceramics Society. Thus, over time, the chronological concerns of the amenity movement have telescoped ever nearer to the present, and the scope of their concerns has continually broadened. A key omission from this list is the National Trust, returned to briefly below.

Within their particular sphere of public life, several of these groups have enjoyed a prominent profile. In their foundation, they have been frequently associated with major figures of their day: SPAB with William Morris, and both the Georgian Group and the Victorian Society with John Betjeman and Nikolaus Pevsner. In the twentieth century, key figures associated with the amenity movement were also often closely linked to government. The most dramatic case was Duncan Sandys, a government minister when he created the Civic Trust, but other notable figures such as Pevsner were involved in myriad advisory capacities. The campaigning influence of amenity groups can be overstated: for example, the development of conservation in the 1940s–60s was not merely about opposition to redevelopment, it was as much about a town-planning system that was gradually evolving more inclusive conceptions of conservation, as discussed in Chapter 3. However, it has been formidable. A number of societies have been formally incorporated into the planning system since the late 1960s. Six are statutory consultees on applications to demolish or partly demolish listed buildings, whereas others, such as the Garden History Society, are consultees on their specific areas of concern. The amenity movement has achieved this status by generally pursuing a 'responsible' approach to participation in planning issues. The conservation movement also seeks to present itself as morally virtuous, not merely as representative of an 'expert discourse' but also as 'speaker for the people' (Law 2004: 87).

Yet it is clear that these bodies do not represent wider public opinion, at least directly. Rather, they are a self-defined elite, not in terms of wealth or power necessarily, but in terms of a particular ideology and set of values and as possessor of a distinct 'cultural capital'; as Matthew Saunders of the Ancient Monuments Society put it (in referring to SPAB and its manifesto), 'sheltering . . . the guttering flame of truth' (Saunders 2002: 1). The membership of these national groups is generally small. The membership of SPAB, for example, stands at around 6000, and the membership of the major national amenity societies as a whole (without accounting for overlapping membership) has been estimated at around 18 000 (Saunders 2002). The alternative history of the amenity bodies, therefore, is of a small group of enthusiasts with a particular set of preoccupations, rather than being an avant-garde movement leading public opinion. Indeed, an alternative view of the early days of SPAB has emphasised how out of tune their ideas were with just about everybody else, and how ineffective many of their early campaigns were (Miele 1996). National amenity groups subscribe to a particularly refined set of 'expert' values about heritage and conservation, 'the Authorized Heritage Discourse' (Smith 2006), and operate within the institutional confines of a highly professionalised planning system, of which they form part. Valuable though their role may be, at best they might be argued to be a link to, rather than representative of, wider public opinion. Indeed, Hobson has demonstrated the deep ambivalence sometimes held by national amenity groups towards public opinion: on the one hand seeking to represent it, on the other, disdainful of the 'subjective' and nostalgic 'heritage' preferences that they perceive the wider public to possess (Hobson 2004).

These membership figures are modest in relation to the national heritage sector as a whole, where it has been claimed by Heritage Link that there are well over a million members of heritage organisations (discounting the National Trust and English Heritage) and an active volunteer force of over 150 000, although it was acknowledged that the methodology used in compiling these figures relied significantly on guesswork (Heritage Link 2003). This wider sector includes, for example, 80 000 members of the National Association of Decorative and Fine Arts Societies, and the Heritage Link report encompassed such diverse organisations as the Almshouse Association, British Sundial Society, English Folk Song and Dance Society, Green Alliance, National Association of Re-enactment Societies, Vintage Wooden Boat Association and the Youth Hostels Association.

It has also been argued that the views of amenity bodies do not necessarily closely reflect the views of their own membership. It is held that amenity bodies may seek broad allegiance to principles rather than active participation in decision-making, and they are often constituted to avoid such active involvement (Coxall 2001).

The one conservation body with a clear mass membership is the National Trust. With over 3 million members, it is claimed to be the largest civil organisation in western Europe (Saunders 2002). This represents a remarkable growth. Established in 1895, its membership in 1929 was just 1000 and was about 7000 just before the Second World War, and it was rebuked by government for not connecting better with the general public (Mandler 1997).

7.2
Palaces of consumption? Waddesdon Manor, one of the National Trust's country houses.
Source: John Sanders.

In the post-war period membership began to grow rapidly, hitting 100 000 in 1964, 1 million by 1980 and 2 million by 1990. A key factor in the growth of the National Trust has been the post-war elevation of the country house as a central component of national heritage and the rise of country house visiting as a leisure pursuit (Mandler 1997). This surely is the principal reason behind the Trust's phenomenal rise in membership. Although it has something like 40 000 active volunteers, it is mostly not an active membership, nor one necessarily particularly actively concerned with conservation issues per se. Membership is sold on the consumption benefits it brings, the free admission to the Trust's properties, although many members are thought to retain their membership in order to support the work of the Trust, rather than calculating whether it will be financially worthwhile (Heritage Link 2003). Furthermore, the Trust's concerns are essentially to do with its estate, rather than the wider conservation planning process with which we are concerned here.

Local groups and their influence

Any assertion that conservation is a national mass movement is dubious. In terms of active participation, local amenity bodies are perhaps more significant. They have been criticised as being unrepresentative of the population as a whole, representing solidly middle-class values and attitudes, self-interest and 'NIMBYism' (cf. Lowe 1977; Rydin 2003; Eversley 1973). It is a long-standing critique that the members of these societies are the vociferous, educated, middle class, 'who by reason of education, training, outlook, social milieu and intellectual persuasion, regard quality of environment not only as important in itself but also as a benevolent influence on others' (Cherry 1975: 3).

Research in the past has certainly tended to show that, typically, their officers possess middle-class occupations and values (Barker 1976) and that they can be deeply unrepresentative of local opinion. Lowe cited the case of the Barnsbury Association in Islington, which, founded by incoming, gentrifying residents, pursued objectives counter to the interests of the majority of the population in the area (Lowe 1977).

Local amenity societies have existed since the nineteenth century. However, their numbers radically expanded in the 1950s, 1960s and 1970s, as part of a wave of civic activism on environmental and conservation issues. This coincided with an official agenda of increasing public participation in planning processes and, it has been argued, as part of increasing economic and political power amongst middle-class groups (Samuel 1994; Urry 1995). The 1969 Skeffington Report (Great Britain. Committee on Public Participation in Planning 1969), which heralded statutory participation rights in the preparation of development plans, was a landmark in this respect, although it has been questioned how much this represented any real sea-change in attitude (Ravetz 1980). It is clear that the amenity movement of the period was extremely heterogeneous in nature. Societies could be quite conservative in outlook and focus purely on historic buildings, or they could link to wider community activism (McKean 1979).

Law used a typology in his research that distinguished between civic trusts (identified in his case studies by their high-profile role), historical groupings (focusing on particular historic periods) and local groups (Law 2004). This latter category was further divided between 'place-based groups', with a broad concern for place, 'space-based groups', with a NIMBY focus and mobilised around resisting development, and 'green-based groups', focused on protecting a particular piece of open space. A similar but simpler distinction made by Rydin (2003) distinguished between short-lived anti-development groups and longer-lived environmental groups, which, while they may oppose individual developments, have a broader and sustained focus on the local environment. Issues of interest around which such groups are formed are very diverse, extending beyond the historic environment and including, for example, various facets of the natural environment. Many local societies interested in the built environment affiliated themselves to the national Civic Trust formed in 1957, hence, the specific term 'civic societies'. Such societies are often characterised as being conservation groups, and, while this may often be central to their purpose, the societies may have wider environmental interests. In 1960 approximately 300 societies were registered with the Trust; by 1967 this was 600, reaching a peak of around 1300 in the late 1970s (Andreae 1996; Larkham 1996).

The heyday of the civic society has often been held to be the 1970s, and it is notable that much of the research referred to in this section was undertaken in this period. This was the era of local development struggles up and down the country, as documented in the various polemical texts mentioned in Chapter 4. However, civic societies and other local amenity groups are still very much with us. Two more recent surveys of societies registered with the Civic Trust (Cairns and Kelly 1994; Civic Trust 1998) showed the number of registered societies had dipped below 900, although they still represented a membership of over 300 000 people. This compares, for example, with a membership of local wildlife trusts that stands at around 560 000 (Wildlife Trusts Partnership 2004). The vast majority of societies were involved in statutory planning processes such as monitoring and commenting upon planning applications, public inquiries and providing written comments on development plan proposals. Interviews carried out for the Civic Trust with individual societies reinforced the heterogeneous nature of societies and their activities, but also a frequent strong desire not to be seen as preservationist, opposing all change.

Law studied local groups in York and Leeds and found distinct differences in the local conservation cultures (Law 2004). The principal groups in York had a very strong planning focus, aimed at strict principles of architectural conservation. In Leeds there was a wider interest in the culture of the city, including, for example, the promotion of new architecture, seen as part of a process of recovery and critical of the conservative 'Leeds-look' style of building that has been popular with the city council (Powell 1989). However, Law also found, in both places, evidence of some of the profound features of the conservation movement touched upon earlier. Conservationists saw themselves as figures of authority, but at the same time constructed an anti-elitist discourse as part of their self-construction as 'the voice of the people'. They tended to stress the importance of a sense of temporal continuity with the past and were critical of 'heritage culture' with its commodifications and tawdry use of architectural symbolism. They also displayed a fierce pride in place, a local patriotism and wish to boost the value of their particular place.

The 1998 Civic Trust report (Civic Trust, 1998) found that, with a few exceptions, societies reported a reasonably good relationship with local authorities. Those societies consulted more by their local authorities generally perceived their relationships to be better. A survey and exploration of the impact of civic societies in the north of England sought to examine some of these issues, looking at the contrasting local authority areas of Newcastle City Council and the deeply rural Tynedale District Council in particular (Cadd et al. 1998; Pendlebury 1999). Officers in both authorities stated they were more likely to respond to opinions that were technically informed. Newcastle officers saw a useful safety-net function for amenity societies. However, councillors and officers in both authorities thought that amenity society input was most likely to have an impact if suggestions were seen to have clarity and to be practical. This reinforces the 'responsible' style of action described by Lowe and Goyder (1983).

Two examples of the influence exerted by amenity bodies in Newcastle upon Tyne can be briefly given. An application put forward for Newcastle Central Station, a Grade I listed building, proposed some alterations to window openings, including the insertion of a Venetian window. At a meeting of the council's Conservation Area Advisory Committee, planning officers were uncertain what view to take. The committee strongly recommended a more modest intervention, in keeping with the existing detailing of the building. The officers subsequently agreed this change with the applicants. A more controversial Newcastle case was the proposal to demolish the listed art deco Wills Building, a range of offices that had been attached to a former tobacco factory (see Figure 7.3). After the building had stood empty for a number of years, the council were minded to grant approval for demolition. However, a sustained campaign against this was fought by a number of bodies. The campaign included the commissioning of a feasibility study on the re-use of the building. Eventually a housing developer acquired it and converted it into flats. The campaign to save the building bought time for a solution to be found.

7.3
The Wills Building, Newcastle upon Tyne, rescued from demolition and converted to apartments.
Source: author.

With both these examples, we see the amenity bodies engaging with the planning system in a 'responsible' way. With the first example, an approach was advocated that was 'correct' in terms of most articulations of conservation principles, and was accepted by an agnostic local authority and applicant. Though the second case involved challenging the local authority, this was done 'responsibly', through the commissioning of a feasibility study.

However, in more routine development control matters, amenity bodies may often lose the argument. Looking in detail at the comments made on planning applications by one society, the Wolverhampton Civic Society, Larkham (1985; 1996) discerned it as having some influence, building good working relationships and trust and achieving detailed changes to planning applications, rather than altering the authority's view in principle. Similar findings were found by Lowe and Goyder (1983) in their study of the Henley Society. They noted a strong alliance between the society and district planning officers, sometimes in conflict with the town council, which was more representative of business and commercial views. A recent analysis has looked at the effect over three years of the successor body to the Newcastle Conservation Area Advisory Committee, the independent Newcastle Conservation Advisory Panel, finding that the council's decision was in line with the panel's recommendation in 61 per cent of cases (Brown 2006). The panel has worked hard to build good relationships with the city council and clearly has some influence. However, this left a substantial number of cases where the council took a different view. In particular, 40 per cent of the cases on which the panel recommended refusal were granted, and 71 per cent of the cases where the panel sought a deferral for amendments or more information were granted conditionally.

Built heritage and everyday life

The importance of demonstrating the assumed public support for conservation policies is something the sector, and English Heritage in particular, have been acutely conscious of. A Gallup poll for English Heritage in 1993 found saving Britain's historic buildings, monuments and gardens to be the public's 'overwhelming heritage priority', ahead of heritage alternatives such as the performing arts, music or sport (English Tourist Board 1994). In subsequent years, the use of opinion poll-based research has become a common tool deployed by English Heritage in marshalling the case for conservation and also in exploring the attitudes of those believed to be disconnected from conventional state representations of heritage, such as ethnic minorities. MORI were commissioned to undertake a report in conjunction with the formulation of *Power of Place* (MORI 2000; English Heritage 2000) and found very strong support for statements such as 'what I love about Britain is its heritage', agreement from most people that their lives were richer for having the opportunity to visit and see heritage, and disagreement that we preserve too much. Interestingly, given the public backlash against redevelopment in the 1960s and 1970s and the controversies of listing modern buildings in the early 1990s, most people were quite happy to regard post-1950 material culture as heritage. Further MORI investigations, undertaken for the *Heritage Counts 2003* report (English Heritage 2003; MORI 2003), produced similar findings and emphasised how people thought of heritage as being something very local, not only grand stately homes, castles and so on. However, while finding positive attitudes towards heritage across the board, the research confirmed that this was especially prevalent amongst the white middle class.

These apparent public preferences for old things and general support for the principle of protecting heritage are perceived as inferring a validation of more specific conservation objectives. However, it can be argued that the terms upon which this appreciation is based are quite different from those that underpin 'modern conservation', with its emphasis upon authenticity of historic fabric. Indeed, it is often argued that more general appreciation of the historic environment is essentially an aesthetic construct (see, for example, Hubbard 1993; Mellor 1991; Zukin 1987; Butler 1997). Different rationales for valuing built heritage lead to quite different approaches to conservation. For example, linked to the stress on buildings as historical documents within orthodox conservation is a sensibility of aesthetic appreciation for decayed, retained fabric, 'the patina of age' (Ruskin 1849 (1886)). From a different perspective, however, Lowenthal (1985) has noted how the wider population often prefers things to look new, including old buildings.

In positing public support for conservation, however broadly defined, there are dangers of over-generalisation. Research by Townshend examined the sort of housing Newcastle students would like to live in post-graduation (Townshend 2000). To some degree this bore out the discussion so far: a general preference for the appearance and character of older buildings without any great interest in their intrinsic historic nature. Thus, the most popular choice was Victorian and Edwardian housing, preferably with some 'features' such as fireplaces, but suitably adapted for modern living, with modern kitchens and bathrooms and so on. More recent housing, inter-war semi-detached, post-war and brand new were all generally unpopular, as was earlier property such as late-Georgian town houses or other converted historic buildings, such as the Wills building mentioned above. Though Victorian and Edwardian housing was liked for its age, equally important were its utility, for example, its spaciousness, and the wider environment in which it was located, leafy inner suburbs – practical attributes the other historic buildings were thought not to possess. Furthermore, there are plenty of other people who place no value on the historic nature of buildings, for example, the resident of Hoxton quoted by Wright in the previous chapter (Wright 1985).

Conservation, suburbia and the public

In considering these issues further, my focus now shifts to the limited empirical evidence that exists on public engagement with the conservation-planning system. Although there are few published comparative data on conservation areas (Pearce *et al.* (1990) is a now out-dated exception), by the mid 1990s rural villages were the most designated type of area, but the fastest-growing type of designation appeared to be the residential suburb (Larkham 1999a). Such areas form the 'anonymous familiar' for many people. It is in such suburbs that many people come into contact with the conservation system on an everyday basis, though, as noted before, the range of people this encompasses is not representative of society as a whole.

Victorian and Edwardian suburbs had been designated from the earliest years of the conservation area system. The designations have grown in number, however, and more recently have extended to encompass 1930s speculatively built suburbs (which were widely criticised by the proto-conservation movement when built). The designation of School Road, Birmingham, in 1988 led to a feature in *The Times* (Franks 1988) (see Figure 7.4). The resulting debate revolved around the extent to which this, an example of the familiar speculative inter-war semi-detached residential area, could qualify for designation, given the legal definition of a conservation area that requires it to possess 'special architectural or historical' interest. What was special about this average, everyday area? Local planners mobilised traditional art-history and authenticity conservation arguments: the area was relatively unaltered since its construction in the late 1930s, with few extensions, PVCu windows, and so on. While other such areas were changing rapidly, the unchanged, original character of School Road was 'special'. Is this how the residents of the School Road view their area though? (Larkham *et al.* 2002).

Residential areas bring a wider part of the population to the formal processes of conservation planning than might commonly be involved for, say, commercial areas, where the role of professional groups in representing interests and conflict mediation is likely to be more prevalent. Furthermore, the pressures within residential areas are likely to be different from, and usually of a smaller scale than, those met in commercial areas and urban centres (Larkham 1996). Residential areas also produce small-scale, but numerous, tensions between the values and aspirations of residents, for example in personalising their homes, and the values embedded in the planning system

7.4
**School Road
Conservation
Area, Birmingham.**
Source: Peter
Larkham.

(Larkham 1999c). For example, the BBC's *Public Eye* programme, 'The Heritage Police' (BBC 1995), showed neighbours arguing over a small doctor's surgery sign, and a landlady pursued for allegedly changing the windows in her property.

Public knowledge and attitudes: some empirical evidence

To review these issues affecting residential conservation, a range of empirical research is discussed that attempts to explore the nature and extent of public involvement in residential conservation area planning; it examines both from the views of the public – residents in these areas – and of the professionals concerned. Little has been written about what people actually perceive to be the aims, objectives and benefits of conserving historic buildings (and environments), and whether these equate in a meaningful way with the priorities and value systems employed by conservation professionals.

Research has been undertaken in suburban conservation areas in the West Midlands (Larkham 1999b), in Chartist villages in Gloucestershire (Larkham and Lodge 1999) and inner-urban areas in Tyne and Wear (Townshend and Pendlebury 1999). In these three studies, the residents' knowledge of, and support for, conservation area status appeared high and was often quite vehement. In one of the north-east studies, respondents rated conservation of the historic environment as second only to crime prevention in terms of the most important local issue, and, in another, when asked how they would feel if the area lost its conservation status, 87 per cent of the respondents said they would oppose this, using phrases such as 'I would fight tooth and nail' (Townshend and Pendlebury 1999: 324).

Beyond this general support, however, there was considerable confusion and misunderstanding. Although there was a general appreciation of the aims and objectives of conservation legislation, few respondents had any idea of the precise scope or nature of that legislation. Most respondents in all the studies thought that conservation area controls were far more draconian than they actually are and, in general, more closely equated them to those applicable to listed buildings.

Residents also encompassed a far wider range of environmental issues within their conception of conservation than is covered by conservation area legislation. In the north-east research, when asked what aspects of the conservation area were most important to residents, six clear themes emerged. In descending frequency of choice these were: architectural appearance (from general styles to details); natural environment (open space, trees etc.); social factors (nice neighbours, the existence of social networks); historical character (referring to distinct historical periods, but also a sense of permanence and continuity); general environmental quality (e.g. peace and quiet); and morphology (size of plots, widths of streets etc.) (Townshend and Pendlebury, 1999). Many of these issues lie outside the direct control of the local planning authority, yet these factors greatly influence the success, or otherwise, of the conservation area as viewed by residents (Larkham, 1999b).

The conservation professionals' views of public involvement

Thus, based on the limited empirical evidence available, there is a general measure of support for the principle of conservation area status from people living in suburban conservation areas, albeit with little precise knowledge about the practical implications. How, then, do the professionals responsible for implementing and managing this system view the wider public? This section is based upon a questionnaire sent to conservation professionals that sought information on the impact of public consultation on decision-making, professionals' views about public comprehension of conservation objectives and, more broadly, the role of public consultation (for a fuller account see Pendlebury and Townshend 1999).

Most local authorities reported making changes to their conservation proposals following public consultation, though mostly these were relatively minor in nature, such as making detailed changes to conservation area boundaries. Respondents were, however, overwhelmingly positive about the benefits of public consultation. The reasons given by respondents for this fell largely into two main themes. First, and most frequently, consultees such as local amenity groups were seen by local authorities as a useful resource in providing conservation staff with information, particularly in terms of historical development. Second, it was seen as part of a process of engendering support for the designation. Sometimes support from public consultation had been important in securing political support for proposals. In one case, a large-scale public consultation was undertaken on ten new proposed areas, because of the councillors' scepticism about the proposals, resulting in 97 per cent support from the public in favour of designation.

Negative responses to public consultation mainly focused on pressure for designations where there was insufficient 'special architectural or historic interest', and, since councillors responded to these pressures, officers perceived that designation became 'political'. The sense of this was nicely conveyed by one respondent who reported that consultation had not in fact changed decisions:

> in my experience the most common approach we receive is people in pleasant, though not necessarily significant, living environments, seeking designation of conservation areas. These proposals are not often justified as they fall short of the qualitative yardstick I apply, but I always judge them carefully.

Though most respondents stressed the importance of public consultation, on closer examination a number of quite different views of the role of 'consultation' could be discerned. At the most participatory end of the spectrum, one respondent stated that, 'we have found it very beneficial to work with the local community in drafting "character statements" and enhancement proposals rather than simply consulting on our ideas. Local ownership has proved very effective in many ways'.

This reply was, however, unusual. More commonly respondents described a process that was less to do with consultation, and more to do with raising awareness and a didactic wish to educate the public in terms of the values of the conservation professionals. A number of respondents explicitly acknowledged a distinction between consultation and information/education, perhaps inevitably returning to issues of 'expert'-defined 'special architectural or historic interest'. For example,

> if an area is of special architectural or historic interest then it should be considered for designation, much in the same way that buildings of special architectural or historic interest are considered for listing, and public debate – as opposed to research – is inappropriate. However, once an area is designated (or a building listed) then education of the public and all other interested parties is the key to conservation success.

More reflexively, from another respondent,

> it's great if you've got support to start off with; v. hard work if you haven't but the only way forward. I probably shouldn't say this but really it's public 'education' here rather than consultation – some may say purveying middle class values?

Thus we see local authority conservation officers displaying similar ambivalence towards their relationship with the wider public to that remarked upon by Hobson with national groups (Hobson 2004). Public support can be useful for achieving professional objectives. However, at this level, it tends to be a rather abstracted form of endorsement. Public influence over the detailed manifestation of conservation objectives and processes is more problematic for conservation professionals, and there is generally an unwillingness to relinquish expert pre-eminence.

Conservation, planning and the public: policy and rhetoric

On the basis of the discussion above, people's engagement with conservation issues can be categorised. The categories identified are by no means purely defined; they are more a spectrum of engagement, based on the premise that nearly all people engage with the historic environment, but in markedly different degrees. First, there is a small group for whom conservation is reasonably central to their 'lifeworld' of personal existence. This includes those for whom conservation is an occupation or part-occupation (including the author of this book) and small numbers of highly motivated activists for whom it is a passion rather than a job. Most of these people, like the professionals, are drawn from higher socio-economic groups, and a combination of this advantage and effective politics has enabled this core conservation movement to achieve its goals to a remarkable degree, one quite disproportionate to the size of the group. This group would generally have a passionate belief in the importance of the conservation of the historic environment for its own sake and are seeking to 'control time' (Castells 2004). To a greater or lesser degree, such conservationists associate themselves with the principles of 'modern conservation' outlined in Chapter 2. This group tends to assume that it has the tacit support of a much larger group within the general population, although, as discussed, it is an ambivalent relationship.

The second distinguishable group consists of those people active in conservation planning processes for more obviously instrumental ends. Like all the groupings suggested here, this involves a spectrum of people. The key point is that any active efforts to conserve historic buildings or protect the character of historic places are intimately linked with personal interest and gain, from an attempt to 'control space' (Castells 2004). At its crudest, this may be an unfettered NIMBYism, for example an attempt to protect property values, or may be a duality of interest, combining sensitivity towards historic buildings with economic self-interest, as noted by Butler (1997). It may also stem from a more rounded attachment to, and passion for, a place (Law 2004). By and large, one might expect such people to have a less well-developed view of what constitutes conservation orthodoxy, and more of a vague conservation aesthetic, a point I expand below. Together, these first two groups make up the rather heterogeneous conservation movement, diverse and diffuse, but capable both at a strategic level and in local case-work of very effective mobilisation.

The third and much larger group that can be defined consists of those who usually play no active part in the protection of the historic environment, but have an active appreciation of it. A key way that this might be expressed is through use of the historic environment as a consumption activity. Most obviously this can be observed through visits to heritage attractions, such as country houses, castles and so on, but it also extends to the enjoyment of historic places more generally, as part of a backdrop to leisure activity. As such, heritage may just be one of many competing consumption possibilities. The Duke of Bedford apparently long ago realised that the main reason why people visited his country house was because they possessed a car and they wanted somewhere to go in it (Ashworth and Howard 1999).

Fourth is the more routine engagement experienced by most people with the typically more modest historic environment encountered as a backdrop to everyday life. Some people may effectively have no contact with the conservation-planning system; others might, if for example they live in a listed building or conservation area. There does appear to be evidence within the wider public domain of a general sympathy towards conservation policies. However, the limited evidence available suggests that this stems from an antipathy towards change, a prevailing attitude that was triggered in the 1960s in reaction to the transformations of modernity that have endured, despite a reappraisal of that period which has allowed some of the buildings of that time to be generally accepted as 'heritage'. Ultimately, this antagonism to change clashes with the values of 'modern conservation', which while seeking to manage change, also embraces it as part of historical continuity. While most conservationists in the first group will advocate that new constructions should be 'of their time', the public mood has been rather more conservative.

Though there does seem to be public sympathy for the retention of old buildings, its underpinnings are not coterminous with orthodox conservation values. Various commentators on conservation issues have referred to a 'heritage aesthetic', a term that is sure to antagonise many within the conservation world with its apparent superficiality. However, to those outside this inner circle of conservation professionals and conservation ideologues, it is a reasonable representation of popular perceptions of conservation issues. Nor, unsurprisingly, is there much evidence that the general public have much knowledge of the mechanics of the conservation-planning system. What they often seem to demonstrate is a holistic view of their environment, but with limited knowledge of the arcane management mechanisms and their failings. This gap between conservationists and the public is evident in Hobson's (2004) work on national groups, and in responses from conservation officers in the author's own research. Though generally core conservationists feel there is support for what they do, ultimately they regard themselves as the keepers of objective values and standards.

Chapter 8

World heritage

Introduction

Much of this book is about the British experience of conservation of heritage. In this chapter, the British experience is more explicitly placed in the context of the wider world. This is done in the context of the concept of 'world heritage' and, in particular, through considering World Heritage Sites, places deemed of 'outstanding universal value'. Looking at world heritage helps illustrate a series of issues about the nature of heritage and the way that it is used and abused. It reveals a broader perspective about issues that are sometimes not very explicit, or even forgotten, in the British context. In particular, it can remind us of the importance of social and economic issues that are not always so obvious in British practice.

The chapter briefly reviews the development of international efforts on conservation before discussing World Heritage Sites. It considers some of the key issues and concerns about World Heritage Sites, drawing upon a range of international examples, before going on to consider sites in the UK. Two of these are discussed in some detail, Blaenavon Industrial Landscape and Liverpool Commercial Centre and Waterfront. The final part of the chapter discusses some of the key lessons to be drawn, focusing in particular on tensions and dissonances that can occur over the symbolic and political role of heritage, over pressures for commodification and over competing ownership claims.

International conservation

Most conservation activity occurs, in the developed western world at least, within the boundary of nation states. That is to say, conservation is framed by national laws and policy and is informed by debates that are internal to the country concerned. However, conservation also exists at a supranational level in a variety of ways and forms. The early phases of modern conservation in the eighteenth and nineteenth centuries were characterised by debates and exchanges of information that crossed national barriers throughout Europe, as was discussed in Chapter 2. For example, one of the early causes taken up by the Society for the Protection of Ancient Buildings was St Mark's, Venice.

International cooperation developed after the Second World War. One arm of the newly founded United Nations dealt with cultural issues, the United Nations Educational, Scientific, and Cultural Organization (UNESCO). In 1956, UNESCO adopted the proposal to found ICCROM in Rome. A key landmark was the production of the International Charter for the Conservation and Restoration of Monuments and Sites, otherwise known as the Venice Charter, in 1964. It was conceived as a revision of the 1931 Athens Charter (Jokilehto 1999). It was adopted as the key doctrinal document by ICOMOS, founded the following year in 1965. ICOMOS has been a key body in international debates about conservation practice and in the articulation of conservation principles through charters, both internationally and within individual countries. It also has a key role in advising UNESCO over the inscription of World Heritage Sites. At a regional level, the Council of Europe, founded in 1949, has also been influential since the early 1960s.

Subsequent to the Venice Charter, a whole raft of supranational developments has occurred at a variety of levels; in Europe principally through the activities of the Council of Europe and at a global level through ICOMOS and UNESCO. Some of the products of this activity take the form of advisory charters, some of legally binding conventions. The United Kingdom is a signatory of the Council of Europe Malta (on the protection of the archaeological heritage) and Granada (on the protection of the architectural heritage) Conventions, though is yet to ratify the more recent Faro Convention (on the Value of Cultural Heritage for Society). It is also a member of the World Heritage Convention. The spirit of these conventions is found within UK law and policy, though neither the legally binding conventions nor advisory charters are usually explicitly referred to. The one exception is the policy weight that has been accorded to World Heritage Sites in planning policy guidance.

World Heritage Sites

Most of the international debate on conservation discussed above has been concerned with appropriate conservation practice, rather than seeking directly to define the heritage to which these principles should be applied. The major exception has been the development of the UNESCO list of World Heritage Sites. In 1972 the UNESCO General Conference adopted the Convention

Concerning the Protection of the World's Cultural and Natural Heritage, otherwise known as the World Heritage Convention. The rationale of the convention was that there were places of 'outstanding universal value', that these were part of the heritage of all humankind and that their protection was therefore a shared responsibility. The most well-known outcome of this was the identification of cultural and natural properties and their inscription as World Heritage Sites. Crucially these were, and still are, considered on the basis of nominations put forward by national governments. Two other key objectives were also established: the publication of a list of 'World Heritage in danger' and the establishment of a World Heritage Fund (Whitbourn 2002).

The first twelve World Heritage Sites were inscribed in seven countries in 1978. By 1982, 137 sites had been inscribed, and by 1992 this had risen to 380. By summer 2006 the total had reached 830 sites (644 cultural, 162 natural and twenty-four 'mixed') across 138 states. By the 1990s, various issues and anxieties were emerging within UNESCO about the nature and status of the list. One outcome of this has been the development of 'mixed' sites, or 'cultural landscapes', where the interaction of the influence of man and nature are deemed to be inextricably linked. This allows for symbolic understandings of cultural significance, rather than relying necessarily on material fabric. Other issues of concern have included anxiety over the large number of applications coming forward, the predominance of certain types of site and the over-representation of western countries already well represented on the list. In order to address and manage these issues, countries are now expected to produce tentative lists of possible future submission for inscription, looking ahead over a five-to-ten year period, and most states are now only allowed to make one submission per year. There has also been a focus on site types; for example, an effort has been made to add more sites related to industrialisation, which has had implications for the UK.

Beyond the internal concerns of UNESCO, a range of other issues are evident. Major issues include the politicisation of World Heritage status, the use of sites as a means of economic and tourism development and tensions over the 'ownership' of heritage between local communities and claims of universality.

Politics and conflict

Though the intention of UNESCO and ICOMOS is to look for 'outstanding universal value' in a dispassionate and scholarly way across the globe, in practice nominations come forward from national governments, which may have a range of rather different motivations. In many countries, having as many sites on the list as possible may be seen to have a positive cachet. Having sites deemed to be of outstanding universal value is seen to proclaim something positive about the culture and status of that individual country.

Conversely, some countries have been suspicious of the concept of World Heritage Sites and reluctant to make nominations. Saudi Arabia, which technically has accepted but not ratified the convention, and with Mecca and Medina within its borders, has no sites (Pocock 1997a). Indeed, according to reports, state-supported Wahhabism, an Islamic doctrine, seems intent on removing the material heritage of these sacred sites for fear that they may give rise to idolatry or polytheism (Howden 2005).

8.1
A necropolis tomb, part of the Paphos World Heritage Site, Cyprus.
Source: author.

Heritage has enormous symbolic power, and the sites chosen by states for nomination as World Heritage Sites are inevitably the product of a particular construction of their own national heritage, as well as aspiring to be deemed of universal significance. Thus, within the confines of a nation-state it might be that the heritage presented as significant and put forward for World Heritage status is that of a dominant group, with less attention paid to other potential heritages of note. This has been argued to be the case in Cyprus. There are three cultural World Heritage Sites, all within the south of the country, with an absence of sites in the archaeologically rich north, isolated as it is by cultural embargoes. Hyland asserted that there are three strong contenders for World Heritage status in the north of the country, but as an unrecognised state, the Turkish Republic of Northern Cyprus is not able to enter the process of nomination and inscription (Hyland 1999). Thus, whatever the rights and wrongs of the political situation in Cyprus, issues of heritage and universal value are inextricably bound up with the construction of the nation-state. Furthermore, in Cyprus there is a sense in which this perpetuates a Greek hegemony over the island's heritage, which dates back before the Turkish invasion in 1974 (for example, in terms of a Greek dominance of the archaeo-logical profession in the country (Scott 2002)). Hopefully, the accession of Greek Cyprus to the European Union will help start a process whereby these issues can be addressed.

The symbolic power of heritage may become a target for a group that considers itself as politically disenfranchised within the state. There are six cultural World Heritage Sites in Sri Lanka, five representing the culture of the Sinhalese Buddhist majority, with the sixth being a fortified city developed by the Portuguese in the sixteenth century. The politicisation of heritage in Sri Lanka has led to the heritage of the majority group becoming a target for the Liberation Tigers of Tamil Eelam, commonly known as the Tamil Tigers, and the principal group from the minority Tamil population fighting for an independent homeland. In 1998, in Kandy, the group bombed the Temple of the Tooth, one of Sri Lanka's holiest Buddhist shrines, in the lead up to Sri Lanka's fiftieth anniversary of independence celebrations. The bomb caused a number of deaths and substantial damage, though not to the main shrine. For the Tamil Tigers, the bomb struck a blow at a major representation of their perceived oppressors in the Sinhalese majority. Moderate Tamil commentators, while condemning the loss of life, saw the targeting of the Temple of the Tooth as the unfortunate consequence of militant Buddhism (Coningham and Lewer 1999).

Similarly heritage can often become a specific focus of attack between states. The shelling of the World Heritage Site of Dubrovnik in Croatia by the Yugoslav/Serbian/Montenegrin army in 1991 was generally considered to be unrelated to any strategic military concerns, but rather an assault on

Croatian (and effectively world) culture. In the words of one contemporary Croatian commentator, 'by destroying our historic heritage . . . Serbia is trying to defeat us retroactively in our past: it is intent on erasing our historical memory and eliminating us from the consciousness of other nations' (Zidic 1991, 2001: 61).

The assault on Dubrovnik had a particular resonance for many in western Europe as it was a city many had visited as part of Dalmatian coast tourism. And even as the war was going on, other commentators were concerned with the future impact of tourism on the character of the city:

> The war is not over. . . . Yet one day it will end, and though Dubrovnik will have peace, *it will face other dangers.* For what the war could not bring about – the mass evacuation of the old town – could happen through a type of urbanism that favours the massive development of tourism.
>
> (Kaiser c.1993/2001: 89, emphasis original)

8.2
The World Heritage Site of Dubrovnik, Croatia, shelled in 1991.
Source: author.

Tourism

There are potential political attractions to World Heritage Site status. However, perhaps even more appealing to many localities is the perceived economic benefits such status might bring, primarily through the development of tourism. Tourism is a major force of commodification, as discussed in Chapter 6. The pressure to present heritage locations in ways deemed suitable by the tourism industry inevitably raise tensions with management objectives centred around notions of cultural authenticity. Van-der-Borg *et al.* (1996) considered seven European 'art cities' and concluded that tourism menaced not only the vitality of their local economies, but also the integrity of their heritage and the quality of life of their residents. Furthermore, sheer weight of visitor numbers can present major problems. For example, the picturesque, but tiny, hill-top city of San Gimignano in Tuscany apparently receives 3 million visitors a year, causing severe environmental problems (Cleere 2006).

It is notable that much of the academic literature concerning World Heritage Sites is to be found in the field of tourism. Much of this, in turn, is concerned with the management problems brought by large influxes of visitors to often sensitive cultural (and natural) sites. Inscription is made on the basis of qualities of 'outstanding universal value', and yet a clear motivation for achieving this status is the economic benefits that ensue; in turn, this raises issues of commodifying for tourist consumption and dealing with the problems of over-use. For,

> the term 'World Heritage Site' is instantly recognised as designating something very special, in tourism terms a definite 'must see'. . . . Needless to say, such sites are magnets for visitors and the enrolment of a new property on the World Heritage List, with the concomitant publicity, is virtually a guarantee that visitor numbers will increase.
>
> (Shackley 1998: Preface)

The desire to achieve these benefits can be found explicitly in the documentation on many sites. Hitchcock has argued that, in the case of Stone Town, Zanzibar, achieving World Heritage Site status in 2000 was equally as important as part of a more existential aspiration to join a world community, and to help mobilise action for preservation and development, over which there has been much concern and international effort (Sheriff 1995; Siravo undated; Hitchcock 2002). However, understandably, tourist development was also a key driver underpinning Zanzibar's successful drive for World Heritage status for Stone Town. Tourist development requires tourist infrastructure. As an article in a publication of the International Finance Corporation (part of the World Bank Group) put it,

8.3
The tourist gaze:
The World
Heritage Site of
Stone Town,
Zanzibar.
Source: author.

sufficient tourism infrastructure is now in place to make Stone Town
a 'destination' rather than merely a faint remembrance of a colorful
historic past . . . Old Stone Town and Zanzibar are together being
crafted and molded through multisegmented imagery to be seen
worldwide on CNN TV travel shows.

(Desthuis-Francis 2002: 4)

The lure of attracting tourists from across the globe can be a
strongly homogenising force. Cash-rich tourists may want an exotic experience,
but rarely *very* exotic. They also want familiarity and good-quality services, the
sort of infrastructure Desthuis-Francis described for Zanzibar as, '15 restaurants
acceptable to the international traveller and a plethora of antique, curio and arts
and crafts shops' (Desthuis-Francis 2000: 4).

Furthermore, Marks argued some time ago that the benefits
of tourism for Zanzibar are socially differentiated, with gentrification

disadvantaging the poor (Marks 1996). While notable buildings are conserved, fragile social and cultural networks and more modest fabric are destroyed. Tourism can thus lead to competing claims over space. Local communities may struggle to compete for what they regard as their own space. It is these issues of 'ownership' that are considered in the next section.

Ownership

What are the implications for local communities of the identification of a place as possessing 'outstanding universal value', such that it becomes a World Heritage Site? Does this global accolade override the wish for people in a place to have their aspirations met in terms of its management? In other words, 'whose heritage' is it?

The desire to construct a location more acceptable to tourists was one of the motivations behind radical changes made to the way the historic centre of Lima was managed, post-inscription as a World Heritage Site, described by Seppanen. The goal was to cleanse the area to 'become a colonial fantasy re-enacted from an imaginary past' (Seppanen 1999: 69). Changes to the fabric and management of the area were effected through the creation of a new agency for the area, *ProLima*, and through changed zoning laws. Physical improvements included works such as restriction of traffic and guidelines on such issues as commercial signage familiar the world over. However, there was also a very particular focus on uses in the area, for example,

> Hotels and bars, the vending of old coins, the fabrication of wigs and the reparation of walking sticks [sic] were allowed. But institutes of higher education, night clubs and schools of martial arts – the typical symbols of modernity and progress of the users of the old centre – were banned.
>
> (Seppanen 1999: 58–9)

A particular issue was the forcible displacement of large numbers of street vendors from the area, apart from small numbers of carefully controlled vendors selling tourist-related items. Seppanen regarded the transformation of the historic centre into a tourist space as being a function of local politics rather than a function of World Heritage Site status per se. However, at the same time, such status was considered to be a fundamental part of the mobilisation that occurred to transform the area.

Kathmandu Valley in Nepal has been inscribed as a World Heritage Site since 1979, focused on a series of religious sites. At the crossroads of the great civilisations of Asia, seven groups of Hindu and Buddhist monuments, as well as the three residential and palace areas of the royal cities of Kathmandu, Patan and Bhadgaon, are held to illustrate Nepalese art at its height.

UNESCO has had serious concerns about the integrity of the World Heritage Site for many years. This has related to various factors, including the demolition, alteration and restoration of historic buildings, uncontrolled new development and an absence of technical personnel and skilled labour (UNESCO 1999). A recommendation was made in 1993 to put the site on the List of World Heritage in Danger. This was finally undertaken in 2003.

Owens described one part of the World Heritage Site, Swayambhu, centred upon a Buddhist shrine (Owens 2002). Broadly speaking, within the wider site the influence of four strands of Buddhism can be seen. Two are local to the area and two originate in Sri Lanka/Thailand/Burma and Tibet/Bhutan. The constant transformation of sacred places through devotional practice is very much a part of South Asian religious tradition, the maintenance of their life and power being dependent upon human intervention and its transformational consequences. Inspired by devotion or desire to acquire merit, people have long restored, improved, decorated, remodelled and rebuilt temples, including ancient ones. This is even more evident in the Kathmandu Valley than elsewhere because of damage caused by frequent earthquakes. Thus, there is nothing new about the transformation of Swayambhu through devotional acts, or about transnational and international involvement; many of the people creating shrines and undertaking devotional acts are not Nepalese. However, the nature of these transformations has changed in other respects.

The introduction of a multi-party democracy in 1990 liberalised a carefully controlled economy and brought great wealth to some, particularly in the Kathmandu Valley (Owens 2002). Some of the newly wealthy, along with other donors, have chosen to spend money on devotional acts of construction. There has been competition between different ethnic and religious groups in this regard. Thus, there has been rapid transformation, often using modern techniques and materials rather than those traditionally employed. Owens quoted two Kathmandu Valley residents:

> This beautiful valley is lost. Twenty years of urban planning have failed. The only thing that would save it would be to tear down everything built over the last twenty years. Though it is a terrible thing to say, and though it would be a terrible thing if it were to happen, the only thing that would save the valley would be an earthquake.

> It used to be that you could put a god wherever you wanted. Nowadays they even tell you what kind of brick to use.

> (Owens 2002: 281)

The first comment was made by a foreign national with twenty-odd years of urban planning and architectural experience in Nepal, the second by an elderly

Nepalese gentleman. Thus, there is an ongoing complex contestation of ownership over Swayambhu and other sites in the Kathmandu Valley. There is a desire for a continuity of religious practice, expressed in devotional transformation of place from people of the Kathmandu Valley but also from far beyond, with tensions between different ethnic and religious groupings. These processes have changed and modernised with changes in the nature of modern Nepal. UNESCO seeks the management of the area around a particular set of ideas about authenticity and integrity. The Nepalese authorities have tried to manage these competing objectives, with, above all, a desire not to lose World Heritage status (Owens 2002).

World Heritage Sites in the United Kingdom

The UK ratified the World Heritage Convention in 1984, and between 1986 and 1988 the first thirteen sites within the UK were inscribed. Eleven of these sites were in the cultural category and displayed a strongly ecclesiastical and archaeological emphasis. Coinciding with Britain's withdrawal from UNESCO between the mid 1980s and 1997, there was a hiatus of activity in nominating new sites, though Edinburgh Old and New Towns were inscribed in 1995, and Maritime Greenwich was inscribed just as Labour came to power in 1997. By summer 2006, ten further sites within the UK had been inscribed, nine of which are cultural. Reflecting the emphasis UNESCO was putting on the theme of industrialisation, five of these new sites have a principally industrial significance (Blaenavon Industrial Landscape, Derwent Valley Mills, New Lanark, Saltaire, Cornwall and West Devon Mining Landscape), whereas only one of the earlier sites fell into this category (Ironbridge Gorge). For now there are no more historic towns to be nominated, such as York or Oxford, nor Royal Palaces such as Hampton Court, nor more great Gothic cathedrals such as Lincoln (Whitbourn 2002). Thus, by 2006, within the UK there were twenty cultural sites and three natural sites, plus the UK had responsibility for a further three sites in dependent territories.

Management issues have been a major concern with UK World Heritage Sites. Some of these have been extremely contentious. Improvements to the surroundings of Stonehenge, probably the most iconic of all British World Heritage Sites, were on the agenda throughout the twentieth century. However, proposals for putting a section of the A303 adjacent to Stonehenge underground and for new visitor facilities have been phenomenally contentious and disputed for over a decade and were dramatically abandoned in late 2007 (Young and Kennet 2000; Save Stonehenge 2007). Though not as contentious, management issues have been a major focus for the Hadrian's Wall World Heritage Site. The sheer size and complexity of the Roman remains, combined

Table 8.1 **UK Cultural World Heritage Sites in order of inscription (not including dependent territories)**

Site	Date of Inscription
Castles and towns of King Edward in Gwynedd	1986
Durham Castle and Cathedral	1986
Ironbridge Gorge	1986
St Kilda (mixed natural and cultural)	1986, 2004, 2005
Stonehenge, Avebury and associated sites	1986
Studley Royal Park, including the ruins of Fountains Abbey	1986
Blenheim Palace	1987
City of Bath	1987
Frontiers of the Roman Empire (previously Hadrian's Wall)	1987, 2005
Westminster Palace, Westminster Abbey and St Margaret's Church	1987
Canterbury Cathedral, St Augustine's Abbey and St Martin's Church	1988
Tower of London	1988
Old and New Towns of Edinburgh	1995
Maritime Greenwich	1997
Heart of Neolithic Orkney	1999
Blaenavon Industrial Landscape	2000
Derwent Valley Mills	2001
New Lanark	2001
Saltaire	2001
Royal Botanic Gardens, Kew	2003
Liverpool – Maritime Mercantile City	2004
Cornwall and West Devon Mining Landscape	2006

Source: author 2006

Table 8.2 **Properties submitted on the Tentative List**

Site	Submission date	To be considered
Lake District (mixed natural and cultural)	1996	
Chatham Naval Dockyard	1999	
Darwin's home and workplace: Down House and environs	1999	Was to be 2007, but withdrawn after controversial ICOMOS evaluation
Manchester and Salford (Ancoats, Castlefield and Worsley)	1999	
Monkwearmouth and Jarrow monastic sites	1999	2010
The New Forest (mixed natural and cultural)	1999	
The Great Western Railway: Paddington-Bristol (selected parts)	1999	
Shakespeare's Stratford	1999	
The Forth Rail Bridge	1999	
Pont-Cysyllte Aqueduct	1999	2009
Mount Stewart Gardens	1999	
Frontiers of the Roman Empire: Antonine Wall	2006	2008

Source: author 2007

with the complexities of ownership and use of the site, including high visitor pressure in some locations, make management a difficult task. Stakeholders include English Heritage, the National Trust, thirteen local authorities, three central government departments, two regional tourist boards, the National Farmers' Union, the Countryside Agency and English Nature (Turley 1998; Young 1999; Pocock 1997b). Hadrian's Wall was one of the first UK World Heritage Sites to produce a management plan in 1996, as now required for new sites by UNESCO, with a revised version emerging in 2002 (Austen and Young 2002). A study by the Getty Conservation Institute has shown how this management process has encompassed and influenced a change in the way the site is valued and understood to encompass more explicitly contemporary-use values (Mason *et al.* 2003). In 2005, matters became even more complex, as Hadrian's Wall was absorbed into the Frontiers of the Roman Empire site, spread also across Germany and Ireland. The management of World Heritage Sites within constantly changing and evolving urban areas brings another layer of complication. A particular concern for UNESCO has been the new wave of tall buildings in much of the developed world in recent years, with, for example, specific concerns about the integrity of the setting of the Tower of London World Heritage Site being raised (World Heritage Centre 2006).

World Heritage Site status is an accolade often sought but can thus bring its own responsibilities and issues. A site such as Stonehenge hardly needs to attract more visitors, if anything the reverse is true. However, becoming a World Heritage Site will have added to the tourism burden and has put the spotlight even more firmly on the efforts of the responsible agencies to improve the management of the site. In the UK it has been the position of successive governments and English Heritage that no additional legislative measures are required for World Heritage Sites (though very modest measures are under discussion at the time of writing). But such status is a material planning consideration and has, for example, helped in fending off hotel and theme park proposals at Avebury and oil drilling and opencast mining of coal near Hadrian's Wall (Pocock 1997b).

Blaenavon Industrial Landscape

For some other UK sites, World Heritage Site status has been seen as vital for economic regeneration. One such is Blaenavon Industrial Landscape, inscribed in 2000. The area demonstrates the pre-eminence of South Wales as the world's first major producer of iron and coal in the nineteenth century. Evidence can be seen of coal and ore mines, quarries, a primitive railway system, furnaces, workers' homes, and the social infrastructure of their community. It is also,

> a torn and ruined landscape that is in stark contrast to the beauty
> of the Welsh Mountains to the north. It is a landscape of worked-

8.4
Logo created for the Blaenavon World Heritage Site by the Blaenavon Partnership.
© Blaenavon Partnership.

out mines, slag heaps and derelict furnaces. It is not a conventional tourist destination.

(Anonymous 2003)

Blaenavon today is one of the most economically and socially disadvantaged areas of the contemporary Welsh economy (Jones and Munday 2001). It has been claimed that the World Heritage designation has had a major effect in changing local peoples' perception of their own area:

> people in Wales were always sure that coal tips, quarries and industrial dereliction were somehow shameful [but] The emerging prospect of World Heritage Status became a vitally persuasive tool, drawing out commitment to a new and honest vision of the landscape.

(Wakelin 2002: 35, 37)

The management plan for the area places heritage-led regeneration to the fore as the cornerstone for socio-economic recovery (Anonymous 2003), giving focus and momentum for ideas of heritage tourism that had been advocated since 1979, at that time principally around what was to become the Big Pit Museum (Edwards and Coit 1996). Investment has come from CADW (the Welsh heritage agency), the HLF and urban regeneration funding. Press estimates at the time of inscription estimated £15 million investment over five years and as many as 250 000 visitors a year (Roberts 2000). Studies have estimated that the operational phase of the Blaenavon regeneration project could support 150 full-time equivalent jobs in the regional economy, with four out of five of these directly within Blaenavon, comprising a significant employment impact for a relatively small and deprived locality. A proportion of the indirect employment associated with tourism development, especially in the service sector of retailing and catering, could also accrue locally (Jones and Munday 2001). In 2003, Blaenavon hit the headlines again when private initiative led to it being launched as a 'book town', following its illustrious neighbour, Hay-on-Wye (Kennedy 2003).

However, Jones and Munday (2001) identified a series of potentially problematic issues for industry-heritage sites, all of which have relevance to Blaenavon. First, such sites can be extensive, needing comparatively large amounts of funds for restoration and repair, and World Heritage Site status emphasises the responsibility of achieving this to an appropriate standard. Second, industrial heritage sites may feature extensive environmental damage and degradation, which might deter non-heritage-tourism investment. Sustaining the landscape may, therefore, narrow the economic options that Blaenavon may have. At the same time, there might be pressure for preference to be given to commercial and economic objectives over core issues of conservation and underlying community sustainability. If the heritage of the area is interpreted solely for the benefit of the incoming consumer, this may alienate the existing community and provide little by way of economic or social benefit. This may be exacerbated by a lack of local entrepreneurs, meaning investment is made by outsiders exploiting relatively cheap labour and subsequently removing profits accrued. Therefore a balance is needed between community involvement and needs and developing an infrastructure for the benefit of visitors.

Liverpool Maritime Mercantile City

The UK's successful nomination for inscription as a World Heritage Site in 2004 was Liverpool Commercial Centre and Waterfront. The value of the status to Liverpool was shown by the funding from 2001, together with English Heritage, of a World Heritage Officer, a degree of commitment that must have helped secure the 2004 nomination. The theme of the nomination was 'The supreme

8.5
**Liverpool
Maritime
Mercantile City
World Heritage
Site: the Albert
Dock and the
'Three Graces'.**
Source: author.

8.5
**Liverpool
Maritime
Mercantile City
World Heritage
Site: the Albert
Dock and the
'Three Graces'.**
Source: author.

example of a port at the time of Britain's greatest global influence' (Liverpool City Council 2002). The World Heritage Site is extensive. It focuses on the earlier surviving docks, with the well-known Albert Dock and Pier Head at their centre, but extends to both the north and south. Also included is the immediate commercial hinterland around the location of the medieval town, a group of major cultural buildings including St Georges' Hall and the Duke Street area of housing and warehousing. The government made it clear when announcing the nomination that it was related to economic development objectives. Arts Minister Tessa Blackstone was quoted as saying,

> Tourism and inward investment in the city would be boosted, and a new range of people would be attracted. Liverpool is already a world famous city; World Heritage status would help bring alive its magnificent industrial heritage to a new international audience.
> (Department for Culture Media and Sport 2003)

The use of the word industrial in this context is slightly curious, as it is primarily as a trading port that Liverpool has been nominated. A crucial component of Liverpool's development was its role in the slave-trade: by the 1760s it was the pre-eminent British slave-trading port, until the abolition of the trade in 1807. A few slaves set foot in Liverpool, but for the most part they did not; they were part of the triangular trade of cheap goods to Africa, slaves to the New World, and sugar and other valuable commodities returned to Liverpool. Wealth generated by this trade was responsible directly or indirectly for a significant part of Liverpool's heritage. For example, the founder of the famous Bluecoat

School, often celebrated as acting out of benevolence, was a slave-merchant. The money that paid for many other buildings at the time, such as wealthy merchants' houses, similarly derived from the slave-trade. The slave-trade and slave-merchants are commemorated by street names in the city: the Goree, a road leading to the former Goree Warehouses, is the name of an island off Senegal where slaves were held, itself inscribed as a World Heritage Site since 1978; Cunicliffe, Hardman and Blundell Streets are examples of streets named after slave-traders (McLernon and Griffiths 2002).

A lack of acknowledgement of this facet of Liverpool's history was identified in the wake of the riots of the 1980s. The 'Gifford Report', *Loosen the Shackles*, on race relations in the city, made constant reference to the city's slaving past (Lord Gifford *et al.* 1989). One of the report's recommendations was that this should be given a much fuller and honest role in interpretations of the city's history. McLernon and Griffiths (2002) documented some of the subsequent efforts to address this issue. They argued that, though some efforts have been made to respond to the city's slaving past, there remained a tendency not to give the issue the full attention it deserved and to gloss over the particular role of Liverpool. For example, the Transatlantic Slave Gallery in the Maritime Museum was criticised for being too neutral and anodyne. Local heritage walks and publications celebrating Liverpool's architectural history were found to focus on the aesthetics of buildings and ignore the processes that produced them and even some of the architectural features that relate directly to the slaving past. For example, the heritage trail, *Liverpool Heritage Walk*, described the 1930s Barclays Bank (formerly Martin's Bank) on Water Street but failed to mention the decorative panels in the bank's porch, which show slave children with bands around their ankles and wrists, the Bank's own acknowledgement of the slave trade as the initial source of banking wealth in the City (see Figure 8.6).

The slave-trade was a major force in Liverpool's rise to prominence, to it becoming 'the supreme example of a port at the time of Britain's greatest global influence', and must therefore be considered part of its world significance. Indeed, Liverpool was pre-eminent in this particular regard, with Liverpool merchants responsible for transporting vastly greater numbers of slaves than the competitor ports of London and Bristol. This is locally reinforced by the significant black population in the city, the origins of which lie in the eighteenth century and domestic servants of wealthy merchant families or black seaman recruited to replace European crew who died or succumbed to disease (McLernon and Griffiths 2002). However, some of the early World Heritage Site documentation appeared to follow the pattern of dealing with slavery identified by McLernon and Griffiths: that is, slavery was not ignored but was compartmentalised. For example, the management plan prepared as part of the nomination documentation (Liverpool World Heritage Liaison Group 2003) very

8.6
The profits of slavery: the former Martins Bank, Liverpool.
Source: author.

directly, but quite fleetingly, addressed issues of slavery. Slavery was not directly mentioned in the proposed inscription criteria (though was added later at the suggestion of UNESCO), but was tackled as part of the statement of significance. There was none of the analysis, such as that by McLernon and Griffiths, about how this was translated into the built fabric and character of the city.

Subsequently the issue of slavery seems to have rise up the agenda in the city and, in 2007, the bicentenary of Britain's ending of the transatlantic slave-trade, an International Slavery Museum opened in the Albert Dock. Furthermore, other projects, such as English Heritage's 'The Historic Environment of Liverpool Project' (H.E.L.P.), launched in 2002, are part of a wider process of broadly based community engagement, including multicultural influences on Liverpool's historic environment (Liverpool City Council 2002; English Heritage 2002a).

World Heritage and universality

The move to define a world heritage of outstanding universal value in recent decades represents a challenge to extreme nationalism and the glorification of national heritages. It has been promoted by UNESCO, the cultural arm of the United Nations, a body more generally charged with mediating between competing national interests and producing global responses to issues facing humanity. The assertion of universality is underpinned by a number of arguments (Graham *et al.* 2000). First, it is held that political frontiers have been and remain highly permeable to aesthetic ideas and cultural movements. Indeed, it can be argued that many heritage sites only have the loosest cultural connection to the country in which they are located and therefore can be more properly claimed by humanity more generically. For example, Stonehenge, in its creation (if not in its subsequent symbolic force), can be considered as quite independent from the modern-day occupiers of the same island space. Second, international concern over the future of heritage sites has been demonstrated many times, whether it be St Mark's Venice in the nineteenth century, the flooding of Venice in the 1960s or the destruction of the Bamiyan Buddhas, Afghanistan, in 2001. Third, a global claim of heritage can be asserted as a consumption activity: the global tourism business that is concerned with experiencing heritage is immense and inherently international.

However, others have found the concept of universality more problematic. For example, Cleere has illustrated the Eurocentric nature of both the idea of universality, rooted in European Enlightenment tradition, and its articulation in practice with the World Heritage process, with its focus on monumental heritage (Cleere 2001). At the time he was writing, over half the inscribed sites were in European countries, a figure that has not changed radically since. For Smith, the World Heritage Convention is representative of an extension of her concept of the Authorised Heritage Discourse, privileging particular European cultural values (Smith 2006).

Furthermore, in practical terms, as the case studies above have illustrated, UNESCO has a problematic task in challenging the supremacy of nation states. As discussed in Chapter 2, the development of modern sensibilities of heritage was integrally linked with the rise of the nation-state in the eighteenth and nineteenth centuries. National governments are still key in defining and managing the heritage and act as the gatekeeper for putting forward sites to be considered for World Heritage status, compromising the aspiration that the list be fully inclusive and representative. The motives of national governments may have little relation to celebrating universal value, but be related to national prestige, economic development and so on.

Though nation-states and their demands for a particular articulation of national heritage create a particular problem for the creation of global heritage, they do not represent the only problem. They are a particularly significant agency in a broader tension over 'ownership' of heritage. For example, this tension may exist between global notions of value and the values of inhabitants of a locality; there are myriad competing claims. According to Lowenthal, 'Too much is now asked of heritage. In the same breath we commend national patrimony, regional and ethnic legacies, and a global heritage shared and sheltered in common.' However, he adds, 'Myopic rivalry is . . . endemic to the very nature of heritage' (Lowenthal 1997: 227, 239).

Heritage and contestation

The above discussion raises themes of relevance to an understanding of heritage, and its identification and management, that are not always obvious in the British context. The discussion stressed some of the tensions and dissonances that can exist, considered through the specific 'window' of World Heritage Sites, which has an interest because of its global construction and its direct applicability to the UK. However, the issues raised apply to the historic environment generally. Cultural heritage can have enormous symbolic power and in some cases can become a focus in armed conflict and a target for destruction. Though, with the major exception of Northern Ireland (Brett 1996), heritage issues have not in modern times led to such extreme conflict within the UK, a number of underlying issues can be identified.

The politics of selection and representation

The definition of heritage categories is an intrinsically selective process. The Sri Lanka and Cyprus cases both demonstrate that World Heritage Sites have emphasised the heritage of one ethnic grouping in those countries, arguably at the expense of the heritage of others. In the UK there was an early emphasis on the ecclesiastical and the archaeological, sites that lie deep within *national* mythologies. Subsequently, other types of site, such as those related to the industrial revolution, have come forward, in part owing to the promptings of UNESCO. In describing the qualities of heritage value, a further selection takes place, where information is assembled to present a particular narrative account of a particular place. In the case of Liverpool this has involved a focus that enables a celebration of the material quality of its heritage. The darker side of the means by which some of this heritage was produced has not been ignored, but has not been a primary focus.

Management, tourism, commodification and ownership

Management issues have been a focus in the UK, and contestation in the management of World Heritage Sites has been evident. In a case such as

Hadrian's Wall (or Frontiers of the Roman Empire), with its diversity of stakeholders, some degree of conflict is inevitable. More controversial has been the case of Stonehenge, where debates about road proposals have become a matter of bitter dispute, relating principally to the adequacy of resources.

Chapter 6 considered issues of the commodification of heritage. This is a huge issue globally, particularly with regard to the tourism industry. The specific badge of World Heritage Site status is firmly linked with the development of tourism, something that is problematic in managing fabric and goals of cultural authenticity in an over-visited site such as Stonehenge. In the case of both Liverpool and Blaenavon the potential economic benefits are clearly a major motivation that underpinned the desire for World Heritage Site status.

However, in neither situation is there necessarily a fundamental conflict between developing tourism and the material heritage of those localities. Rather, the tensions that might arise exist more between different interpretations of the history of the area and how these are presented in such a way to appeal to the market; effectively this is an issue about the 'ownership' of the sites. Discussions of heritage and conservation in the UK rarely address this issue. However, in all the sites discussed in this chapter, there is the potential for a clash of values between how sites are presented to the wider world and how they are valued locally. For example, in Blaenavon, efforts to attract visitors *might* potentially mean a sanitised and romanticised presentation of history of the sort derided by Hewison (1987).

Chapter 9

Postmodern conservation

Introduction

Chapter 2 discussed how deeply ideas of conservation are bound up with the development of modernism, involving a lineage of activity and identity springing from eighteenth-century Enlightenment thought, as it developed in the nineteenth century in particular. Yet it is clear that the role of conservation as a cultural and economic practice has been transformed phenomenally during the course of the last century, and especially over the last thirty or so years. However, this has not been a transformation beyond all recognition. The survival of the nineteenth-century precepts suggests their ongoing relevance; indeed, there are many examples in current debates over their application in the appropriate treatment of historic fabric. However, from being the esoteric concern of a marginal group of intellectual aesthetes, the conservation of the historic fabric of the historic environment has become a central part of the system of town and country planning, with a significant profile in a much wider section of society. It has been actively exploited economically as a commodified good and, as discussed in the next chapter, seen as a means of achieving social goals. As such, conservation has progressed from being an interesting activity with little impact as a cultural and economic practice to one that is woven into the cultural, economic and institutional fabric of much of daily life.

The nature of society has also changed. The intellectual and universalistic certainties of the Enlightenment and the architectural certainties of the Modern Movement have evaporated. These shifts have played a part both in redefining how those at the heart of the conservation movement understand the nature of the activity in which they are engaged and how the role of conservation has shifted from being a narrowly constructed process of discrete selection to being a far more pervading influence. The collapse of modernism and associated events, such as the crash of the UK property market in 1973, undoubtedly had an enormous transformative effect on the significance attributed to the historic environment. In a very short number of years, perceptions of conservation shifted from an association with small numbers of people interested in the artistic and historical merits of relatively small numbers of buildings and rather particular sorts of area, to an issue of much wider concern, such that we can talk of a 'conservation movement' that evolved into a central part of the British town planning system.

However, as discussed in Chapter 4, though the role of conservation in the management of the environment was transformed during this period, this does not mean that it was no longer 'modern'. Though it was a reconfigured modernism, the central tenets of conservation ideology, such as the importance of authenticity, continued. Furthermore, the means of achieving protection was through the further development of the planning system introduced in 1947. Planned redevelopment fired the growth of the conservation movement, but conservationists sought not the abolition of planning but to take control within it.

In general, the loss of faith in modernist architecture and planning is linked to the rise in ideas of postmodernism. It is the impact of these on conservation-planning practice that is the principal focus of this chapter. While it is difficult to have truly postmodern planning, because of the requirement ultimately to make decisions over, for example, whether a development can proceed (Allmendinger 2002), I argue that postmodernism has had a discernable influence on conservation planning. I consider this in terms of such issues as why, what and how we conserve. The penultimate section considers the broader role of heritage as an instrument of power. Other ramifications of a postmodern critique on modern society for issues of heritage are discussed further in Chapter 10. First, though, I briefly consider definitions of postmodernism.

Postmodernism

Discussion of the impact of postmodernism on defining heritage and the nature of conservation practice is made difficult by a lack of consensus over the nature of postmodernism. One general area of agreement is that postmodernity is both a reaction to, and against, modernity. It is clear that there was a reaction in the late 1960s and 1970s against modern architecture and planning. Indeed, one of the problematic questions that lie behind the growth in popularity of conservation is how much this was a response to the loss of familiar and treasured old buildings and how much a reaction against the modern developments that were replacing them. However, it is also clear that this reaction was not merely against the stylistic manifestations of architectural form. It was a loss of faith in the way the built environment was being changed and the mass solutions that had been adopted for social problems, such as housing. So it was also a reaction against rationalist planning and, more broadly, the paternalist and homogenising forms of post-war modernity (Healey 1998).

Dear (1986) discussed postmodernism in terms of style, method and epoch. Considering postmodernism as epoch emphasises the idea of a dramatic break with modernism. Different dates have been given for this fracture: for example, Punter has suggested 1973 as a critical date for the UK, given the collapse of the property market and related events that followed, such as the development of new neo-vernacular housing styles to capture new markets (Punter 1988). Treating postmodernism as method emphasises its anti-avant-gardism, diversity of meaning and pluralist approach. Certainly pluralism and heterogeneity are generally considered integral to postmodernist approaches. Thinking of postmodernism as style is often taken to mean a particular form of artistic expression and is often related to architecture.

The chief chronicler and advocate of architectural postmodernism has been Charles Jencks (1996). For Jencks, modern architecture lost credibility partly because it did not communicate effectively with its ultimate users and partly because it did not make effective links with the city and history. In spite of democratic intentions, Modernism became elitist and exclusivist. On the other hand, he has argued, social purpose has been embedded in post-modernism, evidenced, for example, through an emphasis on pluralism. Crucial to Jencks definition of postmodernism is his concept of double-coding – the combination of modern techniques with something else (often traditional building form and styling) in order for architecture to communicate both with the public and the concerned avant-garde minority, usually other architects.

Implicit within these ideas is the abandonment of the modernist focus on authenticity and honesty in the representation of the built environment. Buildings can legitimately be designed to deceive. The complex chronologies produced by Jencks include such categories as 'historicism', 'straight revivalism' and 'neo-vernacular'. In practice, this has meant new buildings that might appear to be from an earlier era. Very commonly they could conceal their size and try to appear smaller or as the composite form of a number of smaller buildings – a frequent method used for designing new buildings in conservation areas. Jencks' analysis involves a strong relationship and dialogue with the past. Ultimately, however, this is a debate about the creation of new fabric, rather than the retention of the old. The principal connection with conservation debates is over the architectural relationships between new and old fabric. These are of some interest and returned to below.

In exploring the relationship between conservation and postmodernity, I focus on three key issues: first, why we seek to conserve; second, what we seek to conserve through state intervention; and, third, what are regarded as appropriate means of intervening in fabric, i.e. how to conserve. While antecedents can be found for all the shifts described, it is argued that new formulations of conservation and its role developed in this period. Each of the trends discussed grew to become significant issues in the conceptualisation, definition and management of the historic environment.

Why: from morals to marketing

Part of the seismic shift in attitudes towards conservation in the 1960s and 1970s meant that it was opened to, and embraced by, new sectors of society. No longer essentially the preserve of an avant-garde, it was an activity taken up by, and used as a means of, grass-roots activism, and the conceptualisation of the environment as historic was a tool used to resist development proposals, as discussed in Chapter 4. As well as this wider but essentially middle-class public, local authority members and officers and, in due course, entrepreneurs became active supporters of conservation projects. The conservation movement, the promoters of conservation policy and action as an important role of the state, made steady legislative gains during the late 1960s and early 1970s. As discussed in Chapter 5, in the 1980s this was translated into policy and resource gains in an era hostile to state interference with private property and development rights.

The initial development of the conservation-planning system and the rationale for state protection of the historic environment were justified by an assertion of the intrinsic cultural worth presumed to be inherent in protected monuments and buildings. This has been exemplified in such legal definitions as 'special architectural or historic interest'. Official discussions of heritage referred to these qualities; for example, *Preservation and Change* (Ministry of Housing and Local Government 1967) talked in terms of the importance of conservation for sustaining beauty and 'visible history'. However, the wider constituency of engagement with conservation issues brought new arguments about the purpose and benefits of the historic environment. Thus there began a shift in the underlying rationale for conservation action away from the traditional moral precepts passed down from the Ruskinian tradition.

In the 1970s a range of social benefits were attributed to the retention of old buildings. The historic environment was argued to be important in terms of individual and community identity and in terms of peoples' psychological well-being. In 1970, Lionel Brett (Lord Esher) wrote,

> The locality where we belong . . . is the centre of reassurance [identifiable] more by the tenacity of its users than by its architecture: it may even be ugly, will generally be shabby, will invariably be overcrowded. British planners call it the 'historic core', note its tiny extent in relation to the built-up area as a whole, mark it a Conservation Area and hope for the best. Civic societies passionately defend its every cobblestone.
>
> (Brett 1970: 142)

Sometimes this broader rationale began to find its way into official guidance; the Department of the Environment (1973) introduced the phrase 'familiar and cherished local scene' to describe conservation areas. Arguments for the potential of the historic environment to contribute to society in socially progressive ways have continued to grow and develop. The government's statement on the historic environment, *The Historic Environment: A Force for Our Future* (Department for Culture, Media and Sport and Department of Transport, Local Government and the Regions 2001a), was extraordinarily lyrical about the benefits of heritage. For example, the heritage is,

> something from which we can learn, something from which our economy benefits and something which can bring communities together in a shared sense of belonging . . . it can be a stimulus to creative new architecture and design, a force for regeneration and a powerful contributor to people's quality of life.
>
> (Foreword)

During the 1980s and 1990s, the economic role of the heritage assumed a new pre-eminence (Pendlebury 2002). Critics of postmodernity often see it as a manifestation of late capitalism, a means of providing new, differentiated products for consumers (Harvey 1990), part of the post-Fordist era of flexible specialisation. The articulation of the economic value of the built heritage chimed well with both the ideology of Conservative governments in the 1980s and 1990s and the wider public mood. In the 1980s, society seemed to be dominated by the fashionability of the old, a preference that extended far beyond the built environment. The conservation process became fully institutionalised and established as a key town planning objective (see Chapter 5), but this was paralleled by a commercial packaging or commodification of the past that ranged from the scholarly to the ironic (see Chapter 6). In domestic architecture, largely built on greenfield sites, this spawned applied vernacular to speculative housing. Commercial development, however, was more likely to occur in historically sensitive town and city centres. A veneer of historic fabric was used in the practice of 'façadism', or historic forms were reproduced in order to gain planning permission. Historic, or the image of historic, was seen as 'safe' and uncontroversial. This combined with the 'heritage industry', in Hewison's pejorative term (Hewison 1987), and led to the direct economic exploitation of heritage. Thus, in the 1980s, the historic environment became increasingly used to support a range of economic processes, including property speculation and more direct consumption.

The commodification of the historic environment has been subject to much criticism from conservation practitioners. For example, Delafons noted a huge backlash from conservationists when early attempts at commercialisation of sites in state care were made by the Thatcher government (Delafons 1997a). A typical critique of the impact of such commercialisation, from an essentially modernist perspective, was made by Fowler (1989). Lack of authenticity and integrity was central to his critique of what he regarded as postmodernist approaches; his targets included products such as artificially 'antique' furniture (as spotted in an English Heritage magazine) and 'living history' events at English Heritage properties, dismissed as historically inaccurate, populist entertainments; part of the drive to make sites more commercially self-sufficient. Similar critiques were made about interventions in the built environment, which are returned to below.

Thus, economic motivations for valuing heritage have led to postmodern practices. More fundamentally, the more diverse reasons that have developed and assumed prominence for heritage protection form part of the plurality of perspectives ushered in from the 1970s as part of the postmodern critique of modernist architecture and planning.

What: from monuments to the mundane

The emergence of different perspectives on the reasons for the importance of cultural built heritage also contributed to a shift of focus from major buildings as representations of the artistic, economic and political achievements of the nation to the importance of the relatively ordinary and the familiar. This was, of course, intimately linked with the reaction to modernism and the large-scale transformations it was wreaking on familiar environments across the country. Stress on the psychological significance of the historic environment, of the backdrop of familiar environments or 'the familiar and cherished local scene' was a reaction to its loss. It was no longer sufficient to concentrate on the major buildings as isolated monuments; it was the whole environment that was important. Thus changes in perspective about why conservation was important were inextricably linked with questions about what should be conserved.

The statutory framework for the protection of the historic environment, in terms of selection processes and policy guidance, has remained stable and relatively unchanged in its fundamental essence since the 1970s (though with changes anticipated at the time of writing). So, for example, buildings are still listed as of 'special architectural or historic interest' on the basis of criteria concerned with architectural interest, historic interest, historical associations or group value (Department for Culture, Media and Sport undated), much as they were in the 1960s and before. However, the inherently modernist process of scholarly selection has been steadily pushed into new areas. For example, the massive expansion of listed building numbers in the 1980s, as part of the resurvey programme, included large numbers of vernacular buildings (Robertson 1993a). More recently, such modest structures as a pigeon cree in Sunderland have been listed (Howe 1998) (see Figure 9.1). This must be far removed from the idea of 'special architectural or historic interest' as conceived by the post-war legislators. It is the erosion of any grand architectural narrative; although buildings must still officially conform to some measure of national importance, it represents a plurality in valuing different sorts of buildings. The modern frameworks of selection have come under postmodern influence.

The introduction of conservation areas in the 1967 Civic Amenities Act marked a departure in the way in which the historic environment could be defined. Though the language of definition still revolved around 'special architectural or historic interest', and part of the stimulus for the legislation was to secure a better surrounding and setting for listed buildings (Delafons 1997a), it was here that explicit recognition was made that built heritage embraced more than architectural monuments. In other countries, such as France, the introduction of historic area protection remains essentially a highly selective, top-down process. In Britain, power to designate conservation areas was given to local authorities, and it is a power that they have freely used, with

9.1
**Grade 2 listed
pigeon cree,
Ryhope,
Sunderland.**
© Sunderland City
Council.

designation extended to places and in numbers that again cannot have been imagined by legislators. There has been an enormous diversity of practice across the country, and the willingness of local authorities to designate conservation areas ultimately led to conflicts within the conservation movement, and with architectural and development interests. As numbers of designations continued to grow they were, in the argot of the early 1990s, seen to be 'debasing the coinage' (Morton 1991). Designations, such as the suburban areas discussed in Chapter 7, were felt to be too numerous and of insufficient merit. Thus, it was argued, the value of the designation attached to genuinely special places was debased by the inclusion of places that were perhaps pleasant, but unexceptional.

The last forty years have seen a transformation in the value that is placed on the historic environment and the extent and diversity of heritage that we seek to protect. The modernist and universalistic, statutory definitions of the built heritage remain intact but have been bent and twisted into postmodern forms. The extremes of inclusiveness to which listing ('special architectural or historic interest') has been taken has been questioned (for example, Delafons 1997b). The tensions created are seen even more clearly with conservation area designation, however. The conservation officers reported in Chapter 7 showed very different understandings from each other in how to interpret whether or not an area warranted conservation area status. Some equated their designation with the process of selecting listed buildings, and an 'expert' approach of appraisal to universalistic definitions (but without having criteria such as those applied to potential listed buildings), whereas others were open to engagement with 'non-experts' and to areas being defined following a discursive process. The power of local authorities to designate pretty much what they like as a conservation area remains. Thus, competing ideas of modernist selection or more fluid and inclusionary approaches to area identification, less concerned with seeking to establish yardsticks of 'specialness', continue to be resolved at local level.

How: face or fabric?

More catholic and diverse definitions of the historic environment have occasionally been controversial and divided opinion within the conservation movement. However, the tensions created by the synthesis of modern and postmodern approaches to conservation are perhaps most marked in *how* buildings are conserved. Actions seen to lack authenticity and integrity tend to provoke greater concern. Alterations to historic buildings that focus on achieving visual appearance or speculative restoration, rather than material authenticity, or on schemes for public space using bland non-place-specific 'heritage' street furniture and paving can provoke anger and outrage. Indeed, from a 'purist' perspective, such changes may be denied as 'conservation'. However, in the minds of the wider population, encompassing local councillors, architects, developers and planning officers as well as the general public, they may constitute appropriate conservation actions. Indeed, rather than orthodox conservation principles, many people may prefer their old buildings to look new (Lowenthal 1985) and generally have an appreciation of a 'heritage aesthetic' (see Chapter 7).

These issues are now briefly discussed in terms of: first, the radical alteration of buildings through the practice of façadism; second, debates about the appropriate form of new architecture in historic locations; and, third the use of historic buildings.

Façadism

The number of listed buildings grew considerably in the 1980s and 1990s, as detailed in Chapter 5. At the same time, the number of total demolitions of listed buildings declined, making the overall rate of demolition fall enormously. Debate shifted from total demolition to the degree of permissible intervention. In commercial areas, a frequently agreed 'compromise' solution to the tension between the demands of the market and the retention of listed buildings was façadism, the retention of a historic façade or façades as the public face of what were essentially brand new constructions. This was common practice in commercial centres throughout the country. In Newcastle upon Tyne, on Grey Street, described by Pevsner as 'one of the best Streets in England' (Pevsner and Richmond 1957: 249), and, more recently in 2002, voted 'Britain's best street' by BBC Radio 4 listeners (BBC 2002), there were at least four major reconstructions behind façades between 1982 and 1990 (Lovie 1997). Thus, though the number of listed buildings being demolished declined, the use of a technique that constituted as near total destruction of the building as was permissible became more popular. Façadism has continued; for example, a major scheme went ahead in Grey Street in 2001, despite official discouragement of the practice set out in PPG15 (Department of the Environment and Department of National Heritage 1994) (see Figures 9.3 and 9.4).

At the heart of the orthodox, 'conservative repair' tradition of conservation practice is a concern for the historic fabric and 'authenticity' of the cultural object. From this conventional conservation position, the practice of façadism is a destruction of cultural value and a despicable deceit. As noted in Chapter 2, Earl distinguished between the specialist knowledge required to execute schemes of façade retention and 'genuine conservation experts' (Earl 2003: 82). He considered façadism as 'skin-deep' preservation, denying the importance and logic of a building as a whole. He assumed a hypothetical case where the condition of a building, together with every other environmental and

9.2
Crude façadism 1970s style: the retained façade of the British Linen Bank, Princes Street, Edinburgh.
Source: author.

economic circumstance, meant that the preservation of the external appearance was the only practicable option and concluded that a facsimile façade would have as much value as retaining the original, i.e. it might have some townscape merit but none in terms of the material authenticity of the building. From this position, a preferable outcome might be the total demolition of the building and its replacement with a high-quality new building.

Façadism equally has attracted the opprobrium of conservation critiques (Lord Rogers *et al.* 1999; Welsh 1999). Pawley, in his polemic *Terminal Architecture*, linked façadism with what he termed 'stealth architecture'. He described the façading of a Royal Mail sorting office, transformed from a five-storey building to ten, with four storeys underground. He stated that this is 'a veritable "stealth bomber" of a building', and 'post-Modern architecture [can] preserve old buildings, while at the same time utterly destroying their identity' (Pawley 1998: 134).

9.3
**Façadism in
action, Grey
Street, Newcastle
upon Tyne, 2001.**
Source: author.

9.4
**Façadism
completed, Grey
Street, Newcastle
upon Tyne.**
Source: author.

Thus orthodox conservationists and those who consider that conservation is now too extensive an activity concur in their dislike of façadism. However, the latter group see façadism as approved by the conservation world. This is not a message emerging from debates of conservation principles, but is perhaps received through the reality of negotiating for development and the compromises that are offered. For developers, the additional cost of façade retention is presumably still preferable to having to work within the constraints of a retained building. For the public-sector decision-makers, a retained façade presumably is regarded as at least a partial success for the conservation

175

cause, and perhaps as something that will prove more acceptable to wider public opinion. Sparks, the former Chief Planning Officer for Birmingham and Bath, while not necessarily defending façadism, asserted that it is a very popular solution with the wider public (Sparks 1998). This is a 'lighter' view of conservation, one that relates more to the resultant visual appearance, 'the heritage aesthetic', and places little or no stress on the authenticity arguments so fundamental to more orthodox conservation practice.

Stress on authenticity in architecture and conservation coexists with a strong English design tradition that emphasises picturesque composition (Bandini 1992; Esher 1981). Some people working from a conservative repair tradition will occasionally accept façadism as legitimate on these grounds. So, for example, where previous façadism has occurred and the façade has a value as part of a larger, possibly formal, composition, it might prove to be an acceptable logic. These circumstances would obtain in some, but by no means all, of the cases in Grey Street referred to above. An argument favouring façadism has been made by Tugnutt and Robertson along these lines. Though their support was qualified as being 'rarely appropriate for historic buildings with interesting interiors or methods of construction' (Tugnutt and Robertson 1987), they stated, 'there can be little objection to this process' to 'preserve the character of a piece of townscape or the integrity of a group of buildings' (pp. 84–5).

The popularity of the practice during the 1980s generated two books specifically on the subject; both defended the principle and sought to move the debate to when façadism is appropriate and the detailed factors that should come into play in its implementation. Both were written by practitioners with an interest in the subject (Richards 1994; Highfield 1991). Both books considered objections to the practice as coming from 'purists', versus the position advanced by themselves as 'pragmatists'. Both argued the façade to be generally capable of differentiation from the building as a whole and to be usually more important both in architectural terms and in terms of its contribution to the public domain. Furthermore, both argued that users may want the image and perceived prestige of a historic façade combined with modern functionality. Highfield claimed to be part of a large majority: 'despite the "purist" viewpoint, it [façadism] is almost universally accepted by developers, architects, planners and conservationists as a means of re-using historic buildings' (Highfield 1991: x).

Richards sought to place façadism in a broader context of the history of architectural scenery and the use of disguise. He distinguished between façadism and façade retention; the latter was, for him, only one form of façadism. Though he did not conflate façadism with postmodernism, he acknowledged they are clearly linked and that façadism is antithetical to modernism. He had no problem with the 'stage-sets' argument:

> I have encountered the argument that facadism results in nothing
> more than the charade of 'Disneyland' and stage-set architecture
> lacking reality and truth. However, does this constitute valid grounds
> for objection? Is it not one of the roles of buildings to provide an
> enjoyable setting for life's activities?
>
> (Richards 1994: 44)

Façadism is the most radical transformation a building can endure short of total demolition and, for better or worse, is explicitly concerned with creating an artificial, historic backdrop to urban space. Façadism, with its emphasis on show and its disregard for authenticity, is very much a postmodern approach.

New buildings in historic areas

As noted above, for some conservationists total demolition and new building might be preferable to 'inauthentic' conservation, especially façadism. This leads to consideration of what form new construction might take. Again, this is an area where conservation orthodoxy relates more to a modernist rather than a postmodern or anti-modern perspective. Within conservation debates and formal expressions of conservation principles, a strong emphasis is often placed on architecture being 'of its time', and there is an antagonism towards pastiche forms of historic design or more scholarly historic reproduction. It is held that new building, like conservation work, should be honest and authentic and a representation of the age in which it is constructed. This view is not new. It is a fundamental element of the principles of intervention of conservative repair enshrined in the SPAB manifesto, as described in Chapter 2. It is equally evident when applied to the urban level: for example, the attitude towards the construction of new buildings displayed in the 1940s 'reconstruction plans' described in Chapter 3. From this perspective, a postmodern sensibility may be legitimate where it is a cue for intelligent development of new forms of architecture that are cognisant of historic form. However, perhaps more likely, postmodernism may lead to undesirable and inauthentic historicist reproductions or a weak pastiche thereof. Thus, buildings such as those at Richmond Riverside (discussed in Chapter 5) are acknowledged to have an authentic representation of classical architectural form externally, but are ultimately deemed to be inauthentic since the classical façades clothe functional modern offices (Cantacuzino 1998).

This view has long represented conservation orthodoxy, although, as discussed in Chapter 5, historic reproduction and weak interpretations of historic form have perhaps been the dominant form of new construction in practice in our town and city centres over the last twenty-five years. Recent years have seen a renewed attention to advocating more clearly contemporary interventions from the public agencies that have a responsibility for design issues. Publications such as *Building in Context* (English Heritage and CABE 2001) present case-studies that mostly herald architectural solutions that are distinctly modern, albeit a form of modernism much more sympathetic to context than the buildings of the 1960s and 1970s, which became so discredited (see Figure 9.5).

Alternative perspectives exist, however. In the edited collection *Context: new buildings in historic settings* (Warren *et al.* 1998), there was a notable divergence of opinion between a minority of contributors and the majority, who advocated 'of its time' approaches, albeit critically informed by historical precedent. As discussed in Chapter 2, the traditional architect Robert Adam has taken issue with the whole concept of 'of its time' approaches (Adam 1998; and also Adam 2003). He has argued that buildings are *inevitably* of their time, but that what is implicit in this phrase is the self-conscious Modern Movement fracture from historical continuity. This modernism, he argued, as indeed I do in Chapter 2, is deeply embedded in conservation culture and instruments such as conservation charters. It stems from academic archaeological and historical values and a stress on authenticity, which is quite at odds with the experience of place held by most people. He argued instead for a literate continuity of architecture.

Following the theme of a wider public response to architecture, the chapter by the Planning Officer for Canterbury charted the way unpopular postwar buildings have been replaced by others that seek to reproduce historic styles; a major justification for this is their public popularity (Jagger 1998). Though no great evidence was presented to demonstrate this popularity, few,

9.5
Modern infill, Davygate, York – a scheme featured in *Building in Context* (English Heritage and CABE 2001).
Source: author.

including opponents of this architectural approach, would deny that it is probably the case. Hobson (2004), in his case studies, argued that, while conservation professionals advocate contemporary design, planning officers look for conservative, visually acceptable schemes, and councillors seek 'safe' approaches. This conservative public preference seems to have grown stronger through the 1970s, 1980s and 1990s, as discussed in earlier chapters. Sparks, the former Chief Planning Officer in Bath and Birmingham, described how the Bath Preservation Trust once supported distinctly modern architecture, but now advocates neo-classical design for new buildings (Sparks 1998).

Use

With façadism, one can distinguish clear differences between modern conservation orthodoxy and the practices that go on much of the time in the management of the historic environment, which might be considered postmodern. The use to which historic buildings are put presents interesting issues in that such distinctions are not anything like as clear. Although the change of use, for example, of churches can be a very sensitive issue, buildings have historically often changed their use, mostly without any great fuss. In recent decades, the change of use of buildings validated as cultural heritage has not been hugely contentious in principle. Though government guidance has tended to indicate a general preference for sustaining uses, this has been accompanied by an acknowledgement that a building may be better conserved by such a change (Pendlebury 2000). Indeed, the potential for adaptive re-use as an opportunity for exciting and enhancing architectural interventions has been stressed (for example Cantacuzino 1989; 1975b; Latham 2000).

However, in terms of what maybe significant about a building as cultural heritage, and the values that are attributed to it, use may be an important dimension. In 1993, Keeling House in Bethnal Green, London, was the first post-war local authority housing block to be listed. Completed in 1957, it was designed by Denys Lasdun. It follows the form of a cluster, four towers grouped around a central stair and lift tower and it was designed to act as a vertical version of a traditional street. Ultimately unsuccessful as a social housing scheme, it lay empty for many years until it was restored by a private developer, who aimed the refurbished block at style-conscious owner-occupiers (see Figure 9.6). To give purchasers security in an essentially poor neighbourhood, the block has a concierge and is surrounded by a fence. Thus a pioneering piece of welfare state architecture has been rebranded for gated, modish, urban living close to the City of London. Physical improvement has been achieved but by creating a secure island within an area where fundamental problems remain. Whether or not this represents 'good' or 'bad' conservation, the value and meaning of the object have surely changed (although Harwood (2005) has argued that, in practice, the building is occupied by much the same social class

9.6
**Keeling House,
Bethnal Green,
London – welfare
state to modish
urban living.**
Source: author.

for which it was originally intended). Other such incongruities could be detailed. For example, Patrick Wright has described the dissonances involved in the conversion of a large factory in the east of London, famous for a match-girls' strike in the nineteenth century, into upmarket flats (Wright 1992).

The lack of debate over such changes of use serves to emphasise the fabric-focused nature of modern conservation practice. Despite the growing recognition of wider frameworks for valuing heritage, issues of authenticity and meaning still tend to be conflated with architectural integrity.

Conservation and power

One of the central themes of this book is the way that conservation has been accepted over recent decades as a 'public good', virtually without challenge. However, critiques do exist, often of a more theoretical nature and often related to broader, postmodern critiques of the role of culture and cultural institutions more generally.

A very specific attack on conservation and conservationists, made by Eversley (1973) at the very moment that contemporary ascendancy of the conservation movement was gaining momentum, was discussed in Chapter 4. At the heart of his critique was the idea that protecting historic buildings is the imposition on society as a whole of the tastes of a very small, elite minority. Various commentators and theorists have argued that this imposition occurs with specific political purposes, often together with an assertion that heritage policies are intrinsically right-wing (for example, Ascherson 1987). Chapter 5 discussed the surprising insulation and indeed consolidation of conservation from the deregulatory and liberalising efforts of the Conservative governments of the 1980s and 1990s. Hewison has maintained that successive Conservative governments consciously used the past for political purposes. It was perceived as a repository of values and a way of reaffirming national identity (Hewison 1995). Emphasis under the Thatcher governments was on supposedly traditional values that could underpin the idea of 'the enterprise culture', linked to the mission of 'making Britain Great'. Thatcher considered that the heritage of historic buildings and places was part of a (usually specifically English) national culture, important in creating Britain's international standing (Hewison 1995). The importance of the national heritage of buildings and landscapes in reaffirming national identity, both historically and during this period, has been commentated on by, for example, Daniels (1993), Grufford (1995) and Wright (1985). John Major's image of the past has been held to be cosier and more nostalgic, but part of the same process of reinventing the past:

> The past was reinvented, so that the social conflicts of the industrial revolution were consolingly reintegrated into the picturesque and pastoral narrative that became the consumer's version of the national story. Cotton mills and coal mines were painted into a picture-book history as decorative artefacts, redundant relics of lost communities. The machinery still stood, but its brutal *raison d'être* was at best dimly recalled in the act of fantasising 'the way we were'.
>
> (Hewison 1995: 265)

Linked to these ideas is the concept of the dominant ideology thesis, derived from the writings of Marx and Engels (Merriman 1991). Using this thesis, culture is endowed with messages that are deliberately framed by power elites to legitimise the existing dominant regime, perhaps most clearly observed in the former communist regimes in the Soviet bloc (Tunbridge and Ashworth 1996). In the context of conservation, the heritage selected for protection becomes not simply a reflection of the tastes and ideas of elites but part of the apparatus that ensures the maintenance of the present social system (Hoyau 1988, originally published 1980). In a refinement of this argument, Bourdieu argued that the dominated tend to collaborate in their own domination (Merriman 1991). Power relations derive from both symbolic and economic power. Symbolic power derives from mis-recognition of the oppressive basis of hierarchical social relations. So, for example, the popularity of country house visiting and support for organisations such as the National Trust could be interpreted in this way. With this view, visitors to country houses actively affirm historic class relations as they come to marvel at the lifestyle afforded to the aristocracy, while lacking an understanding of how such wealth was created or sustained. Thus, in the context of Conservative governments, sustaining support of, and placing value on, the protection and retention of the heritage could be considered part of a strategy of maintaining existing power structures and social relations, or indeed reasserting a set of social relations perceived to have been eroded by modernism and the welfare state (Gamble 1994).

Tunbridge and Ashworth have criticised the application of the dominant ideology thesis to heritage policy, arguing that, in reality, the ideology of dominant groups is not coherent but heterodox or internally inconsistent (Tunbridge and Ashworth 1996). Furthermore, all these factors probably value heritage in a rather more generalised way than would necessitate the evolution of a sophisticated system of planning control. However, an interesting twist to these ideas has been given by Law (2004). He considered these issues, not in terms of the dominant forces of society as a whole, but in terms of the strategies used by conservationists. He considered that they construct 'self-authority' in much the same way that Bourdieu described the production of symbolic and cultural capital. By positioning their arguments as 'common sense' and patriotic, and by the use of strategies of anger and outrage, they seek to gain both representative authority and populist appeal.

Conservation, heritage and postmodernity

Conservation assumed a new importance in the wake of the collapse of modernism. In part this allowed traditional conservation values to assert themselves more vigorously; in part it opened the gate for more heterogeneous and pluralist conceptions of conservation to develop. In part this shift can be considered an adaptation of modernism (influenced by critiques of modernism) and in part postmodern; precise boundaries between these are difficult and perhaps of academic interest only.

Many of these changes had antecedents. For instance, personal continuity values of nostalgia had coexisted with collective values of the nation and can be found, for example, in Baldwin-Brown (1905). However, in the wake of the fall of modernism, this plurality began to flourish. The postmodern shift allowed a more diverse and individual perspective on valuing historic environments, although this has received only limited formal embodiment in state protection.

The diversity of practice that accompanied some of these changes can be controversial. In achieving official recognition of the architectural and historic merits of large numbers of buildings and areas, the conservation movement has created a situation whereby it becomes difficult, or impossible, to manage change according to the principles that have been held at the heart of this very same movement. Principles of conservative repair, enshrined to a greater or lesser degree in the manifestos of the conservation movement (Morris 1877; ICOMOS 1964) and in official documents (British Standards Institution 1998; Department of the Environment and Department of National Heritage 1994), are only applied in practice in a very dilute way, if at all, in much management of the historic environment. Concepts and techniques for the management of urban areas, such as townscape and urban morphology, are applied equally loosely.

This is partly a question of resources. The expansion of the defined heritage has not been matched by the expansion of finance, or of a skilled conservation movement to proselytise and manage the historic environment in the ways it deems appropriate. In part, however, this is owing to the processes of commodification that have been described. The popularity of things historic has inevitably meant that they become, in a consumer society, an opportunity for consumption. Often a historic image is sufficient for the market, with material authenticity deemed unnecessary or a hindrance. The historic environment becomes postmodern packaging, an aesthetic veneer, for a process of modernisation. This creates inevitable conflicts with an architectural conservation tradition premised on authenticity of fabric.

However, as this chapter has sought to demonstrate, a further source of conflict stems from differences of value and perspective between different people who consider themselves pro-conservation. Postmodernism has produced a flourishing of different perspectives on the value of retaining historic buildings that are quite different from traditional, dominant archaeological and art-historical criteria, which still underpin conservation legislation and policy. Different views about why to protect the historic environment naturally lead to different ideas about what should be protected and how it should be managed. If there is a single particular crux of difference between modern and postmodern perspectives on conservation actions, it is the talismanic concept (to modernists) of authenticity and, specifically, authenticity of fabric. A modernist perspective can embrace broader reasoning for the importance of heritage and can accommodate more generous interpretations of what constitutes the historic environment, as part of the evolution of traditional frameworks of evaluation of importance. This is part of the 'rolling consensus' identified by Hobson (2004) and discussed in Chapter 7. However, the sticking point is often in the way that this heritage is then managed. Modern conservation's moral framework struggles against practices that are, for example, casual with historic evidence and apparently deny 'progressive' architectural form. Postmodern approaches, by contrast, are more concerned with the overall feel and appearance of a place; with the historic environment as a pleasurable setting for urban life, rather than with retained historical documents.

However, it would be overly simplistic to assert that there is a conservation coalition with clearly demarcated modernist and postmodern wings. As discussed, many of those antagonistic to the notion of façadism will accept it as a reasonable solution in some situations, while many people who would be critical of the rigidities of conservative-repair thinking would at the same time identify important cultural monuments where it is perfectly valid. Thus the conservation movement is both modern *and* postmodern, and this combination works both in synthesis and tension.

Using wider postmodern critiques of society also forces us to question the social function of heritage. Assertions that it works neatly as part of an overarching framework to sustain societal power relations are questionable to say the least. However, cultural heritage can have enormous symbolic power, as discussed in Chapter 8. A rigid focus on building fabric and appearance, to the exclusion of other issues, has been characteristic of much modern conservation practice. Such a decontextualised approach, together with the fetishisation of buildings as archaeological or aesthetic objects, ignores the inevitable social, cultural and economic consequences that can flow from conservation actions. It is to the potential of conservation planning to function in a more socially progressive way that the next chapter turns.

Chapter 10

Conservation reformed

Introduction

The principal theme of this chapter is the shift, but not radical transformation, that has occurred in the values espoused by the conservation movement over the relatively recent past. In recent years, there has been an emphasis on the social purpose and function of conservation, which has been largely absent from British debate since the 1970s. In part, this has concerned the use of heritage for socially instrumental purposes paralleling the economic focus developed in the 1980s. In part, it is recognition of the socially constructed nature of heritage and the consequent implication that perhaps conservation experts should not have a monopoly over conservation values. It is argued that these shifts are partly self-generated within the conservation sector and partly, in the English case at least, a response to external political pressures. However, it is highly debateable how much this represents a fundamental broadening-out and new-found institutional reflexiveness on behalf of the heritage sector or conservation community, and how much a tactical shift in standard and authorised conceptions of conservation as part of a process of sustaining expert hegemonies.

Underpinning much of this chapter is a view of heritage that is reformed both as an intellectual construct and a liberal ideology. The prevailing academic view assumes that there is no single narrative of heritage, and different groups and individuals construct their own views of heritage, albeit with perhaps some common meeting points. This pluralisation is not seen necessarily as a potential source of conflict by policymakers, but as a positive social force that can aid social inclusion, community cohesion and so on. Effectively this is the heritage sector seeking to adapt to a prevailing liberal social agenda that seeks to celebrate diversity, pluralism and multiculturalism (though an agenda subject to some challenge in late 2006 when this is being written). This is not seen as a fundamentally transformative shift for the conservation of the historic environment – all those places identified and protected using 'established values' are not suddenly up for review – but is perhaps something of a gloss applied to conservation activity to establish political credibility.

There are, however, significant dangers for the conservation sector in pursuing an agenda of diversity and pluralism, not least where the values of the wider public are found to diverge from those of the professionals. Chapters 7 and 9 highlighted that potentially this is a major issue for the conservation world, as there is reasonable evidence to suggest that while many people might place value on a vague 'heritage aesthetic', this is quite different from the principles espoused by a programme of orthodox modern conservation. In the context of the quite separate but parallel activity of countryside conservation, Goodwin argued that the extension of participation in countryside conservation 'may be bringing about a retreat from the national vision of traditional conservation and a fragmentation of conservation ideas' (Goodwin 1999: 383).

Smith discussed 'the agitation by these [community] groups for greater inclusion and consideration of their own needs, aspiration and values in the way the past is used in present society' (Smith 2006: 35). Waterton, writing about a community project in an archaeologically rich landscape, stated:

> archaeologists, as advocates of the past, are able to validate their esoteric position by asserting control over heritage that represents the past. Those holding a dominant form of knowledge have a greater scope to influence others, to close down other meanings and to arbitrate as to which meanings and values are socially permissible. Questioning this position takes heritage management into a distinctly uncomfortable area that threatens not only the power of the expert but also the loss of scientific knowledge as 'truth'.
>
> (Waterton 2005: 318)

Ultimately, therefore, this is a key test facing the conservation sector. Is the sector prepared to relinquish at least a measure of control, or is the rhetoric of pluralism used as lip-service to sustain control in the face of broader political agendas?

The chapter starts with a discussion of how evolving ideas of heritage have been expressed in the authorised lexicon of heritage charters and so on. The discussion then shifts to the specifically British context provided by a change of government in 1997 and some of the subsequent ways conservation thinking and policy have evolved at national and local levels.

Conservation initiatives at local level have to some degree moved the focus away from the statutorily protected heritage towards a more broadly defined heritage, through such devices as characterisation and local lists. This touches upon the role everyday heritage plays in local identity construction, and, in turn, this connects to the overarching government policy aim of 'social inclusion'. The recent 'public values' debate is then briefly considered. The latter part of the chapter considers an alternative perspective to that set out above: that it is not necessarily evident that communities *want* to be empowered and engaged in the arena of formalised heritage. Finally, the chapter returns to the question of the remaking of conservation narratives.

Shifting orthodoxies

Chapter 1 defined heritage as a fluid phenomenon, rather than a static set of objects with fixed meanings, and as the *contemporary* use of the past. This reading of the nature of heritage is part of the legacy of postmodern critique. Such an understanding of heritage is now broadly accepted in many academic arenas and, in turn, is beginning to influence practice debates. Shifting understandings of heritage have influenced some of the principal official statements on heritage issues over recent decades.

As discussed in Chapter 2, modern conservation values and practice have emphasised the importance of expert knowledge, skills and judgement. This is evident in the British writings discussed and also in the didactic approach and tone of international statements such as the Venice Charter (ICOMOS 1964). However, as also touched upon, when conservation is translated from being applied to monuments to the urban scale and becomes integrated with a process of town planning, the international conservation movement has also long acknowledged the importance of engaging with the wider constituency of people who live in, and use, historic places.

So, the Amsterdam Declaration (Council of Europe 1975), the UNESCO Nairobi statement (UNESCO 1976) and the ICOMOS Washington Charter, (ICOMOS 1987) all extended discussion into areas beyond the traditional concerns of architectural conservation debate to include the wider social relevance of conservation as an activity. All emphasised the importance of integration between conservation and town planning at the urban scale, the significance of public opinion and support and the need for works of conservation to be socially progressive.

A further ICOMOS charter has had great significance in the UK in recent years and, in terms of impact on conservation practice, probably more than the above three documents put together. The Burra Charter is a document specifically drawn up for the conservation of heritage in Australia by Australia

ICOMOS (Australia ICOMOS 1999). First adopted in 1979 and subsequently revised on three occasions (most recently in 1999), its popularity in the UK has principally derived from its recommendations on codifying systematic conservation process, essentially following a sequence of research and analysis before intervention and ensuring proper documentation of interventions. A parallel manifestation of this Australian importation has been the wide-scale adoption of conservation plans as a means of understanding historic sites and informing decision-making. Within this there are some critical concepts useful for an intelligent approach to managing historic assets. Of particular value is the emphasis placed upon defining *significance* – what it is that makes a historic site important – before deciding what can be done with it. However, less commented upon is another crucial facet of the Burra Charter that is of interest here: the question of how conservation knowledge is defined.

The starting premise of the Burra Charter is that *place* is important. To understand the cultural significance of place involves an understanding of familiar elements such as the fabric and its setting and use. But this significance also stems from people's memory and association with place. Thus, judging significance is not just an architectural or archaeological appraisal of fabric, but is also reliant upon incorporating people's experience. How place is valued in conservation terms should not, therefore, be entirely through conventional expert values. Though this is not explicitly stated, the Burra Charter seems to be influenced by the context of a continent with a different inheritance from that familiar in the western world. The living, intangible, Aboriginal heritage, rarely if ever fully understood by non-Aborigines, inevitably gives a different perspective on the limits of conventional expert knowledge and the importance of community ownership.

However, the shift to a more open and inclusive process of conservation-planning is not straightforward. The analysis of the Burra Charter undertaken by Waterton and others (Waterton *et al.* 2006) unpacked the contradictions within the document. They saw no resolution between the rather vague call for democratisation and the continued significance placed upon traditional notions of authority and expertise. What they detected, using Burra Charter terminology, is some willingness to relinquish a degree of control over issues of value and meaning but not over the definition of cultural significance. Cultural significance is closely linked to the physical fabric of buildings and places. Thus, according to Waterton and her colleagues, the ICOMOS conservation experts reserve to themselves judgements over what has been historically the primary focus of conservation activity, in terms of physical fabric, while allowing for some more pluralistic interpretation of the social meaning such fabric might have.

Another more recent international statement on historic environment value and conservation process has come from the Council of Europe with its *Framework Convention on the Value of Cultural Heritage for Society* (or Faro Convention) (Council of Europe 2005a). The convention seeks to square the circle of universalistic notions of heritage with the idea that heritage should be thought of pluralistically. The universalistic claims of cultural heritage are defined in terms of rights; the accompanying commentary claims this to be an innovation of the convention (Council of Europe 2005b). It refers to the 1948 United Nations *Universal Declaration of Human Rights,* asserting, 'Recognising that every person has a right to engage with the cultural heritage of their choice, while respecting the rights and freedoms of others . . .' (Preamble). Emphasis is placed upon pluralist democratic engagement. Thus Article 12a commits signatories to,

> encourage everyone to participate in:
> - The process of identification, study, interpretation, protection, conservation and presentation of the cultural heritage;
> - Public reflection and debate on the opportunities and challenges which the cultural heritage represents.

Cultural heritage is seen as intrinsic to sustainable development, cultural diversity in the face of globalisation and a resource around which to construct dialogue, democratic debate and openness between cultures. On this last point the Convention states that the signatories are, 'Convinced of the soundness of the principle of heritage policies and educational initiatives which treat all cultural heritages equitably and so promote dialogue among culture and religion' (Preamble). The Convention also acknowledges the economic role of heritage and 'without excluding the exceptional, particularly embraces the commonplace heritage of all people' (Explanatory: 4).

In the development of a specifically British discourse on conservation, English Heritage's statement, *Sustaining the Historic Environment,* was a significant document in opening perspectives on heritage issues to include non-expert opinion (English Heritage 1997). This publication sought to conceptualise the historic environment in terms of concepts and vocabulary used in debates about sustainability. Thus, for example, it discussed critical and tradable historic environmental capital. In practice, this has had limited impact on thinking about conservation. However, the wider discussion in the document raised a number of issues that have proved to be of more enduring relevance. It recognised the potential gap between the sort of historic environment that has been validated by conservation values and the types of everyday environment that people may value and that may underpin local distinctiveness and identity. Stemming from this, *Sustaining the Historic Environment* identified the importance of recognising non-expert values and placed an importance on securing wider public participation in conservation debates.

New Labour: new conservation?

Sustaining the Historic Environment was produced before the General Election of 1997, which resulted in a landslide for New Labour. However, its concerns chimed neatly with the political imperatives for the conservation movement that were to arise from a Labour victory. Though a change in government brought no immediate major conservation policy announcements or shifts, there were some signs of a reorientation of approach. An early change was the renaming of the Department of National Heritage as the Department for Culture, Media and Sport (DCMS). Labour wanted to escape the overtly backward-looking associations of 'heritage', and modernising was a common theme of the government's cultural agenda (Smith 1998).

There was immediate concern amongst the conservation lobby over shifts in the government's stance (Venning 1999) and these continue; a DCMS select committee in 2006 reported that 'anxiety pervades the sector', principally over inadequate and declining financial resources (House of Commons Culture Media and Sport Committee 2006: 5). In the early phases of the Labour government particular concern arose from the pronouncements of other organisations created by the government, such as the UTF, which in its *Prospectus* made a reference to historic buildings being a restraint on regeneration (Urban Task Force 1998). This provoked an immediate and well-organised response (English Heritage 1998; SAVE Britain's Heritage 1998).

A recurrent theme in this book is the ability of the conservation sector both to fight its corner and to adapt its arguments to suit the context of the times. Throughout the 1990s English Heritage had been trying to demonstrate its relevance to wider government agendas, particularly in physical regeneration (Pendlebury 2002). The 1997 election of Labour resulted in greater emphasis being placed on the *social* relevance of the historic environment and its protection.

At the request of the government, the heritage sector, coordinated by English Heritage, produced the document *Power of Place* in 2000 (English Heritage 2000) as part of a process of fundamental examination of the historic environment system. This statement encompassed a wide-ranging set of themes including regulatory, policy, technical, management and funding issues. Broader themes considered included the regeneration potential of heritage and the value of characterisation and also the importance of extending public engagement in the historic environment. This included, for example, the importance of education and the removal of barriers to accessing the historic environment and the encouragement of wider participation.

The Labour government's response to *Power of Place*, *A Force for Our Future* (Department for Culture, Media and Sport and Department of Transport Local Government and the Regions 2001a), was criticised in the sector for its lack of specific commitments, but was nevertheless a powerful statement about the significance of the historic environment, with the rather promiscuously long list of benefits ascribed to the heritage that were noted previously. The document placed a heavy emphasis on maximising social access to the historic environment, a theme to which I return below.

Subsequently, the government embarked on a series of reviews of historic environment policy. At the time of writing no major policy shifts are evident; the principal concern is with sorting out the rather messy, incrementally evolved framework for protection, though an intended benefit of this is to make the system less confusing and more accessible to the non-expert. In parallel with this activity, English Heritage produced a first-stage consultation document *Conservation Principles: For the Sustainable Management of the Historic Environment* (English Heritage 2006), intended in the first instance for English Heritage use, though with a hope that it might have a wider influence. In some ways it is remarkable that such a document should be considered necessary, and it reinforces the fluidity or 'rolling consensus' (Hobson 2004) of current orthodox practice. Drawing heavily upon the Burra Charter, *Conservation Principles* emphasised the principles of understanding, maintaining significance and the importance of documentation. *Conservation Principles* was at pains to establish the inclusiveness of heritage across 'multiple communities' and that 'everyone should have the opportunity to contribute to understanding and managing the historic environment' (English Heritage 2006: 23). However, this is an exhortation for practitioners to be accountable rather than an argument for the devolution of decision-making. A second-stage consultation, issued in 2007, developed and expanded this approach without altering the basic philosophy espoused (English Heritage 2007). As with Waterton *et al.*'s analysis of the Burra Charter, this suggests some broadening out of conservation as an activity, but to a limited, cautious extent (Waterton *et al.* 2006).

A new localism?

Characterisation

The idea that places possess a distinct and essentially local character has long been important to conservationists. One of the chief concerns of the campaigners of the 1930s was the impact of chain-store architecture and standardised shopfronts being stamped on settlements across the country; a concern that has never disappeared. In the early 1990s, the charity Common Ground emerged as a new champion for the fight to sustain and celebrate everything that contributes to making places different from one another, with its campaign for local distinctiveness. Local distinctiveness is held to be a quality that is easy to recognise but difficult to define (Clifford and King 1993). This is an approach that emphasises the commonplace alongside the rare; a common-place that forms something that is important for identity and psychological well-being. Common Ground has fronted many campaigns, whether for sustaining local varieties of apple or, perhaps more counter-intuitively, for corrugated iron architecture (see Figure 10.1).

At a similar time to the rise of the notion of local distinctiveness in the 1990s, the Countryside Commission was engaged in a process of refocusing its concerns to put more stress on 'typical' English countryside, as well as on places acknowledged through designated status as National Parks, Areas of Outstanding Natural Beauty and so on. These designated landscapes are unusual and distinct, generally being uplands. Countryside more typical of the English landscape and embedded deep within English mythologies of 'the green and pleasant land' enjoyed no such status. One of the outcomes of this reorientation was a characterisation into landscape types of the whole of England. In parallel to this characterisation programme, the Countryside Commission began promoting the idea of Village Design Statements, produced at community level to identify the character of place and how this should inform future development (Owen 1998).

English Heritage worked closely with the Countryside Commission on these projects and also engaged in debates about how to define the qualities of landscapes and conservation areas. The emphasis on character-isation was picked up and has become a central influence on its work. Much of English Heritage's initial work was rurally based through the Historic Landscape Characterisation (HLC) programme, with a tendency towards an

10.1
Common Ground has campaigned on the importance of corrugated iron chapels: St Mary's, Newton by the Sea, Northumberland.
Source: author.

archaeological focus. Indeed, Turner described HLC as a 'form of landscape archaeology', focusing on the historical development of landscapes (Turner 2006). Drawing loosely from townscape and urban morphological techniques of analysis, character appraisal has been promoted to local authorities as important for conservation area management since the publication of PPG15 (Department of the Environment and Department of National Heritage 1994). Though historic evolution of place is embedded in conservation area character appraisal, greater stress is placed upon contemporary character than is typical with HLC. More recently, English Heritage has been keen to demonstrate the broad applicability of characterisation as a research tool, a means of understanding the 'everyday' and as a participation tool. It has been more directly involved in projects focusing on existing urban fabric, including innovations such as a project on Liverpool 'soundscapes', encompassing the mapping of different music genres and analysing the influence of the urban landscape on music (Cohen 2004/05).

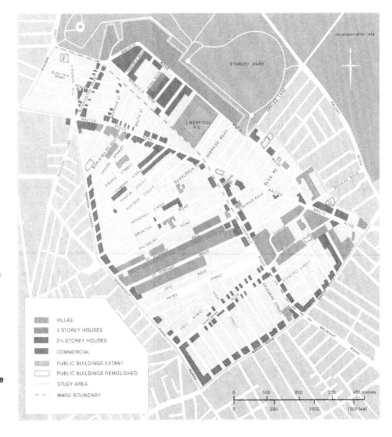

10.2
A characterisation map from the Rapid Area Assessment undertaken by English Heritage of Anfield and Breckfield, Liverpool (Menuge and Taylor 2004).
© English Heritage, NMR.

Housing market renewal

A major stimulus for English Heritage to focus its efforts on characterisation towards urban areas has been the government's housing market renewal programme. In April 2002 the Government announced measures to address low-demand housing as part of its Sustainable Communities Plan. Nine 'Pathfinders' were created to address issues of low demand and abandonment in the Midlands and north of England, with three more designated later in 2005. Typically, the Pathfinder areas cover a mix of terraces of nineteenth-century workers' housing and a variety of types of more modern council housing. One of the products of this process has been the prospect of the large-scale demolition of this housing stock on a scale unparalleled since the slum clearance heyday of the 1950s and 1960s. This has raised the spectre of past mistakes of large-scale slum clearance and has proved controversial on a number of grounds. There are criticisms that demolition on this scale will displace existing low-income residents and destroy existing communities and that it is undesirable on sustainability grounds. There has also been concern regarding the potential impact on the historic character of northern towns and cities.

The official launch of the housing market renewal programme had been preceded by demolition proposals in various places. One such was the Whitefield area of Nelson, Lancashire, an area of nineteenth-century housing. Local groups in the largely Asian community resisted the compulsory purchase and clearance of around 400 houses declared 'unfit' by the local authority. Despite the lack of conservation designations over most of the area, local groups had the support of English Heritage and the Heritage Trust for the North West. As well as arguing in favour of the historic and architectural qualities of

10.3
Looking up Hereford Street, Whitefield, Nelson with Bishop Street and St Mary's Church in the background.
Source: David Webb.

the houses to be demolished and the fundamental soundness of the stock, these bodies stressed the potential impact on community coherence of such an intervention. Locals and conservationists successfully argued at two public inquiries that neighbourhood revitalisation would be accomplished best by working with the existing stock and community.

As the housing market renewal programme has developed momentum it has prompted policy responses from the conservation sector and beyond, and in particular from English Heritage and CABE (English Heritage 2005b; CABE 2005). Conservation issues were also a principal focus for one of the Parliamentary Select Committees that considered Pathfinders (House of Commons Housing Planning 2005). These reports have all stressed the importance of making a positive appraisal of the existing housing stock before concluding that demolition is the best approach. English Heritage has also been engaged in promoting characterisation work to help guide these processes. It has been directly working in the Anfield and Breckfield areas of Liverpool, using techniques it terms 'whirlwind surveys' and rapid area assessment. Through such processes, English Heritage has sought to work more closely with pathfinder bodies and (at the time of writing) some of the heat has been taken out of the situation, although an incendiary report by SAVE Britain's Heritage (Wilkinson 2006) has made sure that conflict has not been smoothed over. The report launched an assault on the heritage impact of proposed demolitions but also on wider issues such as poor public consultation, flawed evidence, the role of registered social landlords and so on.

One of the interesting dimensions to the housing market renewal issue is the role of the heritage sector in defending what, by any definition, is pretty humble heritage. SAVE has a long track record of taking on unfashionable causes, but it is remarkable to see an over-stretched national agency such as English Heritage, which struggles to meet its statutory obligations, becoming so engaged. It is also notable how communities resisting demolition are mobilising heritage arguments, with resonances of the 1960s and 1970s.

Local action

In recent years there also seems to have been an upsurge in local authority initiatives identifying and valorising heritage that sits outside statutorily defined categories such as listing. Some authorities have long had lists of 'locally listed' buildings: buildings that, although not meeting statutory definitions of special architectural or historic importance, are deemed to have a quality or significance worthy of local recognition. A survey in the 1990s estimated that one-third of authorities had such lists (Bolan 1999). The practice of maintaining these seems to date from 1968 when the former statutory category of Grade III listing was abolished; buildings excluded in this way often formed the basis of local lists, sometimes on the explicit recommendation of government listing inspectors. Bolan's work concentrated upon the effectiveness, or lack of it, of designation in controlling development. Local lists were often found to stand up well in appealed planning refusals but ultimately could not prevent destructive works, including total demolition.

There seems to be a new wave of enthusiasm for local lists. English Heritage has made exhortations to local authorities to develop local lists, although this still prompts concerns about the effectiveness of local lists in planning control (Baker 2006). Anecdotal evidence suggests significant numbers of authorities are creating lists for the first time, or are committing resources to revising old and often out-of-date local lists. In part, this may be because consultation documents reviewing the heritage system have hinted at the possibility of an enhanced status for local lists, including demolition control. Interestingly though, in some instances at least, local listing seems to have a subtly altered purpose from its former role. In four cases in the north-east of England, in Gateshead, Newcastle upon Tyne, North Tyneside and the Northumberland National Park, the preparation of local lists has been used as part of a process of community engagement with heritage issues. In all these cases, the process of list compilation has been quite different from the expert-survey methods that underpin statutory listing. All nominations have come from public consultation, with strenuous efforts made to promote the process as widely as possible, albeit in all cases decisions about ultimate inclusion in the list were filtered by invited external panels (a process seemingly common around the country (Baker 2006)). Each local authority has also sought to move away from the idea that local lists are composed of buildings not quite meeting

10.4
Benwell Nature Park, Newcastle upon Tyne, created in the 1980s and included in the City Council's local list.
© Newcastle City Council.

statutory criteria; rather, the emphasis has been on buildings and places important to the distinctiveness of that particular locality. In each case, though it will have a role in development control, the purpose of local listing as a process is seen as much broader. It represents local values and has identified heritage in parts of each of the local authority areas where there was formerly little, or no, recognised heritage (though certainly in Newcastle there were noticeably more nominations for areas with middle-class populations). Local listing is intended to be a celebration of local place by local people.

Identity and inclusion

This focus on local, more humble heritage brings us back to questions about the purpose that its conservation plays in society. In contrast to those who have linked the conservationist cause with sustaining the cultural preoccupations and power relations of a small elite, as described in the previous chapter, other commentators have sought to demonstrate that the benefits attributable to heritage extend widely.

Historically, there has been an argument about the benefits of the complexity typically found in traditional built environments. Benefits have been seen to stem from traditional urban form, with a variety of old buildings, a dense urban morphology organised around streets and public spaces and so on. This does not cover all historic environments as now defined, with, for example, substantial numbers of 1930s suburban conservation areas and the listing of post-war welfare state housing. Hubbard (1993) reviewed a series of academic works that suggested that people find the visual complexity and varied urban form of traditional settlements intrinsically preferable to homogenous modern built form. For example, Lozano suggested that the lack of visual stimuli in modern townscape leads to its general rejection, as the monotony produced creates feelings of oppression and disorientation (Lozano 1974). The stimulus of historic areas, he argued, provides orientation and stability. Hubbard concluded that such studies overplay the significance of sensory inputs rather than investigating the symbolism or meaning ascribed to these forms.

Identity
The meanings and symbolism attached to the heritage have been argued as having psychological importance in the construction of individual and collective identities. This is not a new idea; nearly a century ago Patrick Geddes argued that heritage was important to the memory of a society and its roots of identity (Law 2004). However, ideas about the importance of the past and history, as represented by familiar places, to individual and collective identity became prominent in the 1970s (Tuan 1974) (see also Chapter 4 of this book). This was

prompted by rapid social and economic change manifested as change in the physical environment. Conservation became important as, 'a reaction to anxieties generated by modernist amnesia. We preserve because the pace of change and development has attenuated a legacy integral to our identity and well-being' (Lowenthal 1985: xxiv). Thus, the importance of familiarity and identity has become prominent in benefits argued for protecting the historic environment. Traces of the past 'let us make sense of the present' (Lowenthal 1985: 39).

The association between heritage and identity is now well estab-lished in the heritage literature: for example, 'heritage provides meaning to human existence by conveying the ideas of timeless values and unbroken lineages that underpin that identity' (Graham *et al.* 2000: 41). Symbols of familiarity or identity may be extremely individual and idiosyncratic. However, despite problems with the concept of group or collective identity and its fluid and contingent nature (Hall 2000; Roy 2001), it is also argued that place can still be an important focus of collective identities (Castells 2004) and inherited elements of the built environment important within this (Hubbard 1993). Healey referred to the 'city of cultural identity' that was said to include both grand and more modest collective symbolic reference points, such as grand plazas on the one hand and local football clubs on the other (Healey 2002: 1781).

Thus, it is argued that the meanings attached to the historic environment contribute to people's individual and collective identities, and this embraces not only the symbols within a place that have traditionally been validated by the art-historical perspectives of cultural elites, but many other elements of the built environment, which might mean something to some people. People's relationship to place is tied to its, and their, past, but not necessarily to those buildings and environments currently officially sanctioned as heritage; the two may share attributes but are not coterminous. Historically, heritage has been defined through selecting monuments, buildings and areas considered to have exceptional qualities that distinguish them architecturally or historically and that make them *special*. However, focusing debate on identity and familiarity suggests a shift in emphasis to the environments that form the backdrop for everyday life, and a shift from the special to the *ordinary*. This moves away from the idea that heritage is necessarily a construct of power and an elite. Indeed, as Samuel has documented, political sympathy and interest in heritage are the exclusive preserve neither of the right nor the left (Samuel 1994). Identity may be linked to heritage through standard narratives of heritage, in opposition to such narratives or without reference to them (Smith 2006).

As discussed in Chapter 4, there were conscious efforts in the 1970s to develop a rather more progressive and inclusive idea both of what constituted the cultural built heritage and its relevance to a much wider part of society. These took rather a backseat in the market-dominated 1980s, but since the mid 1990s the potential for the mobilisation of conservation as a progressive social process has gained prominence.

Conservation and inclusion

In the USA, academic commentators such as Dubrow and Hayden have argued, in American terminology, for approaches to historic preservation to represent the community as a whole, including, for example, women, people of colour and the poor. Dubrow (1998: 57) viewed preservation as a powerful tool to be claimed from traditional elites, while lamenting that, 'Planners concerned with issues of social justice have rarely viewed historic preservation as a very engaging issue or considered the tools of preservation to be essential to their practice'.

Hayden developed this line of argument. Social history is embedded in urban landscapes, and urban landscape history can be a unifying framework for urban preservation, replacing 'the old narrative of city building as "conquest"' (Hayden 1995: 45). Such urban landscape history is an empowering process that gives power to communities to define their own collective pasts. Furthermore,

> While a single, preserved historic place may trigger potent memories, networks of such places begin to reconnect social memory on an urban scale. Networks of related places, organised in a thematic way, exploit the potential of reaching urban audiences more fully and with more complex histories . . . People invest places with social and cultural meaning, and urban landscape history can provide a framework for connecting those meanings with contemporary urban life.
>
> (Hayden 1995: 78)

In a British context, debate on such issues has focused around the terms social exclusion and social inclusion, and indeed the issue of social exclusion has been a key policy arena for the Labour government since its election in 1997. All government departments were required to report on their efforts to combat social exclusion. The Department for Culture, Media and Sport was slow to emphasise the role of heritage, focusing instead on sport and the arts (Department for Culture Media and Sport 1999), and a subsequent progress report contained only the briefest of mentions on 'The Built and the Historic Environment' (Department for Culture Media and Sport 2001b). More recently, DCMS produced *People and Places: Social Inclusion Policy for the Built and Historic Environment* (Department for Culture Media and Sport 2002), which was concerned with the wider built environment as well as built heritage. The importance of social inclusion as a political goal has, however, been evident in the policies of bodies such as English Heritage, the HLF and the National Trust.

An examination of this area by the author with colleagues (Pendlebury *et al.* 2004) sought to identify different ways in which conservation and heritage *might* be socially inclusionary. Underpinning the discussion was a distinction we made between cultural built heritage as *historic place* and *opportunity space* within which, for example, to achieve economic and social regeneration. Viewed as historic place, the benefits the historic environment may bring are specifically derived from historic status. Alternatively, the historic environment may bring a physical quality to regeneration that is not easily reproducible, but where the emphasis is not upon intrinsic historic nature. Rather it provides an opportunity space in which regeneration may occur. Physical regeneration might help processes of social inclusion but, conversely, might actively contribute to reinforcing social exclusion, for example through enabling gentrification.

In considering the role of *historic place* we used three categories or levels in which inclusion might be facilitated; each in turn suggested a greater degree of empowerment to people and communities. The first was a widening of access to help more people in society benefit from existing, unchallenged definitions of heritage. Access can be considered in various ways, including physical access, intellectual access and financial access. Extending access is essentially geared to admitting people to the established order on that order's terms. Second, the potential of more pluralistic definitions of heritage was considered; this might include, for example multicultural perspectives and an appreciation of more modest, 'everyday' heritage. Third, we identified the potential for extending involvement in the definition and management of the

10.5
Public engagement: a workshop held as part of the Fish Quay Heritage Economic Regeneration Scheme, North Shields.
© North of England Civic Trust.

historic environment. This runs the risk of residents using conservation processes as exclusionary devices, for example, in efforts to prevent social housing or 'bad neighbour' developments being constructed in their area. Using this spectrum of approach, we can see the potential for a shift from an emphasis on helping poorer groups gain an appreciation of existing conceptions of heritage (which could be considered in terms of the controlling power relationships described in the previous chapter), to one of institutional learning, whereby heritage bodies begin to learn how to question their own values.

Of course, in some circumstances, heritage may be anything but a force of social cohesion, and policy written assuming that a policy of conservation is always socially progressive is perhaps the product of wishful thinking. Ashworth stated that,

> Governments and their agencies have a vested interest in promoting heritage as a reassuringly warm and cuddly blanket, which will soothe away our individual and collective stresses, leaving only contented and well-balanced people in an all-inclusive harmonious society, at ease with its promoted past and predicted future. Is it dismally cynical to point out that the past and the heritage we have made of it was not and is not so?

> (Ashworth 2006: 393)

The public values debate

At the time of writing in 2006, discussions about heritage in policy arenas have become increasingly framed by the idea of 'public values'. Partly this is a logical evolution of 'authorised narratives' of heritage that have been developing since the inception of the Burra Charter, accepting that there can be different and competing ways in which significance and the values attached to heritage may be judged, and seeking to absorb and organise these into systems of state-regulated management. However, like the integration of notions of social inclusion into the conservation arena, the ideas of public value also stem from a wider external discourse permeating throughout government and the public sector.

Moore has been credited with developing ideas of public value, and the idea has been taken up by the Labour government (Kelly *et al*. 2002; Moore 1995). The fundamental concept is the need for an analytical framework for evaluating public services, given the inadequacy of private-sector models based purely around issues of profit and loss. Viewed as a technical device, this is an approach that might be considered as a more sophisticated measuring device from a government obsessed with measurement. Underlying this analysis, however, there may be a political suspicion that some parts of the public sector, including the heritage sector, have traditionally been self-serving, orientating themselves around a closed professional discourse and spending public money accordingly. It is too early to say whether the idea of public values has a positive role to play, or whether it is a merely a response to the managerialism of the political class.

The HLF introduced the idea of public value into the heritage sector through a commissioned report that sought to discuss the impact of ten years of the HLF (Hewison and Holden 2004). It credited the HLF with a move away from a 'culturally conservative approach focused on material evidence of past hegemonies' (p. 12) to something much broader and inclusive, particularly post-1997. By not having a limiting definition of heritage, HLF was also seen as distinct from other heritage bodies 'who use their expert knowledge to identify, manage and advise what is important on behalf of society' (p. 21). This was all regarded as compatible with the emergent discourse of public value. The National Trust has subsequently sought to develop an evaluation methodology around the idea of public value (National Trust and Accenture 2006), and public value and heritage have been the subject of at least one major conference (Clark 2006a).

The development of these ideas has been seen to be very useful in providing a language of communication with politicians and other policy sectors, from a heritage sector not enthusiastic about reductive quantitative approaches (Clark 2006b). Increasingly, discussions about value have used a three-pronged framework of intrinsic values, instrumental values and insti-tutional values, which effectively seek to rationalise the self-justificatory arguments that the heritage sector has developed and deployed in political arenas. The distinction between intrinsic and instrumental values is complex. Two summarised definitions presented at the 2006 Public Values conference are set out in Table 10.1. Superficially, there appeared to be a distinction between values that derive from the heritage itself, and a series of social and economic opportunities that might be wrought from the heritage, in a division not unlike historic space and opportunity space used above. Yet the examples

Table 10.1 **Summary of key words used to define value as advanced at the Capturing Public Value of Heritage Conference (Clark 2006a)**

	Hewison and Holden	Impey
Intrinsic	Individual's experience intellectually, emotionally, spiritually	Evidential, historical, aesthetic, community
Instrumental	Ancillary effects to achieve social or economic purpose	Educational, recreational, economic, social
Institutional	Processes and techniques of organisations	Communicating, listening, mediating

Source: author

of intrinsic values used by different commentators are rather different from each other: Impey's were traditional heritage classifications (Impey 2006), akin to what some refer to as 'established values' (and effectively those values that underpin the system of protection) (Jowell 2006). Hewison and Holden, however, had a rather different focus, with a concentration on attributes that are much more personal than the scientific classifications used by Impey (Hewison and Holden 2006). Ultimately, it is hard to see a meaningful boundary between intrinsic and instrumental value. What are the socially instrumental benefits of heritage if they are not the very things that are defined as intrinsic, such as those concerned with identity or community? Even more profoundly, what sense does it make to discuss intrinsic values if, as is argued here, definitions of heritage are inherently fluid?

Yet clearly heritage does play very different roles in different circumstances, and this can be expressed in terms of values. Building from the heritage places/opportunity spaces distinction made above, another way of conceiving the contingent nature of value is as a spectrum with '*fundamental values*' at one end of the axis and '*incidental values*' or benefits at the other. This recognises the socially constructed nature of heritage values and the degree of instrumentality that is always present, i.e. we value heritage *for* something. It distinguishes between those circumstances where the historic qualities are fundamental to the value, or the gaining of the benefit, such as the evidential values referred to by Impey, and the occasions whereby the historic quality of a place is an incidental, if perhaps necessary, component of the value/benefit. Economic gain might be a typical example of the latter. Values relating to sense of place and identity and architectural merit and beauty come somewhere in between.

Perhaps rather more clear cut is the idea of institutional value. In short, the legitimacy of the heritage sector does not just depend upon the value of heritage but upon the actions of the bodies charged with its care. In addition to general issues of accountability, the focus tends to be upon public engagement and particularly upon more creative and effective means of engagement than some of the sterile participatory activities of the past. One example has been the HLF's adoption of the citizen jury concept, whereby a number of members of the public were asked to undertake an in-depth assessment of a range of heritage projects (Mattinson 2006).

Self-exclusion

Underpinning the drift towards pluralism and inclusion as part of official conservation policy-making is an assumption that communities *want* to be empowered and engaged into the arena of formalised heritage. Two short case studies that challenge this view follow.

Byker, Newcastle upon Tyne

Over the last decade or so in England, validation as cultural heritage has been extended to include the listing of large groups of welfare-state housing. Selected principally on the basis of art-historical criteria, they are significant also for their historical role as part of the mid twentieth-century approach to solving the housing problems of the working class. One such area recommended for listing by English Heritage in 2000, and belatedly ratified by DCMS in January 2007, is Byker, parts of which are only about twenty years old. Famous nationally and internationally, many within Newcastle and Byker itself have a rather less positive view of the estate, related to both the condition of the fabric of the area and perceptions about the very real social and economic problems of the estate. The author, together with colleagues, has undertaken research in the area on the impact of listing, primarily through interviews with a wide variety of stakeholders (Pendlebury *et al.* 2007). In particular, we were interested in how listing might affect perceptions of place.

On the whole, it tends to be middle-class housing that is culturally validated for protection through listed building or conservation area status. For example, in Newcastle upon Tyne, a city generally considered as 'working class', with a smaller middle-class than many British cities, there are nine predominantly residential conservation areas at the time of writing; all are located in essentially middle-class parts of the city. The most recent, in Gosforth, was designated in 2002, after a sustained campaign from residents and local councillors seeking the perceived prestige of conservation area status and concerned about the intensification of residential development in the area, with pressure for flat developments to replace single houses and other uses. Though not always popular with individuals, thwarted by the planning system in their desires to develop their property, it is generally considered that a recognised status as cultural heritage is popular with middle-class homeowners and is actively used by estate agents in their marketing. So, in the case of Byker, what impact might listing have on external and internal perceptions of place? Might it, for example, have a positive effect on community confidence or alter the way external actors, such as the local authority, view the area?

In Byker, a strong identity and pride in place are evident; often particularly so amongst long-standing Byker residents and families, in large part revolving around people rather than bricks and mortar. However, many Byker residents are also aware that it is a special environment, not least from the parties, such as groups of students, who continue to troop round looking at the place, as they have done since its construction. According to our interviewees, when the issue of listing arose, Byker people had no problem in seeing the area as special and even historic, and the voices within the estate that argued for knocking it all down were relatively few. This does not mean the proposed listing was met with acclaim. Indeed, though residents saw the estate as special, listing was viewed with a great deal of suspicion. Our heritage sector interviewees, while acknowledging this, felt that this was largely based on misunderstandings of the implications of listing, often fuelled by grapevine rumours.

Listing was equated with a strict preservation approach and therefore an impediment to improving the estate. While there is probably some misinformation circulating, it is clear, however, that local people will feel

10.6
**'Stop making promises . . .':
an extract from the Byker Conservation Plan (North East Civic Trust 2003).**
© Community Photography for North of England Civic Trust.

"Stop making *promises* and do something *now* before it is too late"

Resident, Raby Cross / South Byker TA area, Summer 2002

prouder about their place if physical and social problems are successfully addressed rather than through heritage valorisation. To most residents, listing is effectively neither here nor there.

Barton and Tredworth, Gloucester

Shore undertook fieldwork in the Barton and Tredworth ward of Gloucester, exploring how people in the locality constructed ideas of heritage and how they engaged, or didn't, with standard representations of the heritage of the city, such as the cathedral (Shore 2007). Barton and Tredworth is an inner suburb of mainly nineteenth-century terraces, immediately to the south-east of the city centre. It is a socially and ethnically very mixed area, with a majority white population, but with a substantial number of people from a variety of ethnic minorities.

The principal focus of Shore's study was, first, the engagement of non-white minorities and the city's heritage and, second, moves by official heritage organisations, such as English Heritage, to engage a wider of sector of society, such as those interviewed in Gloucester, with received definitions of heritage. Inevitably, a wide diversity of views was encountered, but overall he found much scepticism about the reformist intentions of current heritage debates. Indeed, many respondents found something patronising and potentially manipulative about this reformist discourse.

This is not to say that there was no value placed upon the standard representations of the city's heritage; these tended to be accepted and accorded respect. Sometimes there was active engagement with them: 'It's important to maintain your own cultural heritage but not at the expense of your adopted country's heritage . . . We try to show our children the city's historic buildings . . .' (Asian Male, aged 30–49, quoted in Shore (2007: 235)), or they were more passively worked as a backdrop for everyday life:

> Its (Gloucester's) buildings are like a background to day-to-day life . . . you take them for granted and don't give them a lot of thought really . . . but if you're coming back as soon as you see the Cathedral you know you're nearly home.
> (Pakistani Asian female, aged 20–39, quoted in Shore (2007: 232))

However, more commonly, a respectful acknowledgement of the city's history was not accompanied by any such engagement:

> we recognise and value the city's heritage for what it is – a reminder of the past, people and traditions over centuries. That doesn't mean we want to visit or take a closer interest.
> (Asian female, aged 20–39, quoted in Shore (2007: 229))

> It seems a bit patronising to suggest people are excluded because they don't share the same cultural background. . . . What makes you think we want to be included? Not that we don't respect and value buildings for what they are, but to suggest they should have any deeper meaning to people who are not English and are not brought up within an entirely English culture is flawed.
>
> (Asian male, aged 40–59, quoted in Shore (2007: 244))

Indeed, an explicit rejection of the city's heritage sometimes formed part of cultural reinforcement and identity. Furthermore, whatever the attitudes respondents held towards authorised heritage, there was no sense of exclusionary barriers or the need for reformist inclusionary policies. Shore concluded that this perhaps represents as hegemonic a discourse as the one it seeks to replace.

A reformulated modernity?

At the beginning of this chapter, it was baldly stated that heritage is the contemporary use of the past. Heritage is socially constructed; it is what we make it. This understanding of the world moves away from the idea that it is possible to create one master narrative about what constitutes heritage and why we should value it, and is derived from the multiple possibilities of postmodernism. We have seen some acceptance of this principle infusing into conservation practice in efforts to make heritage and conservation more inclusive. We can see this in the emphasis on 'humble heritage' and in the way that the conservation sector has sought, to a degree, to embrace non-expert values into conservation processes. We can see it also in the way that the contemporary utility of heritage has been foregrounded, with traditional concepts of intrinsic worth taking something of a back seat. Most recently, this has been seen in terms of the potential for heritage to contribute to socially progressive policies of social inclusion, but this leads on from the emphasis placed upon the economic and physical regeneration gains that can be extracted from the historic environment.

In a British context, it is possible to conceive of this as a trend driven by the complexion of national politics of the last decade. Clearly this is a factor and has influenced the agenda of national agencies such as English Heritage and the HLF. For conservationists of a conservative hue, there must be an aspiration that all this 'political correctness' will pass. However, that these trends fit in as part of a more international agenda is demonstrated by, for example, the Council of Europe's Faro Convention. There is a wider liberal agenda that is seeking to create a more widely defined and inclusive process of conservation, although the examples given of Byker and Gloucester suggest this is not unproblematic. The work by Waterton and colleagues on the Burra Charter also highlights an important issue: how much control are conservationists really looking to cede to those outside their realm of expertise?

One of the clear dangers of a postmodern view of the world is the potential to plunge into a relativistic morass, where all values are individual rather than collective and any possibility of a shared narrative is illusory. Another, philosophically less extreme issue for the conservation world is that a more pluralistic approach to heritage opens up different sorts of consensus that are in conflict with the dominant values in the sector. The last chapter touched upon some of the tensions that exist between an orthodox conservation perspective and a looser, postmodern approach, in terms of issues such as façadism and reproduction historic architecture. Waterton and colleagues suggested that, although the Burra Charter encourages wider participation in defining meaning in the historic environment, it does not relinquish control from the experts over defining cultural significance, the key measure guiding management decisions. Extending this argument, how much are the efforts of the conservation sector on contemporary agendas of pluralism, inclusion and so on, actually about *retaining* control in the face of political hostility? Indeed, is the public values debate a way of absorbing the pressure for pluralism into a traditional value framework?

The seeds of the current emphasis on pluralism and a diverse heritage were liberally sown in the shifting values of the 1970s, which moved the discussion from issues of architectural excellence to such considerations as community identity and familiarity. These were factors that influenced conservation planning at the time. Conservation areas were designated, and battles were fought over comprehensive redevelopments, urban roads and so on up and down the country. Some conservation *programmes* are influenced by current trends: for example, the way Heritage Lottery funding has shifted priority from large capital projects of physical conservation to greater emphasis upon community benefit and small community-led projects with no physical conservation element. What is less evident is the impact that current reformulations of heritage might have on the conservation-planning process, beyond demonstration *projects*. A more inclusive value framework is not going to have a significant impact on the definition of statutorily protected heritage; it is already so extensive that it is hard to see it growing much more. There has been a rising interest in considering heritage beyond statutorily protected categories; it is perhaps here that the circle between buildings and places marked out as special, and the familiarity of environment argued to be important to identity, can be squared. Characterisation is how English Heritage has sought to analyse and engage with such heritage.

The wider town-planning process is grappling with issues of community participation and engagement and, while there is some potential for this, for example in drawing up conservation area character appraisals, as we saw in Chapter 7, this evokes rather mixed views amongst conservationists. Furthermore, the regulatory planning system, the backbone on which conservation planning is based through law and policy, bases the protection of the historic environment around a particular set of cultural values that can be summarised as 'special architectural or historic interest'. Despite all the current emphasis on wider cultural concerns, such as identity and inclusion, and on the economic potential of the historic environment, these are not embodied in legislation, nor planning guidance, nor are currently at the heart of the decision-making framework (although they may be mobilised in practice). Perhaps this is as it should be, but it will inevitably raise tensions if we argue that the heritage should be protected for one set of reasons and then manage it based upon quite different criteria.

The concept of significance as set out in the Burra Charter is useful in this regard, as is perhaps the idea of fundamental and incidental values and benefits: seeking clarity over the values that derive from historic qualities and those incidental benefits that may be important but are incidental and could be achieved in other ways. Inevitably there will be ongoing debate about which values should prevail in the management of the historic environment. Authorised narratives of heritage can be problematised and critiqued, but they can be argued to have value, if only for the lack of coherent alternatives. I return to this in the next chapter. However, whichever values prevail, we need to be clear about the essence of why we are protecting heritage, and the implications that flow from this for its management.

Chapter 11

Conservation and the challenge of consensus

Introduction

This concluding chapter starts by briefly recapping some of the key features of the evolution of conservation as an activity since the nineteenth century and some of the issues that have gone unresolved in that process. I then discuss my own positionality; my own values necessarily inform my analysis of the challenges that I think face the conservation system and movement. The next part of the chapter discusses sanctioned conservation values and the way they have evolved with, for example, the growth of the idea of historic environment, both as a valuable economic commodity and as a source of individual and community identity. A multiplicity of values exists, and these are important for framing how we conserve. What constitutes 'good' conservation practice is discussed in the next section. While there are clear, authorised sets of principles for managing monuments or sites – the conservative repair approach – no such clarity exists for the management of places, with their multiplicity of buildings (and people). A simple extension of conservative repair principles is both inadequate and impractical. Characterisation, the catch-all term used for a disparate set of methodologies, has perhaps some potential at least in helping to describe and understand place.

The challenges I discuss that face the conservation movement are intimately related to the successful pragmatism of the sector and the issues this conceals, and this forms a significant subtext to the chapter. Though there may be officially sanctioned creeds, the reality is that the activity of conservation is wildly heterogeneous and therefore, inevitably, is not in reality underpinned by any universally agreed values or generally followed practices. At the same time, within the UK, the conservation movement has been very successful as an effective lobby of government and the public and at presenting a united front in doing so. The fuzziness of conservation values and principles has often been of benefit within this process as arguments and cases are mobilised to suit the occasion. Similarly, the pragmatism of the sector has enabled it to move from mid century high modernism and to absorb postmodern influences: sometimes apparently seamlessly, for example with a more diversely defined historic environment, sometimes more contentiously, for example over the nature of legitimate strategies of intervention.

The challenges thus far identified are, at heart, internal to the conservation movement. A much larger issue is the potential for extending processes of definition and management of the historic environment in more pluralistic ways. Changing the nature of conservation planning to respond to this context is admittedly a challenging arena to address, with no simple solutions, and I discuss this briefly in relation to two current, wider theories of democratic debate and place governance: 'inclusionary argumentation' and 'agonistic pluralism'. Finally, I discuss the need for critically reflexive debate that can argue for conservation in intellectually rigorous ways (as well as pragmatically) as an important and diverse practice and as an important goal within a pluralist, democratic society.

Evolution

Given the influence of the SPAB and the principles it formulated, it is easy to forget how modest and lacking in influence its origins were. SPAB, Morris and the preceding prophet, Ruskin, are key figures in the mythological history of the conservation movement. They are credited with unveiling universal truths about the value of the heritage and the appropriate actions to sustain this value. They were also activists and, with the formation of SPAB, created the first major society to fight proactively for the cause. Also, they were outwith the state: the clarion cry for conservation came from concerned citizens, not from government diktat.

From the modest origins of SPAB, the conservation movement had developed considerably by the time of the Second World War, both as a voluntary movement and in terms of the first mild pieces of legislation, particularly in the inter-war period. The impact of twentieth-century modern urbanisation was a strong stimulus. This was a modernity that extended beyond the 'deserts' of nineteenth-century industrialism. The growth of a motor-driven nation impacted on the countryside, and market towns and cathedral cities were affected by corporate capital and chain-store architecture. With its assault on this deep repository of values of Englishness, the impact of such modernisation could no longer be ignored. For the originators of the Georgian Group, rampant speculative development in London was a major source of ire. But many of the conservationists were not anti-modern; rather they sought a *better*, more planned and more sensitive modernism.

As in so many areas of national life, however, the war was a watershed when the role of the state was transformed. On the surface, this period was not necessarily an obvious step forward for the establishment of conservation as an activity, linked as it was with the often competing objective for large-scale planned redevelopment. However, conservation was modestly embedded within the framework of comprehensive planning. In addition, the period produced a series of town- and city-centre plans for historic places, which were the first concerted attempts to plan and manage the process of modernisation and change. As in so many aspects of society, the authority of experts to make rational decisions on conservation and planning issues was barely challenged at this time.

The post-war period was also an important foundation for the next watershed in the 1960s, as the conservation of the historic environment gradually moved from a marginal state activity, acknowledged by, but at the fringes of, town-planning practice, to one of its central objectives. Again, the anti-redevelopment extra-state campaigns of local and national groups form a deeply embedded part of the self-history of the conservation movement, though their ultimate triumph was in winning over the state. Victory involved utilising such tools as the listing of buildings, a mechanism developed for another and more restricted purpose. Legislative strides were made in the late 1960s and early 1970s, but it was, perhaps surprisingly, under the stridently anti-planning Conservative governments of the 1980s and 1990s that conservation's position as a policy objective was fully consolidated. From being an evangelical preoccupation of a small, cultural elite, the conservation of built heritage had become an embedded managerial process. At the same time new issues arose. The principal battleground became, in commercial areas at least, about the extent of permissible change, with developers prepared to work with old buildings if they could be transformed to their perception of the market's wants. They realised that a commodified heritage had economic potential.

Though there are inevitable arguments over cases and resources, virtually no one today challenges the basic premise that the historic environment is important and that the state has a central role to play in its protection and sustenance. Indeed, the same is broadly true on a global scale, with well-established systems of protection throughout most of the western world. Elsewhere, in rapidly modernising countries such as China, rhetoric might often not match reality. However, as touched upon in Chapter 8, the actions of Saudi

Wahhabism in deliberately destroying material heritage seem iconoclastic. The importance of heritage protection is generally a globally agreed goal, with most countries signing up to the World Heritage Convention. This is the age of consensus.

Beneath and beyond consensus

The World Heritage Convention, at a global scale, is an articulation of the orthodox values that have grown up over the nature of conservation practice. It is part of an evolving jigsaw of instruments that exist at national and supranational scales to help define, bind and organise the conservation movement both internally and in terms of carrying its case to the wider world. My own values and aesthetic sensibilities have been honed by my professional experience and relate closely to the modern conservation movement. They help me judge what is important, although this of course is filtered by my own personal experiences. So, for me, old buildings and places are often beautiful, and beauty should be treasured. I am undoubtedly infected by the common English condition of elegiac romanticism for buildings and landscapes lost. I have a belief in the significance of history, for me personally and society generally, and genuine wonder at the survival of things ancient. I have an old-fashioned dislike of waste, which today might be called sustainability. I have respect for the quality of much previous construction and despair at the fumblings of much modern building, and even good new places seem to gain from retaining something old. I have joy in a complex palimpsest of a place with its cheek-by-jowl layerings. I find it difficult to be sanguine looking at PVCu windows inserted into a beautiful old building.

While I might rationalise these responses into frameworks provided by the conservation movement, it is clear to me that they are essentially emotional. Furthermore, the buildings and places I treasure most, as well as being beautiful to my eyes, usually have personal associations with people or a particular time in my life. They are part of *my* narrative, *my* heritage. Furthermore, my attitudes towards the historic environment and its conservation are embedded in my wider values. Thus, although I believe conservation to be an activity that is fundamentally beneficial to our society, and that the state should protect the historic environment and provide resources for so doing, at the same time conservation as a practice does have wider social and economic impacts. While there are dangers of being hijacked by shifting short-term goals, for me these impacts should be compatible with a progressive political agenda.

The understanding of value as a neutral commodity to be revealed by the correct processes of investigation, which can be conducted only by a limited body of experts, is thus problematic. While such experts *may* be able discursively to channel their own responses and preferences into consensual channels internal to their profession, there is a wider issue here: the heritage we define and seek to protect is what we make it. The nature of heritage is that it is socially constructed; value is never an *intrinsic* quality but is externally imposed according to culturally and historically specific frameworks. These may be culturally, or temporally, collective or may be very personal; we each have our own value frameworks. Thus, value becomes an arena for plural interpretations and meaning. What need discussion therefore are conservation values: the reasons why, and what, we seek to conserve and the implications that lead from this as to how we conserve. Finally, we need to think about who decides what happens – whose heritage is it?

Conservation values

Chapter 1 briefly introduced some of the value frameworks that have been evolved by conservation practitioners as part of the process of justifying and framing the importance of conservation as an activity, starting with Riegl and his range of cultural values divided between 'memorial' and 'present-day' (Jokilehto 1999). There is tremendous continuity in these ideas over more than a hundred years. Indeed, some of the central tenets of the conservation-planning system and its emphasis on 'special architectural or historic interest' have shown a similar degree of continuity. Yet, much recent discourse about the desirability of conserving the historic environment has not been driven by traditional conservation values. We need, therefore, to consider further what values might be coming into play.

Governmental descriptions of the benefits said to accrue from our built heritage have expanded dramatically since the early 1970s. For example, the government's statement on heritage issues, *A Force for Our Future* (Department for Culture, Media and Sport and Department of Transport, Local Government and the Regions 2001a), waxed lyrically and extensively about the role of conservation in establishing environmental quality and identity, local distinctiveness and continuity and as an active part of social processes, including community cohesion, social inclusion and as a stimulus for creative new architecture. Furthermore, in addition to these social benefits, conservation was held to aid economic processes and economic regeneration in particular.

From this web of motivations for sustaining heritage, I would like to draw out a number of binary divisions. These are not intended as hard and fast dualisms, but simply as a mechanism for illustrating some significant issues. The first distinction has significant implications for how we think about heritage value. Over recent decades the historic environment has been argued as important for its asserted role in affirming individual and group place-identity.

This rationale was evident in the 1970s but became submerged in the market-driven 1980s, as we can see with the commodification of locales such as Covent Garden. In the last decade or so, such values have begun to re-emerge into a place of prominence. For the first time they are reflected in government policy objectives, highlighting access and inclusion. As was discussed in the previous chapter, the stress that is currently being placed upon the value of continuity and familiarity in the built environment implicitly emphasises the significance of *ordinary* environments, whereas, historically, conservation systems of selection and classification have sought to distinguish what is *special*. Furthermore, an emphasis on continuity implicitly contains an element of social policy; it suggests that the historic environment should sustain existing communities, rather than being an empty, architectural vessel. Thus, displacing effects such as gentrification should be viewed critically.

The second division follows from the distinction made both by Riegl and Feilden and Jokilehto, discussed in Chapter 1 (Jokilehto 1999; Feilden and Jokilheto 1998). Motives for conserving heritage have been separated into those uses that are explicitly concerned with current use values, and those that conceptualise heritage in terms of an inheritance over which we have a short-term custodianship. This resonates with Castells' distinction between groups that seek to control *time* and those that seek to control *space* (Castells 2004) (although, for Castells, controlling space was primarily a defensive impulse, for example, as used by 'NIMBYs'). In understanding the ideology of the conservation movement, the focus on environmental stewardship, on the long term and the rights of subsequent generations, is crucial. This premise was embedded in the founding principles laid down by John Ruskin and William Morris. Heritage was established in a way whereby, it was argued, rights and ownership transcended property ownership and extended temporally to include both the producers of the material heritage and future generations. Though today we might conclude that the nature of heritage is fundamentally the contemporary use of the past, we should recognise the significance of this value framework and that, while heritage as a process exists in the present, it also has a history.

Much of debate over contemporary use values in recent years has distinguished between *cultural* and *socio-economic* motivations for sustaining the historic environment, and this forms my third binary division. These factors are frequently closely intertwined; social or economic exploitation requires a cultural asset, and most defined heritage consists of buildings that require social or economic use to sustain them into the future. The professional activity of conservation, within and without the planning system, is usually linked to cultural concerns, and this is how conservation professionals usually construct their own identity. This is perhaps even more true for those who are committed to conservation through involvement in amenity societies rather than directly working in the sector. Sets of principles, laws and policies have evolved that seek to sustain the cultural value of the object, often held to be embodied in the material fabric. However, we have seen over the last two decades or so that perhaps the key conservation policy discourse has become that conservation is complementary to, first, economic and physical and, more recently, social regeneration. This has involved the heritage sector adopting a heterogeneous pragmatism over ideology as part of the process of sustaining consensus on its political credibility. Indeed, a drive for economic development may clash with sustaining the fabric of material heritage; it is a paradox of World Heritage Site status that recognition of 'outstanding universal value' may immediately place such value under stress. Market processes tend to sanitise and present a simplified narrative to the consumer. From a modern conservation perspective, the lack of regard for the notion of authenticity is particularly troubling.

Somewhat cynically, one might add a fourth distinction: the term *values* is often used to justify conservation activity to other conservationists; the term *benefits* is used to justify to others, such as politicians, why they should value what we do. To use a religious analogy, values are a matter of faith. The conservation faith group then claims instrumental benefits for their belief system, for example, in terms of economic regeneration, but these are not the reasons for belief. Extending the analogy, it is like saying the church is important because it gives a sense of community, rather than because its members believe in God. At the heart of the conservation movement, and the conservation system and planning systems, there is an emphasis on what is identified as special and in seeing this patrimony as intrinsic and timeless, removed from transitory temporal and socio-economic processes. Yet, at the same time, in order to sustain the policy and political significance of conservation planning, arguments are made stressing the importance of the familiar and of the important role of the historic environment in achieving economic and social regeneration.

In practice, the benefits argued to accrue from the conservation of historic environments are sometimes closely tied to the historic status of a place, and sometimes these qualities appear useful but not essential. For example, if we value an old building for its historic evidential value, its historic nature is clearly central, but if we value an old building for the useful role it can play in regeneration, this may be valuable but doubtless could be achieved in some other way. This distinction between *fundamental* and *incidental* values discussed in the previous chapter is the final binary distinction I wish to make. In the same way that the Burra Charter process aims to establish significance, this distinction can help clarify why we seek to conserve a place and, therefore, how we should aim to conserve it.

The binary divisions I have outlined give some of the reasons (although it is by no means an exhaustive list) why we might seek to conserve heritage or what we might seek to achieve in doing so. So, for example, we might want to keep old buildings because they are rare works of an important architect, or because, though they lack any great architectural merit, they form a familiar backdrop in our everyday lives. We might think of them as being valuable for future generations, or for contemporary study. We might see them as saying something about the importance of national cultural achievement, or a useful aid in achieving social and economic regeneration. They might be a useful asset in a wider process or, alternatively, fundamental to our objectives. All these may be perfectly valid goals and motivations. Indeed, as a conservation practitioner I have used them all myself when the occasion has suited. However, it is important to understand our goals in any particular situation, not least as it may dictate the nature of the conservation process we wish to follow.

'Good conservation' and the management of place

Though the discourse over the nature of heritage and the purpose of conservation has undergone transformation, accepted principles about *how* places should be conserved remain rooted in principles that began to be codified in the nineteenth century. The conservation movement and conservation practitioners have stood steadfast by the principles of the founding fathers. Modern conservation practice has thus evolved from the key foundation document of the SPAB manifesto (Morris 1877), and 'modern conservation' has largely prevailed as an ideology over other ways of thinking about material heritage. This dominance has also been replicated on the international stage through the efforts of supra-national bodies such as ICOMOS. Conservation, though it has sought to adapt to the uncertainties of the contemporary world, is an intrinsically 'modern' sensibility, relying on an ethically based rationalism, involving, for example, scientific principles of selection and emphasis on authenticity of material fabric. Though the very notion of an 'ethically based rationalism' is problematic, from my own modern, conservation-informed perspective, these remain meritorious principles and methods of continuing relevance in many situations and, perhaps in particular, for the conservation of the sorts of cultural monument for which they were evolved.

However, the conservation movement has struggled to develop anything as coherent for conservation at the urban scale, as part of a wider process of town planning. British practice has tended enthusiastically to embrace visual ways of seeing places and buildings. Townscape is a term that continues to be very frequently used in discussing the management of historic places, yet little has been written to advance this as a means of urban management since the seminal works of the 1960s. It remains a loose concept applied even more loosely, unfashionable in the domain of urban design for a superficial emphasis on visual composition. Proponents of urban morphology have argued that this concept be applied as a means of urban management of historic places, but, by and large, it remains trapped in academe. Some general sense of the significance of urban form has permeated into practice, but the resource intensity of Conzenian-type studies would seem to preclude them ever becoming a widespread management tool.

In practice, the sheer extensiveness of protection, in the UK in particular, means much 'conservation' takes place removed from any such ethical and considered niceties. It is here that the British emphasis on the visual becomes more problematic. It is evident that much that occurs under the name of conservation management through the British planning system is geared to achieving a visually acceptable result; conservation planning is a bureaucratic system often geared to achieving lowest common denominator minimum standards (Hobson 2004). Façadism is perhaps the starkest example of this. The importance of sustaining our historic environment might be a matter of consensus in planning and development, albeit perhaps only reluctantly accepted by some, but the manner in which this is achieved in practice is often far from the conservation orthodoxies discussed above. There are no generally agreed principles for the management of the wider urban environment, and the sheer extensiveness of protection means that there will *never* be the resources, and *never* the skills, for a modern conservation ideology to prevail in all these cases, even if there was political and societal support for doing so.

The emphasis on appearance produces results that may often dismay many conservationists, including the current author, but often seem to be welcomed and liked by wider society, including many other self-identified conservationists. The core of the conservation movement is often a long way from the wider public, from which it derives legitimacy, in its view of what constitutes proper conservation. As discussed in Chapter 7, ultimately the core conservation community is small. Conservation as a movement relies on a wider group of people active in local conservation planning processes, and on a wider sympathetic public. Beyond the inner circles, conservation carried out with an emphasis on visual appearance may well represent a reasonable balance between historic 'character' and modern functionalism (and, indeed, orthodox practice, which, for example, advocates the introduction of visually identifiable new fabric, may jar with the wider public). The notion of authenticity, so central to conservation thinking, may in reality have little role in much conservation planning. We can view the reduction of orthodox conservation goals to a 'heritage aesthetic' as a postmodern conservation practice, stripped of the carefully constructed ethical framework of modern conservation.

However, perhaps in some circumstances this is legitimate; perhaps it is the sustenance of broad character that matters, rather than the application of fabric-based principles. As Chapter 3 described, the concept of character has long been mobilised as a means of defining the essence of place that should be sustained in a process of change, its vagueness useful to planners able to interpret it to their own purposes. Its formal articulation into the conservation-planning system came with the legislation that introduced conservation areas. Nearly thirty years after the current concept of conservation, area character appraisal was formalised using a combination of townscape analysis together with some basic analysis of historical evolution. Subsequently English Heritage in particular has promoted the process of characterisation as useful in a wide range of places, including those not formally identified as having heritage value. It has been argued as a means of understanding the 'everyday' and as a tool for public participation. In practice, though, characterisation work being undertaken is often reductive in nature and varies wildly in methodology, and it remains to be seen whether, as a technique, it can be developed in ways that accept pluralistic definitions of heritage definition and interpretation. Furthermore, while characterisation may have potential as a tool to achieve a better understanding of place, it does not in itself deal with a critical issue – how decisions are made.

Conservation, community, conflict and control

Chapter 7 suggested a series of different levels of engagement that people might have with built environment conservation. There is a small group for whom it is an occupation or activity central to their identity. Other levels of engagement were suggested: there is a wider group active in conservation planning issues but for more obviously instrumental ends (albeit perhaps connected to a genuine attachment and passion for a place); a much larger group that usually plays no active part in the protection of the historic environment but has an active appreciation of it; and, finally, the more routine engagement most people have with the typically modest historic environment that they encounter as a backdrop to everyday life.

Across the wider heritage sector, there has been a strong emphasis in recent years on increasing engagement; on broadening the constituency for heritage. One strand of this activity has been an access agenda, helping more people in society benefit from established definitions of heritage. Improving access can include physical access, intellectual access and financial access. Whether such moves are part of a liberal progressive process or, as some would argue, part of sustaining existing power relations, is a matter of debate. Either way, ultimately it is a relatively limited agenda. Bigger challenges come from allowing more pluralistic definitions of heritage and from extending some measure of control over decision-making in the historic environment.

Addressing these issues demands institutional learning, whereby heritage bodies begin to learn how to question their own values. To do so is a demanding task for the conservation movement: to sustain its historic trajectory away from patrician elitism while sustaining core meaning and practices where appropriate. Pluralism and diversity, and the partial 'letting go' of power and control they imply, are inevitably a challenge for a practice traditionally expert-defined and -led. This is made more complicated still if we accept the contingent and changing nature of values we attribute to heritage. This is not just an issue of extending access, important though that goal maybe; it is also about a pluralistic widening of who defines heritage, why it is considered important, what should be conserved and how it should be done.

Smith, focusing on indigenous groups in Australia and community-based examples in the UK, has argued cogently about the importance of control over heritage process in terms of creating personal and cultural meaning and the validation of a sense of place, memory and identity to particular and identifiable communities (Smith 2006). In the UK the resources of the HLF have allowed it to support activities developed and controlled by local community initiatives that, in theory at least, might facilitate such empowerment. However, while it *may* be possible to identify a suitable community of ownership for particular projects, when considering the broad activity of the conservation of the historic environment, part of the spatial planning system, these issues become much more difficult.

Literature on heritage management has little to offer on the resolution of these thorny issues. However, in recent years, such concerns have been a major focus in debates concerning the nature of democracy. One major (and contested) statement of such theory, specifically applied to the field of place governance, is the idea of 'collaborative planning' (Healey 2006). At the heart of her argument is a process of 'inclusionary argumentation' within which different forms of knowledge and reasoning and different values and systems of meaning are developed into 'conversations' between stakeholders from different social worlds and cultures. The focus is on the processes through which participants come together, build understanding and trust and develop ownership of whatever strategy evolves. Changing such soft infrastructure of practice should be accompanied by changes to hard infrastructure, to the design of the political, administrative and legal systems that facilitate these processes or 'systematic institutional design'.

An alternative position, which critiques the consensual nature of inclusionary argumentation approaches, has been advanced by Mouffe, amongst others: it is held that such ideas ignore the inherently conflictual nature of democratic society (Mouffe 2000). Mouffe argues instead for an 'agonistic pluralism' that recognises that mutually incompatible positions are a legitimate and necessary part of democratic debate. The democratic challenge is for such differences to occur in a framework of mutual respect rather than, say, violent conflict. The further challenge is to reconstitute the nature of power, inherent in any social relationships, in more democratic, pluralistic ways.

Exploration of these theoretical models may be helpful in developing the nature of conservation planning as a democratic process in a pluralist society. At the same time, some caution must be expressed; it is hard to see immediately how such abstract formulations might translate into practical strategies of action; they also ignore some of the specificities of the conservation-planning story. Discussions about the broadening of control often implicitly, or explicitly, tend to assume the ceding of power from an over-dominant centre to some form of more locally based governance. Yet the establishment of the policy weight enjoyed by the conservation-planning system was due in large part to the top-down interventions of central government overriding recalcitrant local authorities in the 1970s, and the consolidation of this position in national planning policy in the 1980s and 1990s. A 'letting go' of control by a centralised body of experts, away from the accepted regulatory framework, might in practice lead to local development nexuses, generally powerful in local governance, moving in, with consequent traducing or even erasure of the historic environment. Devolving power further to local communities may just result in empowering a NIMBYism that is, in reality, primarily concerned with other issues, such as sustaining property values. The conservation-planning system and the principles that apply to its management may be part of a wider hegemonic discourse, sustaining the power of a cultural elite, but is this necessarily worse than ceding power to an economic elite or to an exclusionary local politics? It is a difficult circle to square: devolving power – but to the 'right' recipients.

Addressing the concerns raised here does not necessarily suggest rapid institutional change. In the short term, it might be the same professionals administering the same systems but in a more critically reflexive way, more systematically engaging wider stakeholders and cultural communities. The ethical framework of the conservation practitioner becomes redefined to extend from a concern with the material fabric of the historic environment to include a duty to attend to the views of all those people who might have a cultural claim to that place. Gradually systems can be redesigned to facilitate this. This is not just about seeking to empower local communities. Often people outside a locality, outside the region or outside the country will have a legitimate voice that should be heard. And of course, this should include the right not to engage. As Shore has shown, not all the wider public wishes to engage with professionals over issues of heritage definition and management (Shore 2007).

Closing words

There is much to celebrate in the history of conservation. The transformation of conservation from the marginal preoccupation of an artistic elite to being an important consideration in the management of the environment is a remarkable and, I believe, fundamentally positive achievement. Yet we should not forget the patrician origins of the activity, nor their ongoing significance that, for me personally, does not always sit comfortably with the wider values I hold. Many in the conservation movement *are* part of a self-defined cultural elite (Hobson 2004), while often spuriously claiming to be 'the voice of the people' (Law 2004).

Ultimately, I believe, conservation should also be compatible with (but not driven by) a progressive modern liberal political agenda, corresponding with my own wider value framework. If as conservationists we believe that the goals we pursue have a relevance to society as a whole (and are not just our hobby) and should be embedded in an extensive system of state regulation, we need to accept both the social and economic consequences that follow and that these are not inherently beneficial or benign. British conservation has been guilty of over-fetishising the object. Conservation strategies that inextricably link physical and social regeneration, such as that tried in Bologna in the 1960s and 1970s, have not been common. However, conversely, the need for cultural programmes to contribute to social and public policy outcomes, such as regeneration, has put increasing pressure on policy arenas, such as conservation, to respond to government objectives. The need for the conservation of historic environments to be more plural and democratic in nature should not be synonymous with slavish responses to shifting political imperatives.

Acknowledging that conservation can have regressive consequences should be part of a more reflexive conservation debate. The heritage sector should be *critically* researching and examining the benefits it claims for the activity of conservation. Benefits asserted, such as the contribution of the historic environment towards personal or collective identity, towards regeneration or towards a process of social inclusion, often have weak underpinnings in terms of theoretical and empirical evidence. Much of what passes for conservation research seeks uncritically to affirm predetermined outcomes. Indeed, the British conservation movement's mobilisation to prove the value of conservation has been matched by its denial of the negative social consequences that may derive from conservation actions, albeit these may be unintended. Physical transformation *may* engender gentrification, displace non-powerful groups and suppress narratives of place that do not sit easily with new commodifications. At times these outcomes have been directly facilitated by conservation policies and programmes. Since the 1970s the conservation movement as a whole has, at best, been disinterested in these potential consequences of conservation actions; this stands in marked contrast to a pragmatic willingness to assert its relevance to achieving benefits of any kind, including social inclusion.

New understandings of the world brought about by postmodernism, or the 'cultural turn' with its revealing of the socially constructed nature of heritage and conservation, the power relations this embodies, the critique this presents to the authority of expert knowledge and values and its dissipation of grand narratives, challenge the essentially modernist practice of conservation. These perspectives provide a clear critique, often effective in puncturing our sense of self-righteousness, but they are less good at providing alternative frameworks capable of practical implementation. The after-modernist challenge is about finding coherent routes through this fuzziness.

One outcome of this should be more explicit discussion of what we are doing as conservationists and why. The hazy consensus that exists over the desirability of conservation, which enables arguments over its benefits to be opportunistically presented and at the same time hides underlying tensions and unresolved issues, has a utility in practical politics. Yet the ambiguities this creates should be of concern to conservationists, because they help conceal destructive and inappropriate acts and create problems for conservation as a justifiable and coherent practice. This surface consensus masks difficult political, philosophical and technical issues about what to do in specific cases.

If there are multiple reasons why we might wish to conserve, and multiple views about which reasons are relevant or irrelevant in any one case, these emphasise the importance for those experts in control of decision-making processes to be both open and receptive to these different perspectives and to be clear and explicit about the basis upon which decisions are made. In doing so we should not smooth over conflict but, as the agonists argue, accept it as a necessary part of democratic negotiation. At the same time, we should try to make our systems and processes open to those who wish to engage in such debate.

Linked to this should be a clearer acknowledgement of the heterogeneous nature of what falls within the ambit of the historic environment and the diverse principles and techniques that might then be applied to its management. There *is* a difference between an artistic masterwork and a local landmark; or between an uninhabited architectural monument and a large-scale social-housing development, which might also happen to be a modernist icon. This makes for a multilayered heritage, and the ways we seek to manage this should be qualitatively different. For example, local lists *shouldn't* just be a record of buildings that didn't quite match the criteria for statutory listing. This does involve empowering different groups in decisions over the definition and management of the historic environment. There will be mess, mistakes and bad decisions, but then these are all features of the current system.

Finally, in the not so distant future, circumstances may be such as to provide challenges of a radically different scale and order to anything thus far discussed. Climate change may not just affect our everyday conservation practices, but also our sense of the progression of history and the evolution of hybrid, palimpsest landscapes. The decades ahead may prove to be an era of literally letting go of cultural built heritage.

References

Abercrombie, P. (1943) *Town and Country Planning,* London: Oxford University Press.

Abercrombie, P. (1945) *Greater London Plan 1944,* London: HMSO.

Abercrombie, P. and Abercrombie, L. (1923) *Stratford upon Avon: Report on Future Developments,* Liverpool: University Press.

Abercrombie, P. and Nickson, R. (1949) *Warwick: Its Preservation and Redevelopment,* London: Architectural Press.

Abercrombie, P. and Plumstead, D. (1949) *A Civic Survey and Plan for the Royal Burgh of Edinburgh,* Edinburgh: Oliver & Boyd.

Abercrombie, S. P., Owens, J. and Mealand, H. A. (1945) *A Plan for Bath: The Report Prepared for the Bath and District Joint Planning Committee,* Bath: Bath and District Joint Planning Committee.

Adam, R. (1998) 'Tradition: the driving force of urban identity', in J. Warren, J. Worthington and S. Taylor (eds.) *Context: new buildings in historic settings,* Oxford: Architectural Press, pp. 30–9.

Adam, R. (2003) 'Does heritage dogma destroy living history?' *Context,* 79: 7–11.

Adshead, S. D., Minter, C. J. and Needham, C. W. C. (1948) *York: A Plan for its Progress and Preservation,* York: Ben Johnson & Co.

Aldous, T. (1972) *Battle for the Environment,* London: Fontana.

Aldous, T. (1975) *Goodbye Britain?* London: Sidgwick & Jackson.

Allmendinger, P. (2002) *Planning Theory,* Basingstoke: Palgrave.

Allmendinger, P. and Thomas, H. (eds.) (1998) *Urban Planning and the British New Right,* London: Routledge.

Amery, C. and Cruikshank, D. (1975) *The Rape of Britain,* London: P. Elek.

Anderson, C. and Green, R. (1992) *Save the Jubilee Hall!,* London: Random Thoughts.

Andreae, S. (1996) 'From comprehensive development to Conservation Areas', in M. Hunter (ed.) *Preserving the Past,* Stroud, Gloucester: Alan Sutton, pp. 135–55.

Anonymous (2003) *Industrial World Heritage Sites in the United Kingdom.* Online. Available at www.worldheritagereview.org (accessed: 21 July 2003).

Anonymous (2007) *Shikinen Sengu Ceremony in Ise Jingu.* Online. Available at www.isejingu.or.jp/shosai/english/sikinen/sikinen.htm (accessed 12 June 2007).

Anson, B. (1981) *I'll Fight You For It! Behind the Struggle for Covent Garden,* London: Jonathan Cape.

Appleyard, D. (ed.) (1979) *The Conservation of European Cities,* London: MIT Press.

Architectural Review (1970) 'Dropping the Pilot?', *Architectural Review,* CXLVIII (886): 340–8.

Architectural Review (1973) 'Bath: City in Extremis', *Architectural Review,* 153 (915): 280–306.

Arnold, G. (1987) 'Circular 8/87 and all that', *Context,* 15: 11–12.

Ascherson, N. (1987) 'Why Heritage is Right Wing', *Observer,* 8 November 1987.

Ashworth, G. and Howard, P. (eds.) (1999) *European Heritage, Planning and Management,* Exeter: Intellect.

Ashworth, G. and Tunbridge, J. (1990) *The Tourist-Historic City,* Chichester: John Wiley & Sons.

References

Ashworth, G. J. (2006) 'Editorial: On Icons and ICONS', *International Journal for Heritage Studies*, 12 (5): 392–3.

Ashworth, G. J. and Voogd, H. (1990) *Selling the City: marketing approaches in public sector urban planning*, London: Belhaven.

Assi, E. (2000) 'Searching for the Concept of Authenticity: Implementation Guidelines', *Journal of Architectural Conservation*, 3: 60–9.

Atkinson, D., Cooke, S. and Spooner, D. (2002) 'Tales from the Riverbank: place-marketing and maritime heritages', *International Journal of Heritage Studies*, 8 (1): 25–40.

Atkinson, R. (2003) 'Misunderstood Saviour or Vengeful Wrecker? The Many Meanings and Problems of Gentrification. Introduction to Special Issue', *Urban Studies*, 40 (12): 2343–50.

Austen, P. and Young, C. (2002) *Hadrian's Wall World Heritage Site Management Plan 2002–2007*, London: English Heritage.

Australia ICOMOS (1999) *The Burra Charter*. Online. Available at www.icomos.org/australia/burra.html (accessed 30 April 2007).

Avrami, E., Mason, R. and Torre, M. d. l. (2000) *Values and Heritage Conservation*. Los Angeles: The Getty Conservation Institute.

Bailly, G. H. (1975) *The Architectural Heritage: Local Authorities and the Policy of Integrated Conservation*: Council of Europe/Stanley Thornes.

Baker, L. (2006) 'Listings create local shield', *Planning*, 8 December 2006: 17.

Baldwin-Brown, G. (1905) *The Care of Ancient Monuments*, Cambridge: University Press.

Bandarin, F. (1979) 'The Bologna Experience: Planning and Historic Renovation in a Communist City', in D. Appleyard (ed.) *The Conservation of European Cities*, London: MIT, pp. 178–202.

Bandini, M. (1992) 'Some Architectural Approaches to Urban Form', in J. Whitehand and P. Larkham (eds.) *Urban Landscapes: International Perspectives*. London: Routledge, pp. 133–69.

Barker, A. (1976) *The Local Amenity Movement*, London: Civic Trust.

Bath City Council (1975) *Yesterday's Tommorrow: Conservation in Bath*, Bath: City Council.

Baumann, N. (1997) 'Townscape in urban conservation: the impact of the theory of townscape on conservation planning'. DPhil thesis, University of York.

BBC (1995) *Public Eye: The Heritage Police*, Broadcast 14 March.

BBC (2002) *Streets of Shame*. Online. Available at www.bbc.co.uk/radio4/today/reports/archive/features/sos1.shtml (accessed 16 February 2004).

Beacham, P. (2001) 'The Urban Panel: Urban Regeneration', *Conservation Bulletin*, 41, September 2001: 4–7.

Bianchini, F. and Parkinson, M. (eds.) (1993) *Cultural policy and urban regeneration: The West European experience*, Manchester: University Press.

Binney, M. (2005) *SAVE Britain's Heritage 1975–2005: Thirty Years of Campaigning*, London: Scala.

Birmingham City Council (1999) *Regeneration Through Conservation*, Birmingham: City Council.

Blain, D. (1989) 'A Brief and Very Personal History of the Spitalfields Trust', in M. Girouard, D. Cruickshank, R. Samuels *et al.* (eds.) *The Saving of Spitalfields*, London: The Spitalfields Historic Buildings Trust, p. 174.

Bolan, P. (1999) 'The role of local lists', *Context*, 61: 26–8.

Booker, C. (1980) *The Seventies: Portrait of a Decade*, London: Allen Lane.

Bosma, J. E. (1990) 'Planning the Impossible: History as the Fundament of the Future – the Reconstruction of Middelburg, 1940–4', in J. M. Diefendorf (ed.) *Rebuilding Europe's Bombed Cities*, Basingstoke: MacMillan, pp. 64–76.

Bott, O. (1987) 'Historic Buildings: The Statutory Lists in Cheshire', *Context*, 15: 3–4.

Boyer, M. C. (1996) *The City of Collective Memory*, London: MIT Press.

Brett, D. (1996) *The Construction of Heritage*, Cork: University Press.

Brett, L. (1970) *Parameters and Images: Architecture in a Crowded World*, London: Weidenfield and Nicolson.

British Standards Institution. (1998) *Guide to the principles of the conservation of historic buildings, BS 7913*, London: BSI.

Brown, J. (2006) *NCAP: Research Into Recommendations,* Newcastle upon Tyne: NCAP.

Brunskill, R. W. (1971) *Illustrated Handbook of Vernacular Architecture,* London: Faber & Faber.

Buchanan, C. (1958) *Mixed Blessing: The Motor In Britain,* London: Leonard Hill.

Buchanan, C., Cooper, G., MacEwen, A., Crompton, D., Crow, G., Michell, G., Dallimore, D., Hills, P. and Burton, D. (1963) *Traffic in Towns: A study of the long term problems of traffic in urban areas. Reports of the Steering Group and Working Group appointed by the Minister of Transport,* London: HMSO.

Burke, G. (1976) *Townscapes,* Harmondsworth: Pelican.

Burrows, G. S. (1968) *Chichester: A study in conservation: report to the Ministry of Housing and Local Government and Chichester Borough Council,* London: HMSO.

Buswell, R. J. (1984) 'Reconciling the past with the present: Conservation policy in Newcastle upon Tyne', *Cities,* 1 (5): 500–14.

Butler, T. (1997) *Gentrification and the Middle Classes,* Aldershot: Ashgate.

Butler, T. (2003) 'Living in the Bubble: Gentrification and its 'Others' in North London', *Urban Studies,* 40 (12): 2469–86.

Butler, T. (2005) 'Gentrification', in N. Buck, I. Gordon, A. Harding and I. Turok (eds.) *Changing Cities: Rethinking Urban Competitiveness, Cohesion and Governance,* Basingstoke: Palgrave Macmillan, pp. 172–87.

CABE (2005) *Creating successful neighbourhoods: Lessons and actions for housing market renewal,* London: CABE.

Cadd, J., Jennings, L., Jones, D., McCafferty, J., Rounce, P., Smith, M. and Zainuddin, Z. (1998) *Local Amenity Societies and Public Participation.* Newcastle upon Tyne: Newcastle University, Department of Town and Country Planning.

Cairns, T. and Kelly, C. (1994) *Access to Action Survey Report,* London: Civic Trust.

Cantacuzino, S. (ed.) (1975a) *Architectural Conservation in Europe,* London: Architectural Press.

Cantacuzino, S. (1975b) *New Uses for Old Buildings,* London: Architectural Press.

Cantacuzino, S. (1989) *Re-Architecture, Old Buildings/New Uses,* London: Thames & Hudson.

Cantacuzino, S. (1998) 'Assessing quality: the pertinent criteria for designing buildings in historic settings', in J. Warren, J. Worthington and S. Taylor (eds.) *Context: new buildings in historic settings,* Oxford: Architectural Press, pp. 83–94.

Castells, M. (2004) *The Power of Identity,* 2nd edn, Malden, Mass: Blackwell.

Cherry, G. (1975) *Environmental Planning 1939–1969 Volume 2: National Parks and Recreation in the Countryside,* London: HMSO.

Cherry, G. (1996) *Town Planning in Britain since 1900,* Oxford: Blackwell.

Cianci, G. (2001) 'Tradition, Architecture and *Rappel a L'Ordre*: Ruskin and Eliot (1917–21)', in G. Cianci and P. Nicholls (eds.) *Ruskin and Modernism,* Basingstoke: Palgrave, pp. 133–52.

Ciborowski, A. and Jankowski, S. (1962) *Warsaw Rebuilt,* Warsaw: Polonia Publishing.

City and County of Newcastle upon Tyne (1963) *Development Plan Review,* Newcastle upon Tyne: City of Newcastle upon Tyne.

City and County of Newcastle upon Tyne (c. 1964) *Central Redevelopment: The Eldon Square Area,* Newcastle upon Tyne: City of Newcastle upon Tyne.

Civic Trust (c. 1966) *Conservation Areas: Preserving the architectural and historic scene,* London: The Civic Trust.

Civic Trust (1970) *Conservation Progress No 20,* London: The Civic Trust.

Civic Trust (1972) *Conservation in Action,* London: The Civic Trust.

Civic Trust (1998) *The Relationship between Civic Societies and Local Authorities,* London: Civic Trust.

Clark, K. (ed.) (2006a) *Capturing the Public Value of Heritage: the proceedings of the London Conference,* London, 25–26 January 2006.

Clark, K. (2006b) 'From significance to sustainability', in K. Clark (ed.) *Capturing the Public Value of Heritage: The proceedings of the London Conference,* 25–26 January 2006, London: English Heritage, pp. 59–60.

References

Cleere, H. (2001) 'The uneasy bedfellows: Universality and cultural heritage', in R. Layton, P. G. Stone and J. Thomas (eds.) *Destruction and Conservation of Cultural Property*, London: Routledge, pp. 22–9.

Cleere, H. (2006) *ICOMOS-UK International Briefing*, London: ICOMOS-UK (Number 1).

Clifford, S. and King, A. (eds.) (1993) *Local Distinctiveness: Place, Particularity and Identity*, London: Common Ground.

Coard, P. and Coard, R. (1973) *Vanishing Bath*, Bath: Kingsmead Press.

Cocks, R. (1998) 'The mysterious origin of the law for conservation', *Journal of Planning and Environment Law*, March: 203–9.

Cohen, S. (2004/05) 'Liverpool and music', *Conservation Bulletin*, 4: 29.

Colin Buchanan & Partners (1965) *Bath: A Planning and Transport Study*, London: HMSO.

Colin Buchanan & Partners (1968) *Bath: A Study in Conservation: report to the Ministry of Housing and Local Government and Bath City Council*, London: HMSO.

Collins, G. R. and Collins, C. C. (1986) *Camillo Sitte: The Birth of Modern City Planning*, New York: Rizzoli.

Coningham, R. and Lewer, N. (1999) 'Paradise Lost: the bombing of the Temple of the Tooth – a UNESCO World Heritage site in Sri Lanka', *Antiquity*, 73 (282): 857–66.

Conzen, M. R. G. (1960) *Alnwick, Northumberland: A Study in Town-Plan Analysis*, London: Institute of British Geographers.

Conzen, M. R. G. (1975) *Anglo-German Symposium in Applied Geography, Giessen-Wurzburg-Munchen, 19*, Giessener Geographische Schriften.

Cormack, P. (1976) *Heritage in Danger*, London: Quartet Books.

Council of Europe (1963) *The preservation and development of ancient buildings and historical or artistic sites*, Strasbourg: Council of Europe.

Council of Europe (1973) *EAHY 1975: Aims, Organisations and Activities*, Strasbourg: Council of Europe.

Council of Europe (1975) *European Charter of the architectural heritage*, Amsterdam: Council of Europe.

Council of Europe (1987) *Convention for the Protection of the Architectural Heritage of Europe*, Granada: Council of Europe.

Council of Europe (2005a) *Council of Europe Framework Convention on the Value of Cultural Heritage for Society*, Faro: Council of Europe.

Council of Europe (2005b) *Council of Europe Framework Convention on the Value of Cultural Heritage for Society: Explanatory Report*. Faro: Council of Europe.

Cowen, H. (1990) 'Regency Icons: marketing Cheltenham's built environment', in M. Harloe, C. Pickvance and J. Urry (eds.) *Place Policy and Politics*, London: Unwin Hyman, pp. 128–45.

Coxall, B. (2001) *Pressure Groups in British Politics*, Harlow: Longman.

Croot, P. (1985) 'Islington Growth: Barnsbury and King's Cross', in T. F. T. Baker (ed.) *A History of the County of Middlesex: Volume VIII Islington and Stoke Newington parishes*, London: Victoria County History, pp. 24–9.

Cullen, G. (1961) *Townscape*, London: The Architectural Press.

Cummin, D. (ed.) (1973) *York 2000: People in protest*, York: York 2000.

Curl, J. S. (1977) *The Erosion of Oxford*, Oxford: Oxford Illustrated Press.

Daniels, S. (1993) *Fields of Vision: Landscape Imagery and National Identity in England and the United States*, Cambridge: Polity Press.

Dartmouth, Countess of (1975) *What is Our Heritage?*, London: HMSO.

Davies, J. G. (1972) *The Evangelistic Bureaucrat*, London: Tavistock.

Dear, M. J. (1986) 'Postmodernism and planning', *Environment and Planning D*, 4: 367–84.

Delafons, J. (1993) 'Viewpoint', *Town and Country Planning*, 62 (9): 226–8.

Delafons, J. (1997a) *Politics and Preservation*, London: E & FN Spon.

Delafons, J. (1997b) 'Sustainable Conservation', *Built Environment*, 23 (2): 111–20.

Dellheim, C. (1982) *The face of the past: The Preservation of the Medieval Inheritance in Victorian England,* Cambridge: University Press.

Dennier, D. A. (1976) 'Chester: Conservation in Practice', in J. Reynolds (ed.) *Conservation planning in town and country,* Liverpool: University Press, pp. 37–48.

Dennis, N. (1970) *People and Planning: the sociology of housing in Sunderland,* London: Faber.

Department for Culture, Media and Sport (undated) *What Listing Means: A Guide for Owners and Occupiers.* Online. Available at www.culture.gov.uk/ (accessed 26 February 2004).

Department for Culture, Media and Sport (1999) *Policy Action Team 10; A Report to the Social Exclusion Unit.* London: DCMS.

Department for Culture, Media and Sport and Department of Transport Local Government and the Regions (2001a) *The Historic Environment: A Force for Our Future,* London: DCMS.

Department for Culture, Media and Sport (2001b) *Building on PAT 10: Progress Report on Social Inclusion,* London: DCMS.

Department for Culture, Media and Sport (2002) *People and Places: Social Inclusion Policy for the Built and Historic Environment,* London: DCMS.

Department for Culture, Media and Sport (2003) *Pier Head Set to Join Pyramids as World Heritage Site.* Online. Available at www.culture.gov.uk/global/press_notices/archive_2003 (accessed 24 July 2003).

Department for Culture, Media and Sport (2004) *Culture at the Heart of Regeneration,* London: DCMS.

Department of the Environment (1973) *Circular 46/73: Conservation and Preservation,* London: HMSO.

Department of the Environment (1977) *Circular 23/77: Historic Buildings and Conservation Areas – Policy and Procedure,* London: HMSO.

Department of the Environment (1980) *Circular 22/80: Development Control: Policy and Practice,* London: HMSO.

Department of the Environment (1985) *Circular 31/85: Aesthetic Control,* London: HMSO.

Department of the Environment (1987) *Circular 8/87: Historic Buildings and Conservation Areas – Policy and Procedures,* London: HMSO.

Department of the Environment and Department of National Heritage (1994) *Planning Policy Guidance 15: Planning and the Historic Environment,* London: HMSO.

Desthuis-Francis, M. (2000) *Tourists and Cities: Friend or Foe?* Online. Available at www.ifc.org/publications/pubs/impact/spring00/tourists/tourists.html (accessed 29 May 2004).

Diefendorf, J. M. (ed.) (1990) *Rebuilding Europe's Bombed Cities,* Basingstoke: Macmillan.

Dobby, A. (1978) *Conservation and Planning,* London: Hutchinson & Co.

Donald Insall and Associates (1968) *Chester: A study in conservation: report to the Ministry of Housing and Local Government and Chester City Council,* London: HMSO.

Drivas Jonas. (c. 2006) *Heritage Works: The use of historic buildings in regeneration,* London: Royal Institute of Chartered Surveyors, British Property Federation, English Heritage.

Dubrow, G. L. (1998) 'Feminist and Multicultural Perspectives on Preservation Planning', in L. Sandercock (ed.) *Making the Invisible Visible: A Multicultural Planning History,* London: University of California Press, pp. 57–77.

Earl, J. (2003) *Building Conservation Philosophy*, 3rd edn, Shaftesbury: Donhead.

ECOTEC (2003) *The Economic Impact of the Restoration of the Kennet and Avon Canal,* Watford: British Waterways.

ECOTEC (2004) *The Economic and Social Impacts of Cathedrals in England,* London: English Heritage & Association of English Cathedrals.

EDAW (1996) *Grainger Town Regeneration Strategy,* Newcastle upon Tyne: Newcastle City Council, English Partnerships.

Edwards, J. A. and Coit, J. C. L. i. (1996) 'Mines and Quarries: Industrial Heritage Tourism', *Annals of Tourism Research,* 23 (2): 341–63.

References

English Heritage (1988) 'Shopping in Historic Towns: A Policy Statement', *Conservation Bulletin*, 5: 1–2.

English Heritage (1991) *Principles of repair*, London: English Heritage.

English Heritage (1997) *Sustaining the historic environment: new perspectives on the future*, London: English Heritage.

English Heritage (1998) *Conservation-led regeneration: The work of English Heritage*, London: English Heritage.

English Heritage (1999) *The Heritage Dividend: Measuring the Results of English Heritage Regeneration 1994–1999*, London: English Heritage.

English Heritage (2000) *Power of Place: The future of the historic environment*, London: English Heritage.

English Heritage (2002a) *H.E.L.P. Arrives for City on the Brink of Change*. Online. Available at www.english-heritage.org.uk (accessed: 24 July 2003).

English Heritage (2002b) *The Heritage Dividend 2002*, London: English Heritage.

English Heritage (2003) *Heritage Counts 2003: The State of England's Historic Environment*, London: English Heritage.

English Heritage (2005a) *The Heritage Dividend Methodology: Measuring the Impact of Heritage Projects*, London: English Heritage.

English Heritage (2005b) *Low Demand Housing and the Historic Environment*, London: English Heritage.

English Heritage (2005c) *Regeneration and the Historic Environment: Heritage as a catalyst for better social and economic regeneration*, London: English Heritage.

English Heritage (2006) *Conservation Principles for the Sustainable Management of the Historic Environment, First Stage Consultation*, London: English Heritage.

English Heritage (2007) *Conservation Principles: Policies and Guidance for the Sustainable Management of the Historic Environment, Second Stage Consultation*, London: English Heritage.

English Heritage and CABE (2001) *Building in Context: New Development in Historic Areas*, London: English Heritage, CABE.

English Heritage and DEFRA (2005) *Building Value: Public benefits of historic farm building repair in the Lake District*, London: English Heritage & DEFRA.

English Historic Towns Forum (1992) *Townscape in Trouble: Conservation Areas – The Case for Change*, Bristol: EHTF.

English Tourist Board (1994) *English Heritage Monitor*, London: English Tourist Board.

Erten, E. (2002) 'From Townscape to Civilia: The Evolution of a Collective Project', paper presented at Cities of Tomorrow: the 10th International Planning History Conference, London & Letchworth, July 2002.

Esher, L. (1968) *York: a study in conservation: report to the Ministry of Housing and Local Government and York City Council*, London: HMSO.

Esher, L. (1981) *A Broken Wave: The Rebuilding of England 1940–1980*, Harmondsworth: Penguin.

Essex County Council (1973) *A Design Guide for Residential Areas*, Chelmsford: Essex CC.

Eversley, D. (1973) *The Planner in Society: The Changing Role of a Profession*, London: Faber & Faber.

Feilden, B. (1994) *Conservation of Historic Buildings*, Oxford: Butterworth-Heinemann.

Feilden, B. (2003) *Conservation of Historic Buildings*, 3rd edn, Oxford: Butterworth-Heinemann.

Feilden, B. and Jokilheto, J. (1998) *Management guidelines for world cultural heritage sites*, Rome: ICCROM.

Fergusson, A. (1973) *The Sack of Bath*, Salisbury: Compton Russell.

Foucault, M. (2000) 'Introduction to "The use of Pleasure"', in P. du Gay, J. Evans and P. Redman (eds.) *Identity: A Reader*. London: Sage, pp. 360–70.

Fowler, P. (1989) 'Heritage: A Post-Modernist Perspective', in D. Uzzell (ed.) *Heritage Interpretation Volume 1: The Natural and Built Environment,* London: Belhaven, pp. 57–63.

Franks, A. (1988) 'The Street They Froze in Time', *The Times,* July 15: 11.

Gamble, A. (1994) *The Free Economy and the Strong State: The Politics of Thatcherism,* London: Macmillan.

Garcia, B. (2005) 'Deconstructing the City of Culture: The Long-term Cultural Legacies of Glasgow 1990', *Urban Studies,* 42 (5/6): 841–68.

Gibson, L. and Stevenson, D. (2004) 'Urban Space and the Uses of Culture', *International Journal of Cultural Policy,* 10 (1): 1–4.

Giedion, S. (1941) *Space, Time and Architecture: the growth of a new tradition,* Oxford: University Press.

Girouard, M., Cruickshank, D., Samuel, R. and others (1989) *The Saving of Spitalfields,* London: The Spitalfields Historic Buildings Trust.

Glancey, J. (2003) 'Goodbye to Berlin', *The Guardian,* May 12, G2: 12–13.

GLC (1978) *Covent Garden Action Area Plan.* London: GLC.

Glendinning, M. (2000) 'A cult of the modern age', *Context,* 68: 13–15.

Glendinning, M. (2001a) 'Beyond the cult of the monument', *Context,* 70: 15–18.

Glendinning, M. (2001b) 'Conservation at war', *Context,* 69: 7–10.

Godfrey, W. H. (1944) *Our Building Inheritance: are we to use it or lose it?,* London: Faber & Faber.

Gold, J. (2004) 'York: A Suitable Case for Conservation', *Twentieth Century Architecture: The Journal of the Twentieth Century Society,* 7: 89–100.

Goodman, R. (1972) *After the Planners,* Harmondsworth: Penguin.

Goodwin, P. P. (1999) 'The end of consensus? The impact of participatory initiatives on conceptions of conservation and the countryside in the United Kingdom', *Environment and Planning D: Society and Space,* 17: 383–401.

Graham, B., Ashworth, G. J. and Tunbridge, J. E. (2000) *A Geography of Heritage,* London: Arnold.

Great Britain. Committee on Public Participation in Planning. (1969) *People and Planning: Report of the Committee on Public Participation in Planning,* London: HMSO.

Greenwood, C. (1945) *Chester: A Plan for Redevelopment,* Chester: Phillipson & Golder.

Gruffudd, P. (1995) 'Heritage as National Identity: Histories and Prospects of the National Pasts', in D. Herbert (ed.) *Heritage, Tourism and Society,* London: Mansell, pp. 49–67.

Haddleton, M. (2003) 'How I survived the regeneration process', *Context,* 78: 28–32.

Hague, C. (1984) *The Development of Planning Thought: A critical perspective,* London: Hutchinson.

Hall, P. (1969) 'Salvaging Our Historic Towns', *New Society,* 349: 872–4.

Hall, P. (1997) 'The View From London Centre: Twenty-five years of planning at the DoE', in A. Blowers and B. Evans (eds.) *Town Planning into the 21st Century,* London: Routledge, pp. 119–36.

Hall, S. (2000) 'Who needs "identity"?' in P. du Gay, J. Evans and P. Redman (eds.) *Identity: A Reader,* London: Sage, pp. 15–30.

Hanna, M. (annual) *English Heritage Monitor,* London: English Tourist Board.

Hardill, I., Crampton, A. and Ince, O. (2003) *Nottingham's Urban Renaissance: An Exploration of the Role of Housing and Labour Markets. Report 2, The changing urban form of central Nottingham,* Nottingham: The Nottinghamshire Research Observatory (5).

Hargreaves, J. (1964) *Historic Buildings: Problems of Their Preservation,* York: York Civic Trust.

Harvey, D. (1990) *The Condition of Postmodernity,* Oxford: Blackwell.

Harwood, E. (2005) Interview with author, 24 November 2005.

Hasegawa, J. (1999) 'The Rise and Fall of Radical Reconstruction in 1940s Britain', *Twentieth Century British History,* 10 (2): 137–61.

Hayden, D. (1995) *The Power of Place: Urban Landscapes as Public History,* London: MIT Press.

Healey, P. (1998) 'Collaborative planning in a stakeholder society', *Town Planning Review,* 69 (1): 1–21.

References

Healey, P. (2002) 'On Creating the 'City' as a Collective Resource', *Urban Studies,* 39 (10): 1777–92.

Healey, P. (2006,) *Collaborative Planning: Shaping Places in Fragmented Societies,* 2nd edn, Basingstoke: Macmillan.

Heighway, C. M. (ed.) (1972) *The Erosion of History: Archaeology and Planning in Towns,* London: Council for British Archaeology.

Heritage Link (2003) *Volunteers and the Historic Environment.* London: Heritage Link, English Heritage.

Heritage Link (2004) *Heritage Link Homepage.* Online. Available at www.britarch.ac.uk/ heritagelink/index.asp (accessed 23 April 2004).

Heritage Lottery Fund, (2004) *New Life: Heritage and Regeneration,* London: HLF.

Hewison, R. (1987) *The Heritage Industry: Britain in a Climate of Decline,* London: Methuen.

Hewison, R. (1995) *Culture and Consensus: England, art and politics since 1940,* London: Methuen.

Hewison, R. and Holden, J. (2004) *Challenge and Change: HLF and Cultural Value,* London: HLF.

Hewison, R. and Holden, J. (2006) 'Public value as a framework for analysing the value of heritage: the ideas', in K. Clark (ed.) *Capturing the Public Value of Heritage: The proceedings of the London Conference,* 25–26 January 2006, London: English Heritage, pp. 14–18.

Highfield, D. (1991) *The Construction of New Buildings Behind Historic Facades,* London: E & F Spon.

Hillier, B. and Hanson, J. (1984) *The social logic of space,* Cambridge: University Press.

Hirst, C. (1996) 'An avenging angel of the Tory right', *Planning Week,* 4 (27): 12–13.

Hitchcock, M. (2002) 'Zanzibar Stone Town Joins the Imagined Community of World Heritage Sites', *International Journal for Heritage Studies,* 8 (2): 153–66.

Hobson, E. (2004) *Conservation and planning: changing values in policy and practice,* London: Spon Press.

Home, R. and Loew, S. (1987) *Covent Garden,* London: Surveyors Publications.

Hooper, J. (2004) 'The major and the minor miracle that saved a historic town', *The Guardian,* April 28: 7.

House of Commons Culture Media and Sport Committee (2006) *Protecting and Preserving Our Heritage: Third Report of Session 2005–06: Volume 1,* London: The Stationery Office.

House of Commons ODPM: Housing Planning and Local Government and the Regions Committee (2005) *Empty Homes and Low Demand Pathfinders,* London: The Stationery Office.

Howden, D. (2005) 'The destruction of Mecca', *The Independent,* 6 August: 1–2.

Howe, J. (1998) 'Not a cree – more a listed building', *Newcastle Journal,* 27 March: 9.

Hoyau, P. (1988, originally published 1980) 'Heritage and 'the conserver society': the French case', in R. Lumley (ed.) *The Museum Time Machine,* London: Routledge, pp. 27–35.

HRH Prince of Wales (1989) *A Vision of Britain: a personal view of architecture,* London: Doubleday.

Hubbard, P. (1993) 'The value of conservation: A critical review of behavioural research', *Town Planning Review,* 64 (4): 359–73.

Hyland, A. D. C. (1999) 'Ethnic Dimensions to World Heritage: Conservation of the Architectural Heritage of the Turkish Republic of Northern Cyprus', *Journal of Architectural Conservation,* 5 (1): 59–74.

ICOMOS (1964) *International Charter for the Conservation and Restoration of Monuments and Sites: 'The Venice Charter',* Paris: ICOMOS.

ICOMOS (1987) *Charter on the Conservation of Historic Towns and Urban Areas: 'The Washington Charter',* Paris: ICOMOS.

ICOMOS (1994) *The Nara Document on Authenticity,* Paris: ICOMOS.

Impey, E. (2006) 'Why do places matter? The New English Heritage *Conservation Principles*', in K. Clark (ed.) *Capturing the Public Value of Heritage: The proceedings of the London Conference,* 25–26 January 2006, London: English Heritage, pp. 79–84.

Institute of Historic Building Conservation (2005) 'Valuing historic places', *Context,* 89: 30.

Jacobs, J. (1961) *The Death and Life of Great American Cities: The Failure of Town Planning,* New York: Random House.

Jacobs, J. M. (1992) 'Cultures of the past and urban transformation: the Spitalfields Market redevelopment in East London', in K. Anderson and F. Gale (eds.) *Inventing Places,* Melbourne: Longman Cheshire, pp. 194–214.

Jacobs, J. M. (1996) *Edge of Empire: Postcolonialism and the City,* London: Routledge.

Jagger, M. (1998) 'The planner's perspective: a view from the front', in J. Warren, J. Worthington and S. Taylor (eds.) *Context: new buildings in historic settings,* Oxford: Architectural Press, pp. 71–82.

Jankowski, S. (1990) 'Warsaw: Destruction, Secret Town Planning, 1939–44, and Postwar Reconstruction', in J. M. Diefendorf (ed.) *Rebuilding Europe's Bombed Cities,* Basingstoke: MacMillan, pp. 77–93.

Jeffrey, A. (1975) 'A Future for New Lanark', in S. Cantacuzino (ed.) *Architectural Conservation in Europe,* London: Architectural Press, pp. 61–70.

Jencks, C. (1996) *What is Post-Modernism?,* Chichester: Academy Editions.

Jenkins, S. (2007) 'Not just a building but a joy to behold – Ken Livingstone must hate St Pancras', *The Guardian,* 9 November Online. Available at www.society.guardian.co.uk (accessed: 29 November 2007).

Jiven, G. and Larkham, P. J. (2003) 'Sense of Place, Authenticity and Character: A commentary', *Journal of Urban Design,* 8 (1): 67–81.

Johnson, J. (2000) 'Rebuilding of a Historic Polish Town: "Retroversion" in Action', *Journal of Architectural Conservation,* 6 (2): 63–71.

Jokilehto, J. (1998) 'Organisations, charters and world movements – an overview', in J. Warren, J. Worthington and S. Taylor (eds.) *Context: new buildings in historic settings,* Oxford: Architectural Press, pp. 40–9.

Jokilehto, J. (1999) *A History of Architectural Conservation,* Oxford: Butterworth-Heinemann.

Jones, A. and Larkham, P. (1993) *The Character of Conservation Areas,* London: Royal Town Planning Institute.

Jones, C. and Munday, M. (2001) 'Blaenavon and United Nations World Heritage Site Status: Is Conservation of Industrial Heritage a Road to Local Economic Development', *Regional Studies,* 35 (6): 585–90.

Jordan, A. G., Kimber, R. H. and Richardson, J. J. (1975) 'Participation and Conservation: The Chester Conservation Area Advisory Committee', *Local Government Studies,* 1 (4): 1–11.

Jowell, T. (2006) 'From consultation to conversation: the challenge of *Better Places to Live*', in K. Clark (ed.) *Capturing the Public Value of Heritage: The proceedings of the London Conference,* 25–26 January 2006, London: English Heritage, pp. 7–13.

Kaiser, C. (c.1993/2001) 'Dubrovnik: When the War is Over', in M. Hrvatska (ed.) *Dubrovnik in War,* Dubrovnik: Matica Hrvatska, pp. 87–91.

Kearns, G. and Philo, C. (eds.) (1993) *Selling places: the city as cultural capital, past and present,* Oxford: Pergammon Press.

Keeble, L. (1964) *Principles and Practice of Town and Country Planning,* London: Estates Gazette.

Kelly, G., Mulgan, G. and Meurs, S. (2002) *Creating Public Value: An Analytical Framework for Public Service Reform,* London: Strategy Unit, Cabinet Office.

Kennedy, M. (2003) 'Books could help town to turn a new leaf', *The Guardian,* March 10. Online. Available at www.society.guardian.co.uk (accessed: 21 July 2003).

Kennet, W. (1972) *Preservation,* London: Temple Smith.

Larkham, P. J. (1985) *Voluntary Amenity Societies and Conservation Planning,* Birmingham: Department of Geography, University of Birmingham (Working Paper 30).

Larkham, P. J. (1996) *Conservation and the City,* London: Routledge.

References

Larkham, P. J. (1999a) 'Preservation, Conservation and Heritage: Developing Concepts and Applications', in B. Cullingworth (ed.) *British Planning: 50 Years of Urban and Regional Policy,* London: The Athlone Press, pp. 105–22.

Larkham, P. J. (1999b) *Residents' Perceptions of Conservation: Case Studies in the West Midlands,* Birmingham: School of Planning, UCE (Working Paper 74).

Larkham, P. J. (1999c) 'Tensions in Managing the Suburbs: Conservation versus Change', *Area,* 31 (4): 359–71.

Larkham, P. J. and Barrett, H. (1998) 'Conservation of the built environment under the conservatives', in P. Allmendinger and H. Thomas (eds.) *Urban Planning and the British New Right,* London: Routledge, p. 287.

Larkham, P. J. and Chapman, D. W. (1996) 'Article 4 Directions and Development Control: Planning Myths, Present Uses and Future Possibilities', *Journal of Environment and Planning Management,* 39 (1): 5–20.

Larkham, P. J. and Lodge, J. (1999) *Do residents understand what conservation means?,* Birmingham: School of Planning, UCE (Working Paper 71).

Larkham, P. J., Pendlebury, J. and Townshend, T. (2002) 'Public Involvement in Residential Conservation Planning: Values, Attitudes and Future Directions', in Y. Rydin and A. Thornley (eds.) *Planning in the UK: Agendas for the New Millennium,* Aldershot: Ashgate, pp. 237–56.

Larsen, K. (ed.) (1995) *Nara Conference on Authenticity, 1994,* Nara: UNESCO World Heritage Centre, Government of Japan Agency for Cultural Affairs, International Centre for the Study and Preservation and Restoration of Cultural Property & ICOMOS.

Latham, D. (2000) *Creative Reuse of Buildings,* Shaftesbury: Donhead.

Laurier, E. (1993) ' "Tackintosh": Glasgow's Supplementary Gloss', in G. Kearns and C. Philo (eds.) *Selling Places: The City as Cultural Capital, Past and Present,* Oxford: Pergamon Press, pp. 267–90.

Law, A. (2004) 'The Built Heritage Conservation Movement: landscapes of Englishness and social class.' PhD thesis, Newcastle University.

Lees, L. (2003) 'Visions of "urban renaissance": the Urban Task Force report and the Urban White Paper', in R. Imrie and M. Raco (eds.) *Urban Renaissance? New Labour, community and urban policy,* Bristol: The Policy Press, pp. 61–82.

Ley, D. (1989) 'Modernism, post-modernism, and the struggle for space', in J. Agnew and J. Duncan (eds.) *The Power of Place: Bringing Together Geographical and Sociological Imaginations,* London: Unwin Hyman, pp. 44–65.

Ley, D. (1996) *The New Middle Class and the Remaking of the Central City,* Oxford: University Press.

Lichfield, N. and Proudlove, A. (1976) *Conservation and Traffic: A Case Study of York,* York: Ebor Press.

Liverpool City Council (2002) 'Maritime Mercantile City Liverpool World Heritage Bid: Newsletter No2', in Liverpool City Council: Liverpool, p. 4.

Liverpool World Heritage Liaison Group (2003) *Nomination of Liverpool – Maritime Mercantile City for Inscription on the World Heritage List,* Liverpool: Liverpool City Council.

London Borough of Camden (1974) *Bloomsbury: the case against destruction.* London: London Borough of Camden.

Lord Gifford, Brown, W. and Bundey, R. (1989) *Loosen the Shackles: First Report of the Liverpool 8 Inquiry into Race Relations in Liverpool,* London: Karia Press.

Lord Rogers, MacCormac, R. and Coleman, R. (1999) 'Facade retention: the case against', *Property Week,* 22/10/99, pp. 24, 28.

Lovie, D. (1997) *The Buildings of Grainger Town: Four Townscape Walks Around Newcastle,* Newcastle upon Tyne: NEEEF.

Lowe, P. (1977) 'Amenity and equity: a review of local environmental pressure groups in Britain', *Environment and Planning A,* 9 (1): 35–8.

Lowe, P. and Goyder, J. (1983) *Environmental Groups in Politics*, London: George Allen & Unwin.

Lowenthal, D. (1985) *The Past Is a Foreign Country*, Cambridge: Cambridge Press.

Lowenthal, D. (1997) *The Heritage Crusade and the Spoils of History*, London: Viking.

Lozano, E. (1974) 'Visual needs in the built environment', *Town Planning Review*, 45 (3): 351–74.

McLernon, P. and Griffiths, S. (2002) 'Liverpool and the Heritage of the Slave Trade', in A. Phelps, G. J. Ashworth and B. O. H. Johannson (eds.) *The Construction of the Built Heritage: A north European perspective on policies, practices and outcomes*, Aldershot: Ashgate, pp. 191–206.

Mageean, A. (1998) 'Urban Conservation Policy Development: Character Appraisal and Analysis', *Journal of Architectural Conservation*, 4 (3): 59–77.

Mageean, A. (1999) 'Assessing the impact of urban conservation policy and practice: the Chester experience 1955–96', *Planning Perspectives*, 14 (1): 69–97.

Mandler, P. (1994) 'John Summerson (1904–1992): The architectural critic and the quest for the Modern', in S. Pedersen and P. Mandler (eds.) *After the Victorians: Private conscience and public duty in modern Britain*, London: Routledge, pp. 229–46.

Mandler, P. (1997) *The Fall and Rise of the Stately Home*, London: Yale University Press.

Marks, R. (1996) 'Conservation and community: The contradictions and ambiguities of tourism in the Stone Town of Zanzibar', *Habitat International*, 20 (2): 265–78.

Mason, R., MacLean, M. and Torre, M. d. l. (2003) *Hadrian's Wall Heritage Site*, Los Angeles: Getty Conservation Institute.

Matless, D. (1998) *Landscape and Englishness*, London: Reaktion Books.

Mattinson, D. (2006) 'The value of heritage: what does the public think?' in K. Clark (ed.) *Capturing the Public Value of Heritage: The proceedings of the London Conference*, 25–26 January 2006, London: English Heritage, pp. 86–91.

McKean, C. (1979) 'Community Action in Britain', in D. Appleyard (ed.) *The Conservation of European Cities*, London: MIT Press, pp. 269–81.

Mellor, A. (1991) 'Enterprise and heritage in the dock', in J. Corner and S. Harvey (eds.) *Enterprise and Heritage*, London: Routledge, pp. 93–115.

Menuge, A. and Taylor, S. (2004) *Anfield and Breckfield, Liverpool: A Rapid Area Assessment of the Built Environment*. York: English Heritage (B/006/2004).

Merriman, N. (1991) *Beyond the Glass Case*, Leicester: University Press.

Miele, C. (1996) 'The first conservation militants: William Morris and the Society for the Protection of Ancient Buildings', in M. Hunter (ed.) *Preserving the Past: The Rise of Heritage in Modern Britain*, Stroud: Alan Sutton, pp. 17–37.

Miles, S. and Paddison, R. (2005) 'Introduction: The Rise and Rise of Culture-led Urban Regeneration', *Urban Studies*, 42 (5/6): 833–39.

Ministry of Housing and Local Government (1967) *Preservation and change*, London: HMSO.

Mitchell, D. (2000) *Cultural Geography: A Critical Introduction*, Oxford: Blackwell.

Montgomery, J. (2003) 'Cultural Quarters as Mechanisms for Urban Regeneration. Part 1: Conceptualising Urban Quarters', *Planning Practice and Research*, 18 (4): 293–306.

Montgomery, J. (2004) 'Cultural Quarters as Mechanisms for Urban Regeneration. Part 2: A Review of Four Cultural Quarters in the UK, Ireland and Australia', *Planning Practice and Research*, 19 (1): 3–31.

Moore, M. (1995) *Creating Public Value: Strategic Management in Government*, Cambridge MA: Harvard University Press.

MORI (2000) *Attitudes Towards the Heritage*, London: English Heritage.

MORI (2003) *Making Heritage Count?* London: English Heritage, DCMS & Heritage Lottery Fund.

Morris, W. (1877) *Restoration, reprinted by the Society for the Protection of Ancient Buildings as their Manifesto*, London: SPAB.

Morton, D. (1991) 'Conservation areas: has saturation point been reached?' *The Planner*, 77 (17): 5–8.

Mouffe, C. (2000) *The Democratic Paradox*, London: Verso.

References

Mynors, C. (1994) 'Planning and the Historic Environment: The Final Version of PPG 15', *Context*, 44: 20–2.

Mynors, C. (1999) *Listed Buildings, Conservation Areas and Monuments*, London: Sweet and Maxwell.

Nairn, I. (1960) 'Superlative Newcastle upon Tyne', *The Listener*, July 28 1960.

National Park Service (1992) *Lowell: The Story of an Industrial City*, Washington D C: National Parks Service.

National Trust and Accenture (2006) *Demonstrating the Public Value of Heritage*, London: The National Trust.

Negussie, E. (2001) 'Dublin, Ireland', in R. Pickard (ed.) *Management of Historic Centres*, London: Routledge, pp. 133–61.

Newcastle City Planning Department (1962) *A Plan for the Preservation of Buildings of Architectural or Historic Interest*, Newcastle upon Tyne: City and County of Newcastle upon Tyne.

North East Civic Trust (2003) *A Byker Future: The Conservation Plan for the Byker Redevelopment, Newcastle upon Tyne*, Newcastle upon Tyne: English Heritage & Newcastle City Council.

Nuttgens, P. (1976) *York: The Continuing City*, London: Faber & Faber.

Oliver, P. (1975) *English Cottages and Small Farmhouses*, London: Arts Council of Great Britain.

Ousby, I. (1990) *The Englishman's England*, University Press: Cambridge.

Owen, S. (1998) 'The Role of Village Design Statements in Fostering a Locally Representative Approach to Village Planning and Design in UK', *Journal of Urban Design*, 3 (3): 359–80.

Owens, B. M. (2002) 'Monumentality, Identity and the State: Local Practice, World Heritage, and Heterotopia at Swayambhu, Nepal', *Anthropological Quarterly*, 75 (2): 269–316.

Palliser, D. M. (1974) 'Preserving our heritage: the historic city of York', in R. Kimber and J. J. Richardson (eds.) *Campaigning for the environment*, London: Routledge & Kegan Paul, pp. 6–26.

Pawley, M. (1998) *Terminal Architecture*, London: Reaktion Books.

Pearce, G., Hems, L. and Hennessy, B. (1990) *Conservation Areas in the North of England*, London: Historic Buildings and Monuments Commission for England.

Pendlebury, J. (1999) 'Civic Societies and Conservation Area Advisory Committees: Children of the 1960s at the End of the Century', paper presented at XIII AESOP Congress, Bergen, Norway, July 1999.

Pendlebury, J. (2000) 'Conservation, Conservatives and Consensus: The Success of Conservation Under the Thatcher and Major Governments, 1979–1997', *Planning Theory and Practice*, 1 (1): 31–52.

Pendlebury, J. (2001) 'Alas Smith and Burns? Conservation in Newcastle upon Tyne city centre 1959–68', *Planning Perspectives*, 16: 115–41.

Pendlebury, J. (2002) 'Conservation and Regeneration: Complementary or Conflicting Processes? The Case of Grainger Town, Newcastle upon Tyne', *Planning Practice & Research*, 17 (2): 145–58.

Pendlebury, J. (2003a) 'Planning the Historic City: 1940s Reconstruction Plans in Britain', *Town Planning Review*, 74 (4): 371–93.

Pendlebury, J. (2003b) 'The Reconstruction Planners' in P. J. Larkham and J. Nasr (eds.) *The Rebuilding of British Cities: Exploring the Post-Second World War Reconstruction*, Birmingham: School of Planning & Housing, University of Central England (Working Paper), pp. 15–22.

Pendlebury, J. (2004) 'The Function of Cultural Built Heritage', paper presented at Planning Academics Conference, Aberdeen, March/April 2004.

Pendlebury, J. (2005) 'The Modern Historic City: Evolving Ideas in Mid-20th-century Britain', *Journal of Urban Design*, 10 (2): 253–73.

Pendlebury, J. (2006) 'Planning the Historic City: 1960s Plans for Bath and York', in J. Monclus and M. Guardia (eds.) *Culture, Urbanism and Planning*, Abingdon: Ashgate, pp. 149–64.

Pendlebury, J. and Townshend, T. (1999) 'The Conservation of Historic Areas and Public Participation', *Journal of Architectural Conservation*, 5 (2): 72–87.

Pendlebury, J., Townshend, T. and Gilroy, R. (2004) 'The Conservation of English Cultural Built Heritage: A Force for Social Inclusion?' *International Journal for Heritage Studies,* 10 (1): 11–32.

Pendlebury, J., Townshend, T. and Gilroy, R. (2007) 'Social Housing as Heritage: The Case of Byker, Newcastle upon Tyne', paper presented at Heritage, Housing and Home conference. Newcastle upon Tyne April 2007.

Pevsner, N. (1956) *The Englishness of English Art,* Harmondsworth: Penguin.

Pevsner, N. (1960) *Pioneers of Modern Design,* Harmondsworth, Middlesex: Pelican.

Pevsner, N. and Richmond, I. (1957) *Northumberland,* Harmondsworth, Middlesex: Penguin.

Pocock, D. (1997a) 'Some reflections on world heritage', *Area,* 29 (3): 260–8.

Pocock, D. (1997b) 'The UK World Heritage', *Geography,* 357: 380–5.

Powell, K. (1981) 'Leeds: 'Obsolesence' and the Destruction of the Inner City', in D. Lowenthal and M. Binney (eds.) *Our Past Before Us: Why Do We Save It?,* London: Temple Smith, pp. 143–57.

Powell, K. (1989) 'The Offence of the Inoffensive', *Architects' Journal,* 3/5: 24–9.

Powell, K. (2003) 'Squaring up', Architects' Journal, 30/10: 28–45.

Powys, A. R. (1929, reprinted 1995) *Repair of Ancient Buildings,* London: SPAB.

Punter, J. (1988) 'Post-Modernism', *Planning Practice and Research,* 2 (4): 22–8.

Punter, J. (1990) 'The Ten Commandments of Architecture and Urban Design', *The Planner,* 76 (39): 10–14.

Punter, J. (1991) 'The long term conservation programme in central Bristol, 1977–1990', *Town Planning Review,* 62 (3): 341–64.

Punter, J. and Carmona, M. (1997) *The Design Dimension of Planning,* London: E & FN Spon.

Raban, J. (1974) *Soft City,* Glasgow: Fontana.

Ravetz, A. (1980) *Remaking Cities: Contradictions of the Recent Urban Environment,* London: Croom Helm.

Richards, J. (1994) *Facadism,* London: Routledge.

Richards, P. (1993) 'Impact of the Resurvey on Different Areas: A County Council View', *Transactions of the Ancient Monuments Society,* 37: 40–2.

Richardson, J. (1993) 'Interest Group Behaviour in Britain: Continuity and Change', in J. Richardson (ed.) *Pressure Groups,* Oxford: University Press, pp. 86–99.

Roberts, P. (2000) *Iron Town granted world status.* Online. Available at http://news.bbc.co.uk/1/hi/wales/1047398.stm (accessed 21 July 2003).

Robertson, M. (1993a) 'Listed Buildings: The National Resurvey of England', *Transactions of the Ancient Monuments Society,* 37: 21–38.

Robertson, M. (1993b) 'Public Reaction to the Resurvey', *Transactions of the Ancient Monuments Society,* 37: 50–1.

Roy, A. (2001) '"The Reverse Side of the World": Identity, Space and Power', in N. AlSayyad (ed.) *Hybrid Urbanism: On the Identity Discourse and the Built Environment,* London: Praeger, pp. 229–46.

Royal Fine Art Commission (1967) Letter to Newcastle City Council, 20/10/67.

Ruskin, J. (1849, 5th edn 1886) *The Seven Lamps of Architecture,* Orpington: George Allen.

Rydin, Y. (2003) *Urban and Environmental Planning in the UK,* 2nd edn, Basingstoke: Palgrave MacMillan.

Rypkema, D. (1992) 'Rethinking Economic Values', in A. Lee (ed.) *Past Meets Future: Saving America's Historic Environment,* Washington D. C.: The Preservation Press, pp. 205–12.

Rypkema, D. D. (2001) 'The Economic Power of Restoration', paper presented at Restoration & Renovation Conference, Washington DC, 15 January 2001.

Sadler, D. (1993) 'Place Marketing, Competitive Places and the Construction of Hegemony in Britain in the 1980s', in G. Kearns and C. Philo (eds.) *Selling Places: The City as Cultural Capital, Past and Present,* Oxford: Pergamon Press, pp. 175–92.

Saint, A. (1996) 'How listing happened', in M. Hunter (ed.) *Preserving the Past: The Rise of Heritage in Modern Britain,* Stroud: Alan Sutton, pp. 115–34.

References

Samuel, R. (1989) 'The Pathos of Conservation', in M. Girouard, D. Cruickshank, R. Samuels *et al.* (eds.) *The Saving of Spitalfields,* London: The Spitalfields Historic Buildings Trust, pp. 133–70.

Samuel, R. (1994) *Theatres of Memory,* London: Verso.

Saunders, M. (1996) 'The Conservation of Buildings in Britain since the Second World War', in S. Marks (ed.) *Concerning Buildings,* Oxford: Architectural Press, pp. 5–33.

Saunders, M. (2002) 'The Role of the Amenity Societies', paper presented at The Planning and the Historic Environment Conference, Oxford, May 2002.

National Trust and Accenture (2006) *Demonstrating the Public Value of Heritage,* London: The National Trust.

SAVE Britain's Heritage (1975) 'SAVE Report', *The Architects' Journal,* 17–24 December: 1279–313.

SAVE Britain's Heritage (1978) *Preservation Pays: Tourism and the Economic Benefits of Conserving Historic Buildings,* London: SAVE.

SAVE Britain's Heritage (1979) *Satanic Mills,* London: SAVE.

SAVE Britain's Heritage (1998) *Catalytic Conversion,* London: SAVE.

Save Stonehenge. Online. Available at htpp://www.savestonehenge.org.uk/ (accessed 20 December 2007).

Scott, J. (2002) 'World Heritage as a Model for Citizenship: the case of Cyprus', *International Journal for Heritage Studies,* 8 (2): 99–115.

Scottish Civic Trust (1970) *The conservation of Georgian Edinburgh: An outcome of a conference,* Edinburgh: The Scottish Civic Trust.

Seppanen, M. (1999) *Global Scale, Local Place? The Making of the Historic Centre of Lima Into a World Heritage Site,* Helsinki: Interkont Books.

Shackley, M. (ed.) (1998) *Visitor Management: Case studies from World Heritage Sites,* Oxford: Butterworth-Heinemann.

Sharp, T. (1932) *Town and Countryside: Some Aspects of Urban and Rural Development,* Oxford: University Press.

Sharp, T. (1937) 'The North East – Hills and Hells', in C. Williams-Ellis (ed.) *Britain and the Beast,* London: Readers' Union, pp. 141–59.

Sharp, T. (1945) *Cathedral City: A Plan for Durham,* London: Architectural Press.

Sharp, T. (1946a) *The Anatomy of the Village,* Harmondsworth, Middlesex: Penguin.

Sharp, T. (1946b) *Exeter Phoenix: A Plan for Rebuilding,* London: Architectural Press.

Sharp, T. (1948) *Oxford Replanned,* London: Architectural Press.

Sharp, T. (1949a) *Georgian City: A Plan for the Preservation and Improvement of Chichester,* Brighton: Southern Publishing Corporation.

Sharp, T. (1949b) *Newer Sarum: A Plan for Salisbury,* London: Architectural Press.

Sharp, T. (1952) *Oxford Observed,* London: Country Life.

Sharp, T. (1968) *Town and Townscape,* London: John Murray.

Sheail, J. (1981a) 'Changing perceptions of land-use controls in inter-war Britain', in R. Kain (ed.) *Planning for Conservation,* London: Mansell Publishing, pp. 141–58.

Sheail, J. (1981b) *Rural Conservation in Inter-War Britain,* Oxford: Clarendon Press.

Sheriff, A. (ed.) (1995) *The History and Conservation of Zanzibar Stone Town,* London: James Currey.

Shore, N. (2007) 'Whose Heritage? The Construction of Cultural Built Heritage in a Pluralist, Multicultural England' PhD thesis, Newcastle University.

Siravo, F. (undated) *A Plan for the Historic Stone Town.* Online. Available at www.akdn.org/aktc/hcsp_zanzibar5.html (accessed 29 May 2004).

Sitte, C. (1889) *The Art of Building Cities: City building according to artistic fundamentals,* trans. Charles T. Stewart (1945), New York: Reinhold.

Smith, C. (1998) *Creative Britain,* London: Faber & Faber.

Smith, D. L. (1974) *Amenity and Urban Planning,* London: Crosby Lockwood Staples.

Smith, L. (2006) *The Uses of Heritage,* London: Routledge.

Smith, N. and Williams, P. (eds.) (1986) *Gentrification of the City,* London: Allen & Unwin.

Smithson, A. and Smithson, P. (1968) *The Euston Arch and the Growth of the London, Midland and Scottish Railway,* London: Thames & Hudson.

Sparks, L. (1998) 'Historicism and public perception', in J. Warren, J. Worthington and S. Taylor (eds.) *Context: new buildings in historic settings,* Oxford: Architectural Press, pp. 61–70.

Stamp, G. (1996) 'The art of keeping one jump ahead: conservation societies in the twentieth century', in M. Hunter (ed.) *Preserving the Past: The Rise of Heritage in Modern Britain,* Stroud, Gloucestershire: Alan Sutton, pp. 77–98.

Stedall, J. (Director) *Bath* (1962), in the series *The Lost Betjemans,* UK: Green Umbrella.

Strange, I. and Whitney, D. (2003) 'The Changing Roles and Purposes of Heritage Conservation in the UK', *Planning Practice and Research,* 18 (2–3): 219–29.

Stratford on Avon District Council (2001) *Stratford-on-Avon District Design Guide,* Stratford: District Council.

Summerson, J. (1949) 'The Past in the Future', in J. Summerson (ed.) *Heavenly Mansions,* London: Cresset Press, pp. 219–42.

Tarn, J. N. (1976) 'The Derbyshire Heritage. The conservation of ordinariness', in J. Reynolds (ed.) *Conservation planning in town and country,* Liverpool: University Press, pp. 103–117.

Tewdwr-Jones, M. (2005) ' "Oh, the planners did their best": the planning films of John Betjeman', *Planning Perspectives,* 20: 389–411.

Thornley, A. (1991) *Urban Planning under Thatcherism: the Challenge of the Market,* London: Routledge.

Thornley, A. (1998) 'The ghost of Thatcherism', in P. Allmendinger and H. Thomas (eds.) *Urban Planning and the British New Right,* London: Routledge, pp. 211–35.

Tibbalds, F. (1992) *Making people-friendly towns: improving the public environment in towns and cities,* London: Spon.

Tiesdell, S. (1995) 'Tensions between revitalization and conservation: Nottingham's Lace Market', *Cities,* 12 (4): 231–41.

Tiesdell, S., Oc, T. and Heath, T. (1996) *Revitalizing Historic Urban Quarters,* Oxford: Architectural Press.

Torre, M. d. l. (2002) *Assessing the Values of Cultural Heritage,* Los Angeles: Getty Conservation Institute.

Townshend, T. (2000) 'But would you live here? Researching attitudes towards Newcastle upon Tyne's urban area', in J. Benson and M. Roe (eds.) *Urban Lifestyles: Spaces, Places, People,* Rotterdam: Balkema, pp. 221–8.

Townshend, T. and Pendlebury, J. (1999) 'Public Participation in the Conservation of Historic Areas: Case studies from North East England', *Journal of Urban Design,* 4 (3): 313–31.

Tuan, Y.-F. (1974) *Topophilia,* New Jersey: Prentice-Hall.

Tugnutt, A. and Robertson, M. (1987) *Making Townscape: A contextual approach to building in an urban setting,* London: Mitchell.

Tunbridge, J. and Ashworth, G. (1996) *Dissonant Heritage: the management of the past as a resource in conflict,* Chichester: Wiley.

Turley, S. (1998) 'Hadrian's Wall, UK', in M. Shackley (ed.) *Visitor Management: Case studies from World Heritage Sites,* Oxford: Butterworth-Heinemann, pp. 100–20.

Turner, S. (2006) 'Historic Landscape Characterisation: A Landscape Archaeology for Research, Management and Planning', *Landscape Research,* 31 (4): 385–98.

UNESCO (1976) *Recommendation concerning the Safeguarding and Contemporary Role of Historic Areas,* Nairobi: UNESCO.

UNESCO (1999) *World Heritage Committee: Twenty-Third Session,* Marrakesh, Morroco: UNESCO.

Unwin, R. (1909, reprinted 1971) *Town Planning in Practice: An Introduction to the Art of Designing Cities and Suburbs,* New York: Benjamin Blom.

Urban Task Force (1998) *Prospectus,* London: UTF.

References

Urban Task Force (1999) *Towards an Urban Renaissance,* London: E & FN Spon.

Urry, J. (1995) *Consuming Places,* London: Routledge.

Van-der-Borg, J., Costa, P. and Gotti, G. (1996) 'Tourism in European Heritage Cities', *Annals of Tourism Research,* 23 (2): 306–21.

Venning, P. (1999) 'The Government turning its back on the historic environment', *Context,* 61: 7.

Wakelin, P. (2002) 'Celebrating Industrial Landscapes: The New Blaenavon World Heritage Site and Its Implications', in *Institute of Historic Buildings Conservation Handbook,* 2002, pp. 35–8.

Warburton, D. (2002) 'Raising the stakes in the Jewellery Quarter', *Context,* 75: 9–10.

Ward, P. (ed.) (1968) *Conservation and Development in Historic Towns and Cities,* Newcastle upon Tyne: Oriel Press.

Ward, S. (1994) *Planning and Urban Change,* London: Paul Chapman.

Ward, S. (1998) *Selling Places: The Marketing and Promotion of Towns and Cities 1850–2000,* London: E & FN Spon.

Warren, J. (1996) 'Principles and problems: Ethics and aesthetics', in S. Marks (ed.) *Concerning Buildings,* Oxford: Architectural Press, pp. 34–54.

Warren, J., Worthington, J. and Taylor, S. (eds.) (1998) *Context: new buildings in historic settings,* Oxford: Architectural Press.

Warwickshire County Council (1951) *Development Plan for the Administrative County of Warwick,* Warwick City Council.

Waterton, E. (2005) 'Whose Sense of Place? Reconciling Archaeological Perspectives with Community Values: Cultural Landscapes In England', *International Journal for Heritage Studies,* 11 (4): 309–25.

Waterton, E., Smith, L. and Campbell, G. (2006) 'The Utility of Discourse Analysis to Heritage Studies: The Burra Charter and Social Inclusion', *International Journal for Heritage Studies,* 12 (4): 339–55.

Wates, N. (1976) *The Battle for Tolmers Square,* London: Routledge & Kegan Paul.

Welsh, J. (1999) 'Behind the facade of the preservation argument', *Property Week,* 17/9/99: 23.

Wenger, E. (1998) *Communities of Practice: Learning, Meaning and Identity,* University Press: Cambridge.

Whistler, W. and Reed, D. (1994) 'Townscape as a Philosophy of Urban Design', *Urban Design Quarterly,* 52: 15–30.

Whitbourn, P. (2002) *World Heritage Sites – the First Thirty Years.* Online. Available at www.sal. org.uk/lectures (accessed: 8 July 2003)

Whitehand, J. W. R. (ed.) (1981) *The Urban Landscape: Historical Development and Management: Papers by M R G Conzen,* London: Academic Press.

Wiener, M. J. (1981) *English Culture and the Decline of the Industrial Spirit 1850–1980,* Cambridge: University Press.

Wildlife Trusts Partnership (2004) *The Wildlife Trusts partnership.* Online. Available at www. wildlifetrusts.org/ (accessed: 26 April 2004).

Wilkinson, A. (2006) *Pathfinder,* London: SAVE Britain's Heritage.

Williams-Ellis, C. (1978) *Around the World in Ninety Years,* Portmeirion: Golden Dragon Books.

Williams, R. (1976) *Keywords: A Vocabulary of Culture and Society,* London: Croom Helm.

Wirth, R. and Freestone, R. (2003) *Tourism, Heritage and Authenticity: State-Assisted Cultural Commodification in Suburban Sydney, Australia.* Online. Available at www.etsav.upc.es/ urbpersp/ (accessed 13 January 2004).

World Heritage Centre (2006) Annex to the Information Paper on Safeguarding the Historic Urban Landscape Planning Meeting: World Heritage Cities under pressure from contemporary urban development, including hi-rise development. Paris: UNESCO.

Worskett, R. (1969) *The Character of Towns: An Approach to Conservation,* London: The Architectural Press.

Worskett, R. (1975) 'Great Britain: Progress in Conservation', in S. Cantacuzino (ed.) *Architectural Conservation in Europe*, London: Architectural Press, pp. 17–26.

Worskett, R. (1982) 'Conservation: the missing ethic', *Monumentum*, 25 (2): 151–61.

Wright, P. (1985) *On Living in an Old Country: the national past in contemporary Britain*, London: Verso.

Wright, P. (1992) *A Journey Through Ruins: A keyhole portrait of British postwar life and culture*, London: Flamingo.

York 2000 (1972) *People in Protest*, York: York 2000.

Young, C. (1999) 'Hadrian's Wall', in G. Chitty and D. Baker (eds.) *Managing Historic Sites and Buildings*, London: Routledge, pp. 35–48.

Young, E. and Kennet, W. (2000) 'Stonehenge: The Saga Continues', *Journal of Architectural Conservation*, 6 (3): 70–85.

Zancheti, S. M. and Jokilehto, J. (1997) 'Values and Urban Conservation Planning: Some Reflections on Principles and Definitions', *Journal of Architectural Conservation*, 3 (1): 37–51.

Zidic, I. (1991, 2001) 'The Siege of Dubrovnik and City's Wounds (Letter to an Italian Friend)', in M. Hrvatska (ed.) *Dubrovnik in War*. Dubrovnik: Matica Hrvatska, pp. 59–63.

Zukin, S. (1987) 'Gentrification: Culture and Capital in the Urban Core', *Annual Review of Sociology*, 13: 129–47.

Index

Note: References to figures are in *italic* print and references to tables are in **bold** print.

Printed in Great Britain
by Amazon

55639267R00150